4th Workshop on Building and Using Comparable Corpora: Comparable Corpora and the Web 2011

(BUCC 2011)

Held at ACL HLT 2011

Portland, Oregon, USA
24 June 2011

ISBN: 978-1-61839-249-7

Printed from e-media with permission by:

Curran Associates, Inc.
57 Morehouse Lane
Red Hook, NY 12571

Some format issues inherent in the e-media version may also appear in this print version.

Printed by Curran Associates, Inc. (2011)

Association for Computational Linguistics
209 N. Eighth Street
Stroudsburg, Pennsylvania 18360

Phone: 1-570-476-8006
Fax: 1-570-476-0860

acl@aclweb.org

Additional copies of this publication are available from:

Curran Associates, Inc.
57 Morehouse Lane
Red Hook, NY 12571 USA
Phone: 845-758-0400
Fax: 845-758-2634
Email: curran@proceedings.com
Web: www.proceedings.com

Introduction

Comparable corpora are collections of documents that are comparable in content and form in various degrees and dimensions. This definition includes many types of parallel and non-parallel multilingual corpora, but also sets of monolingual corpora that are used for comparative purposes. Research on comparable corpora is active but used to be scattered among many workshops and conferences. The workshop series on "Building and Using Comparable Corpora" (BUCC) aims at promoting progress in this exciting emerging field by bundling its research, thereby making it more visible and giving it a better platform.

Following the three previous editions of the workshop which took place at LREC 2008 in Marrakech, at ACL-IJCNLP 2009 in Singapore, and at LREC 2010 in Malta, this year the workshop was co-located with ACL-HLT in Portland and its theme was "Comparable Corpora and the Web". Among the topics solicited in the call for papers, three are particularly well represented in this year's workshop:

- Mining word translations from comparable corpora, an early favorite, continues to be explored;
- Identifying parallel sub-sentential segments from comparable corpora is gaining impetus;
- Building comparable corpora and assessing their comparability is a basic need for the field.

Additionally, statistical machine translation and cross-language information access are recurring motivating applications.

We would like to thank all people who in one way or another helped in making this workshop a particularly successful. This year the workshop has been formally endorsed by ACL SIGWAC (Special Interest Group on Web as Corpus) and FLaReNet (Fostering Language Resources Network). Our special thanks go to Kevin Knight for accepting to give the invited presentation, to the members of the program committee who did an excellent job in reviewing the submitted papers under strict time constraints, and to the ACL-HLT workshop chairs and organizers. Last but not least we would like to thank our authors and the participants of the workshop.

Pierre Zweigenbaum, Reinhard Rapp, Serge Sharoff

Organizers:

Pierre Zweigenbaum (LIMSI, CNRS, Orsay, and ERTIM, INALCO, Paris, France)
Reinhard Rapp (Universities of Leeds, UK, and Mainz, Germany)
Serge Sharoff (University of Leeds, UK)

Invited Speaker:

Kevin Knight (Information Sciences Institute, USC)

Program Committee:

Srinivas Bangalore (AT&T Labs, USA)
Caroline Barrière (National Research Council Canada)
Chris Biemann (Microsoft / Powerset, San Francisco, USA)
Lynne Bowker (University of Ottawa, Canada)
Hervé Déjean (Xerox Research Centre Europe, Grenoble, France)
Kurt Eberle (Lingenio, Heidelberg, Germany)
Andreas Eisele (European Commission, Luxembourg)
Pascale Fung (Hong Kong University of Science & Technology, Hong Kong)
Éric Gaussier (Université Joseph Fourier, Grenoble, France)
Gregory Grefenstette (Exalead, Paris, France)
Silvia Hansen-Schirra (University of Mainz, Germany)
Hitoshi Isahara (National Institute of Information and Communications Technology, Kyoto, Japan)
Kyo Kageura (University of Tokyo, Japan)
Adam Kilgarriff (Lexical Computing Ltd, UK)
Natalie Kübler (Université Paris Diderot, France)
Philippe Langlais (Université de Montréal, Canada)
Tony McEnery (Lancaster University, UK)
Emmanuel Morin (Université de Nantes, France)
Dragos Stefan Munteanu (Language Weaver, Inc., USA)
Reinhard Rapp (Universities of Leeds, UK, and Mainz, Germany)
Sujith Ravi (Information Sciences Institute, University of Southern California, USA)
Serge Sharoff (University of Leeds, UK)
Michel Simard (National Research Council, Canada)
Monique Slodzian (INALCO, Paris, France)
Richard Sproat (OGI School of Science & Technology, USA)
Benjamin T'sou (The Hong Kong Institute of Education, Hong Kong)
Yujie Zhang (National Institute of Information and Communications Technology, Japan)
Michael Zock (Laboratoire d'Informatique Fondamentale, CNRS, Marseille, France)
Pierre Zweigenbaum (LIMSI-CNRS, and ERTIM, INALCO, Paris, France)

Table of Contents

Invited Presentation

Oral Presentations

Poster Presentations

Conference Program

Friday June 24, 2011

Session 1: (09:00) Bilingual Lexicon Extraction From Comparable Corpora

9:00 *Learning the Optimal Use of Dependency-parsing Information for Finding Translations with Comparable Corpora*
Daniel Andrade, Takuya Matsuzaki and Junichi Tsujii

9:20 *Building and Using Comparable Corpora for Domain-Specific Bilingual Lexicon Extraction*
Darja Fišer, Nikola Ljubešić, Špela Vintar and Senja Pollak

9:40 *Bilingual Lexicon Extraction from Comparable Corpora Enhanced with Parallel Corpora*
Emmanuel Morin and Emmanuel Prochasson

10:00 *Bilingual Lexicon Extraction from Comparable Corpora as Metasearch*
Amir Hazem, Emmanuel Morin and Sebastian Peña Saldarriaga

Session 2: (11:00) Extracting Parallel Segments From Comparable Corpora

11:00 *Two Ways to Use a Noisy Parallel News Corpus for Improving Statistical Machine Translation*
Souhir Gahbiche-Braham, Hélène Bonneau-Maynard and François Yvon

11:20 *Paraphrase Fragment Extraction from Monolingual Comparable Corpora*
Rui Wang and Chris Callison-Burch

11:40 *Extracting Parallel Phrases from Comparable Data*
Sanjika Hewavitharana and Stephan Vogel

12:00 *Active Learning with Multiple Annotations for Comparable Data Classification Task*
Vamshi Ambati, Sanjika Hewavitharana, Stephan Vogel and Jaime Carbonell

Friday June 24, 2011 (continued)

Session 3: (14:00) Invited Presentation

14:00	*Putting a Value on Comparable Data / The Copiale Cipher* Kevin Knight (in collaboration with Beáta Megyesi and Christiane Schaefer)

Session 4: (14:50) Poster Presentations (including Booster Session)

14:50	*Unsupervised Alignment of Comparable Data and Text Resources* Anja Belz and Eric Kow
14:55	*Cross-lingual Slot Filling from Comparable Corpora* Matthew Snover, Xiang Li, Wen-Pin Lin, Zheng Chen, Suzanne Tamang, Mingmin Ge, Adam Lee, Qi Li, Hao Li, Sam Anzaroot and Heng Ji
15:00	*Towards a Data Model for the Universal Corpus* Steven Abney and Steven Bird
15:05	*An Expectation Maximization Algorithm for Textual Unit Alignment* Radu Ion, Alexandru Ceauşu and Elena Irimia
15:10	*Building a Web-Based Parallel Corpus and Filtering Out Machine-Translated Text* Alexandra Antonova and Alexey Misyurev
15:15	*Language-Independent Context Aware Query Translation using Wikipedia* Rohit Bharadwaj G and Vasudeva Varma

Session 5: (16:00) Building and Assessing Comparable Corpora

16:00	*How Comparable are Parallel Corpora? Measuring the Distribution of General Vocabulary and Connectives* Bruno Cartoni, Sandrine Zufferey, Thomas Meyer and Andrei Popescu-Belis
16:20	*Identifying Parallel Documents from a Large Bilingual Collection of Texts: Application to Parallel Article Extraction in Wikipedia.* Alexandre Patry and Philippe Langlais
16:40	*Comparable Fora* Johanka Spoustová and Miroslav Spousta

Putting a Value on Comparable Data

Kevin Knight
USC Information Sciences Institute
4676 Admiralty Way
Marina del Rey, CA, 90292 USA
knight@isi.edu

Invited Talk

Abstract

Machine translation began in 1947 with an influential memo by Warren Weaver. In that memo, Weaver noted that human code-breakers could transform ciphers into natural language (e.g., into Turkish)

- without access to parallel ciphertext/plaintext data, and
- without knowing the plaintext language's syntax and semantics.

Simple word- and letter-statistics seemed to be enough for the task. Weaver then predicted that such statistical methods could also solve a tougher problem, namely language translation.

This raises the question: can sufficient translation knowledge be derived from comparable (non-parallel) data?

In this talk, I will discuss initial work in treating foreign language as a code for English, where we assume the code to involve both word substitutions and word transpositions. In doing so, I will quantitatively estimate the value of non-parallel data, versus parallel data, in terms of end-to-end accuracy of trained translation systems. Because we still know very little about solving word-based codes, I will also describe successful techniques and lessons from the realm of letter-based ciphers, where the non-parallel resources are (1) enciphered text, and (2) unrelated plaintext. As an example, I will describe how we decoded the *Copiale* cipher with limited "computer-like" knowledge of the plaintext language.

The talk will wrap up with challenges in exploiting comparable data at all levels: letters, words, phrases, syntax, and semantics.

Proceedings of the 4th Workshop on Building and Using Comparable Corpora, page 1,
49th Annual Meeting of the Association for Computational Linguistics,
Portland, Oregon, 24 June 2011. ©*2011 Association for Computational Linguistics*

The Copiale Cipher*

Kevin Knight

USC Information Sciences Institute
4676 Admiralty Way
Marina del Rey, CA, 90292, USA
knight@isi.edu

SDL Language Weaver, Inc.
6060 Center Drive, Suite 150
Los Angeles, CA 90045
kknight@sdl.com

Beáta Megyesi and Christiane Schaefer

Department of Linguistics and Philology
Uppsala University
Box 635, S-751 26 Uppsala, Sweden
beata.megyesi@lingfil.uu.se
christiane.schaefer@lingfil.uu.se

Abstract

The Copiale cipher is a 105-page enciphered book dated 1866. We describe the features of the book and the method by which we deciphered it.

1. Features of the Text

Figure 1 shows a portion of an enciphered book from the East Berlin Academy. The book has the following features:

- It is 105 pages long, containing about 75,000 handwritten characters.
- The handwriting is extremely neat.
- Some characters are Roman letters (such as a and b), while others are abstract symbols (such as ð and Δ). Roman letters appear in both uppercase and lowercase forms.
- Lines of text are both left- and right-justified.
- There are only a few author corrections.
- There is no word spacing.

There are no illustrations or chapter breaks, but the text has formatting:

- Paragraphs are indented.
- Some lines are centered.
- Some sections of text contain a double-quote mark (") before each line.
- Some lines end with full stop (.) or colon (:). The colon (:) is also a frequent word-internal cipher letter.
- Paragraphs and section titles always begin with Roman letters (in capitalized form).

The only non-enciphered inscriptions in the book are "Philipp 1866" and "Copiales 3", the latter of which we used to name the cipher.

The book also contains preview fragments ("catchwords") at the bottom of left-hand pages. Each catchword is a copy of the first few letters from the following (right-hand) page. For example, in Figure 1, the short sequence ʒâʌ floats at the bottom of the left page, and the next page begins ʒâʌomı... In early printing, catchwords were used to help printers validate the folding and stacking of pages.

2. Transcription

To get a machine-readable version of the text, we devised the transcription scheme in Figure 2. According to this scheme, the line

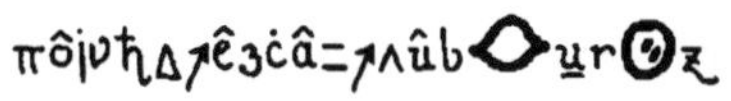

is typed as:

```
pi oh j v hd tri arr eh three c. ah
ni arr lam uh b lip uu r o.. zs
```

—

*This material was presented as part of an invited talk at the 4th Workshop on Building and Using Comparable Corpora (BUCC 2011).

Proceedings of the 4th Workshop on Building and Using Comparable Corpora, pages 2–9,
49th Annual Meeting of the Association for Computational Linguistics,
Portland, Oregon, 24 June 2011. ©2011 Association for Computational Linguistics

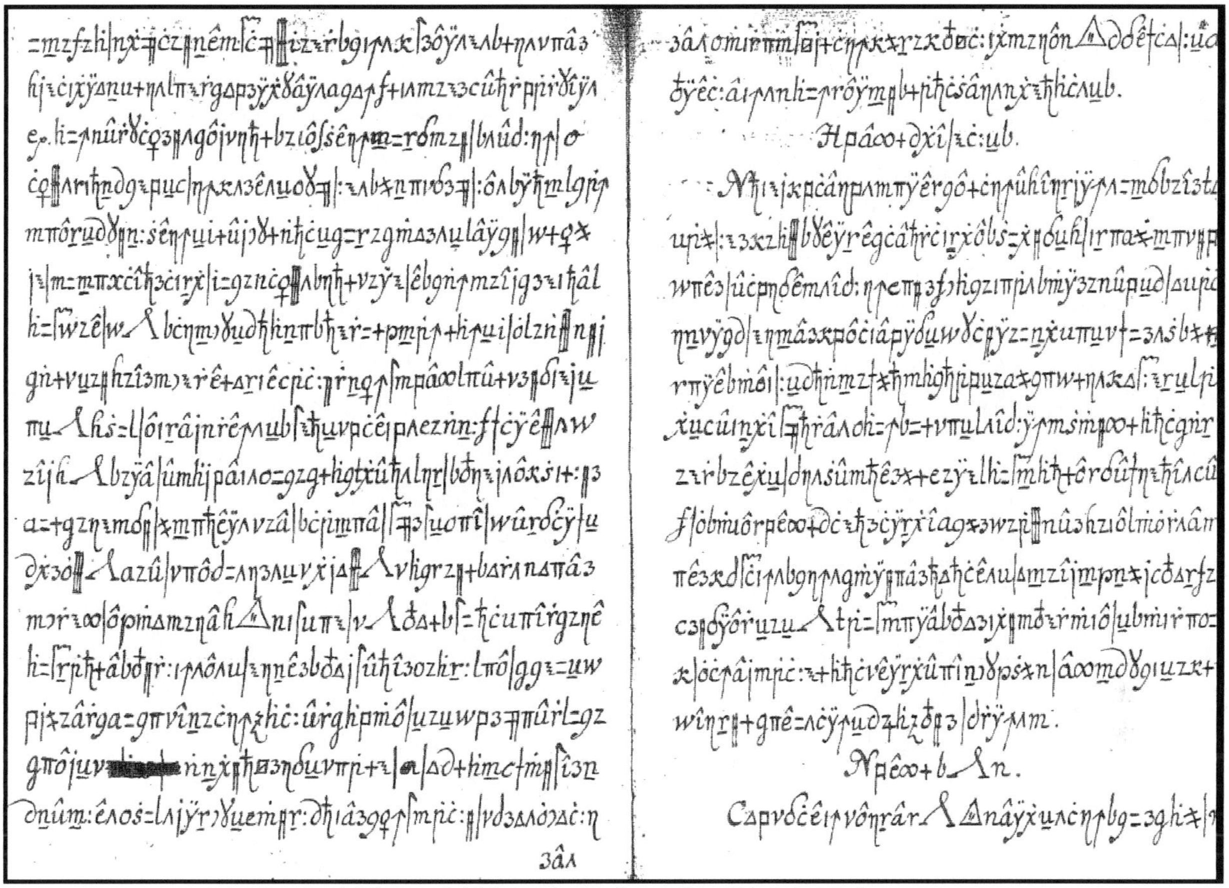

Figure 1. Two pages from the Copiale cipher.

The transcription uses easy-to-reach keyboard characters, so a transcriber can work without taking his/her eyes off the original document.

There are approximately 90 cipher letters, including 26 unaccented Roman letters, a-z. The letters c, h, m, n, p, r, s, and x have dotted forms (e.g., ċ), while the letter i also has an un-dotted form. The letters m, n, r, and u have underlined variants (e.g., m̲), and the vowels have circumflexed variants (e.g., â). The plain letter y does not appear unaccented until page 30, but it appears quite frequently with an umlaut (ÿ).The four Roman letters d, g, n, and z appear in both plain (d, g, n, z) and fancy forms (∂, ɡ, η, ʑ). Capitalized Roman letters are used to start paragraphs. We transcribe these with A-Z, though we down-case them before counting frequencies (Section 3). Down-casing D, G, N, and Z is not trivial, due to the presence of both plain and fancy lowercase forms.

The non-Roman characters are an eclectic mix of symbols, including some Greek letters. Eight symbols are rendered larger than others in the text: λ, ⊙, Δ, ✕, ◇, ▲, ∞, and Π.

We transcribed a total of 16 pages (10,840 letters). We carried out our analysis on those pages, after stripping catchwords and down-casing all Roman letters.

3. Letter Frequencies and Contexts

Figure 3 shows cipher letter frequencies. The distribution is far from flat, the most frequent letter being ^ (occurring 412 times). Here are the most common cipher digraphs (letter pairs) and trigraphs, with frequencies:

ɔ ħ	99	ɔ ħ ʌ	47
ċ :	66	ċ : u̲	23
ħ ʌ	49	η ɔ ħ	22
: u̲	48	ÿ ɔ ħ	18
z ʀ	44	ĥ ċ |	17

a	a	â	ah			δ	del
b	b					Δ	tri
c	c			ċ	c.	ɣ	gam
d	d					ι	iot
e	e	ê	eh			ʌ	lam
f	f					π	pi
g	g					↗	arr
h	h	ḣ	h.	ħ	hd	ɂ	bas
i	i	î	ih			ŧ	car
į	j					+	plus
ϰ	k					†	cross
l	l					♀	fem
m	m	ṁ	m.	m̲	mu	♂	mal
n	n	ṅ	n.	n̲	nu	ꝼ	ft
o	o	ô	oh	ȯ	o.	⊠	no
p	p	ṗ	p.			ꝕ	sqp
q	q					ʓ	zzz
r	r	ṙ	r.	r̲	ru	ʄ	pipe
s	s	ṡ	s.			ſ	longs
t	t					Ħ	grr
u	u	û	uh	u̲	uu	Ħ	grl
v	v					▮	grc
w	w			Δ̇	tri..	ɼ	hk
x	x	ẋ	x.	◇	lip	Γ	sqi
y	y	ÿ	y..	ᴧ	nee	:	:
z	z			ʘ	o..	·	.
∂	ds	=	ni	☆	star	…	...
ℊ	gs	ǂ	ki	X	bigx	│	bar
ƶ	zs	(:	smil	Π	gat	ɜ	three
ɳ	ns	:)	smir	⏝	toe	∞	inf

Figure 2. Transcription scheme. Columns alternate between the cipher letters and their transcriptions.

The full digraph counts reveal interesting patterns among groups of letters. For example, letters with circumflexes (â, ê, î, ô, û) have behaviors in common: all five tend to be preceded by z and π, and all five tend to be followed by ɜ and į. To get a better handle on letter similarities, we automatically clustered the cipher letters based on their contexts. The result is shown in Figure 4. We did the clustering as follows. For each distinct letter x, we created a

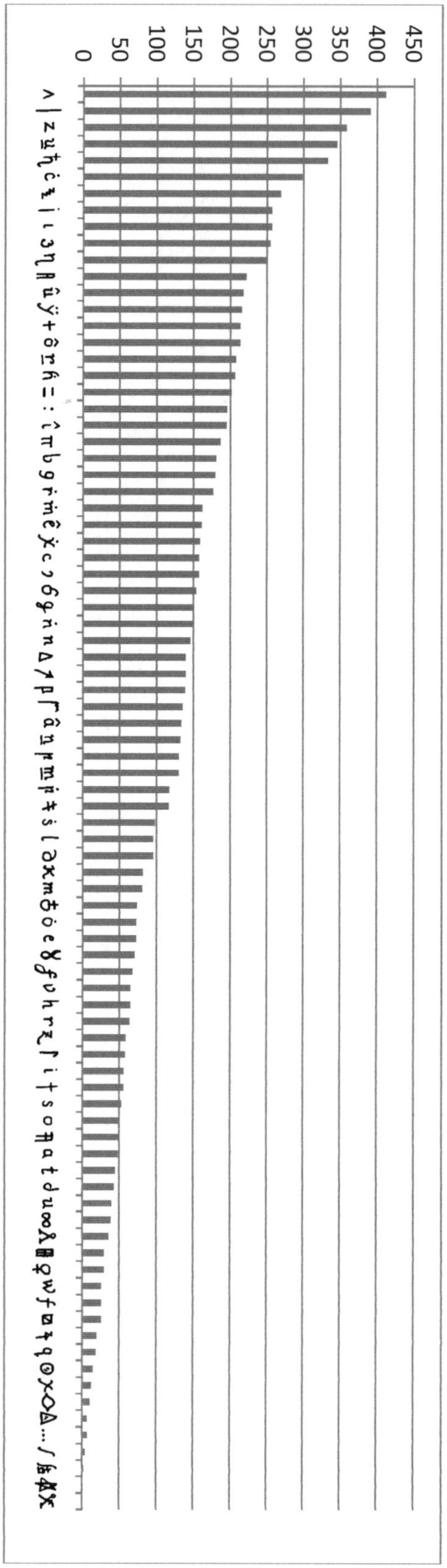

Figure 3. Cipher letter frequencies.

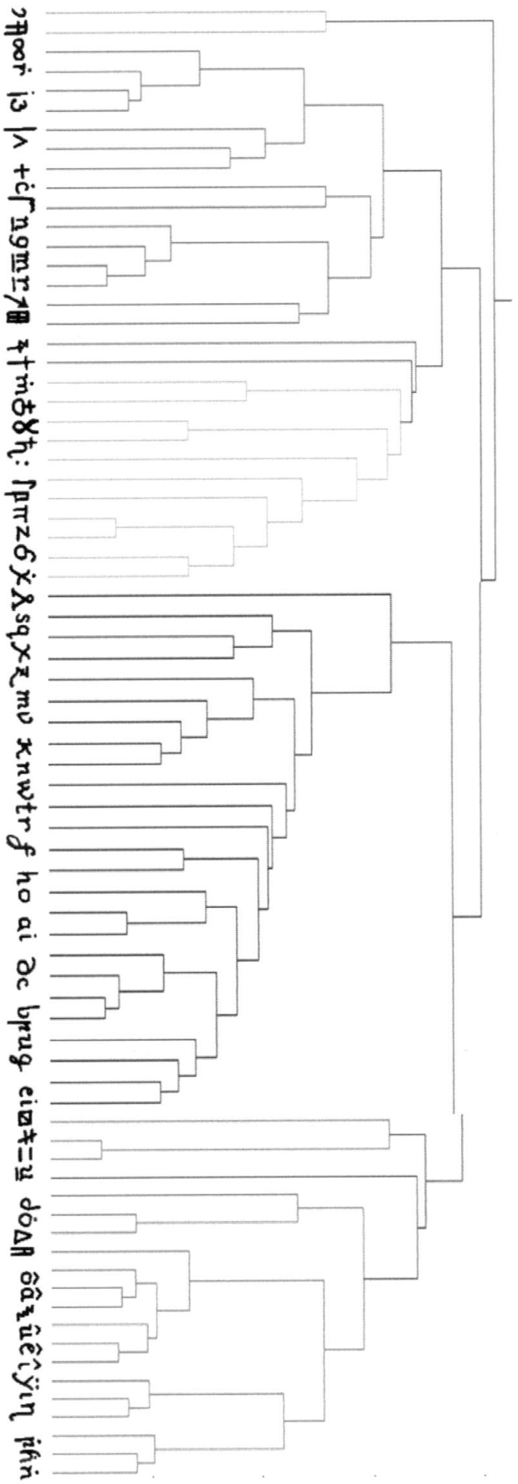

Figure 4. Automatic clustering of cipher letters based on similarity of contexts.

co-occurrence vector of length 90, to capture the distribution of letters than precede x. For example, if x is preceded 12 times by π, 0 times by û, 4 times by ÿ, 1 time by 6, etc, then its vector looks like this: [12, 0, 4, 1, …]. For the same letter x, we created another vector that captures the distribution of letters than follow x, e.g., [0, 0, 7, 2, …]. Then we concatenated the two vectors to create v(x) = [12, 0, 4, 1, …, 0, 0, 7, 2, …]. We deemed two letters a and b to be similar if the cosine distance between v(a) and v(b) is small, indicating that they appear in similar contexts. We used the Scipy software (http://users.soe.ucsc.edu/~eads/cluster.html) to perform and plot a clustering that incrementally merges similar letters (and groups of letters) in a bottom-up fashion.

The cluster diagram confirms that circumflexed letters (â, ê, î, ô, û) behave similarly. It also shows that the unaccented Roman letters form a natural grouping, as do underlined letters. Merges that happen low in the cluster map indicate very high similarity, e.g., the group (ÿ, ι, η).

4. First Decipherment Approach

Building on the self-similarity of Roman letters, our first theory was that the Roman letters carry all the information in the cipher, and that all other symbols are NULLs (meaningless tokens added after encipherment to confuse cryptanalysis). If we remove all other symbols, the remaining Roman letters indeed follow a typical natural language distribution, with the most popular letter occurring 12% of the time, and the least popular letters occurring rarely.

The revealed sequence of Roman letters is itself nonsensical, so we posited a simple substitution cipher. We carried out automatic computer attacks against the revealed Roman-letter sequence, first assuming German source, then English, then Latin, then forty other candidate European and non-European languages. The attack method is given in [Knight et al, 2006]. That method automatically combines plaintext-language identification with decipherment. Unfortunately, this failed, as no language identified itself as a more likely plaintext candidate than the others.

We then gave up our theory regarding NULLs and posited a homophonic cipher, with each plaintext letter being encipherable by any of several distinct cipher letters. While a well-executed homophonic cipher will employ a flat letter frequency distribution, to confound analysis, we guessed that the Copiale cipher is not optimized in this regard.

We confirmed that our computer attack does in fact work on a synthetic homophonic cipher, i.e., it correctly identifies the plaintext language, and yields a reasonable, if imperfect, decipherment. We then loosed the same attack on the Copiale cipher. Unfortunately, all resulting decipherments were nonsense, though there was a very slight numerical preference for German as a candidate plaintext language.

5. Second Decipherment Approach

We next decided to focus on German as the most likely plaintext language, for three reasons:

- the book is located in Germany
- the computer homophonic attack gave a very slight preference to German
- the book ends with the inscription "Philipp 1866", using the German double-p spelling.

Pursuing the homophonic theory, our thought was that all five circumflexed letters (â, ê, î, ô, û), behaving similarly, might represent the same German letter. But which German letter? Since the circumflexed letters are preceded by z and π, the circumflexed letters would correspond to the German letter that often follows *whatever* z *and* π *stand for*. But what do they, in turn, stand for?

From German text, we built a digraph frequency table, whose the most striking characteristic is that C is almost always followed by H. The German CH pair is similar to the English QU pair, but C is fairly frequent in German. A similar digraph table for the cipher letters shows that ʒ is almost always followed by ђ. So we posited our first two substitutions: ʒ=C and ђ=H. We then looked for what typically precedes and follows CH in German, and what typically precedes and follows ʒђ in the cipher. For example, ʒђʌ is the most frequent cipher trigraph, while CHT is a common German trigraph. We thus hypothesized the further substitution ʌ=T, and this led to a cascade of others. We retracted any hypothesis that resulted in poor German digraphs and trigraphs, and in this way, we could make steady progress (Figure 5).

The cluster map in Figure 4 was of great help. For example, once we established a substitution like ÿ=I, we could immediately add η=I and ι=I, because the three cipher letters behave so similarly. In this way, we mapped all circumflexed letters (â, ê, î, ô, û) to plaintext E. These leaps were frequently correct, and we soon had substitutions for over 50 cipher letters.

Despite progress, some very frequent German trigraphs like SCH were still drastically under-represented in our decipherment. Also, many cipher letters (including all unaccented Roman letters) still lacked substitution values. A fragment of the decipherment thus far looked like this (where "?" stands for an as-yet-unmapped cipher letter):

?GEHEIMER?UNTERLIST?VOR?DIE?GESELLE
?ERDER?TITUL
?CEREMONIE?DER?AUFNAHME

On the last line, we recognized the two words CEREMONIE and DER separated by a cipher letter. It became clear that *the unaccented Roman letters serve as spaces in the cipher*. Note that this is the opposite of our first decipherment approach (Section 4). The non-Roman letters are not NULLs -- they carry virtually all the information. This also explains why paragraphs start with capitalized Roman letters, which look nice, but are meaningless.

We next put our hypothesized decipherment into an automatic German-to-English translator (www.freetranslation.com), where we observed that many plaintext words were still untranslatable. For example, ABSCHNITL was not recognized as a translatable German word. The final cipher letter for this word is colon (:), which we had mapped previously to L. By replacing the final L in ABSCHNITL with various letters of the alphabet (A-Z), we hit on the recognized word

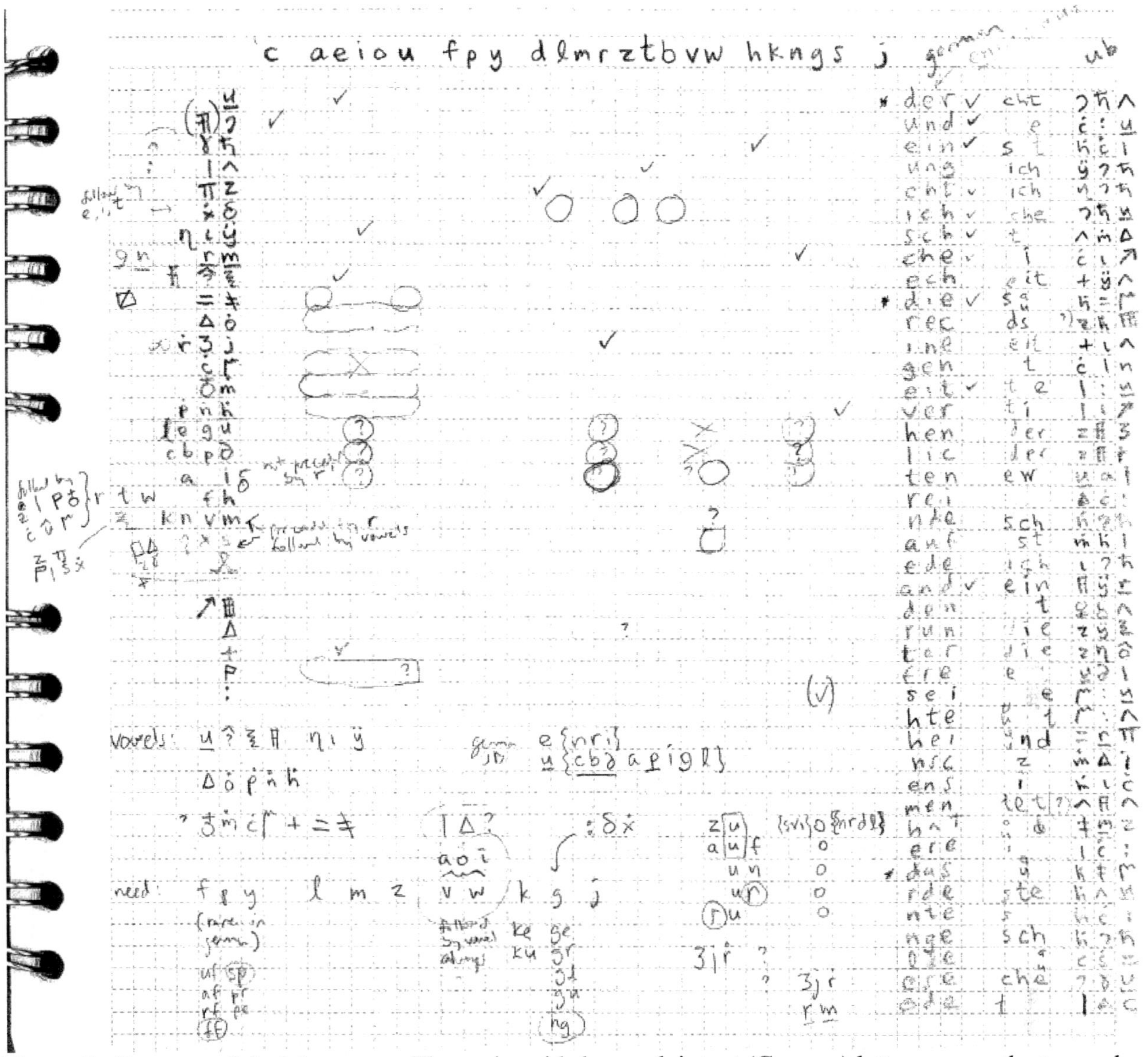

Figure 5. Progress of decipherment. The main grid shows plaintext (German) letters across the top and ciphertext letters down the left side. The ciphertext letters are grouped into clusters. To the right of the main grid are frequent German trigraphs (der, und, ein, …) and frequent cipher trigraphs (ɔħʌ, ċ:ɥ, ɦċ|, …), with the two columns being separated by hypothesized trigraph decipherments.

ABSCHNITT (translated as "section"). We then realized that the function of colon (:) is to double the previous consonant (whether it be T, L, F, or some other letter). Old German writing uses a stroke with the same function.

The cipher letter † was still unknown, appearing in partially deciphered words like †AFLNER, †NUPFTUCHS, and GESELL†AFLT. We tried substituting each of the letters A-Z for †, but this did not yield valid German. However, we found GESELLSCHAFLT in a German dictionary, so we concluded that † stands for SCH. This opened the door for other multi-plaintext-letter substitutions.

Finally, we brought full native-German expertise to bear, by taking hypothesized decipherments (hyp) and correcting them (corr):

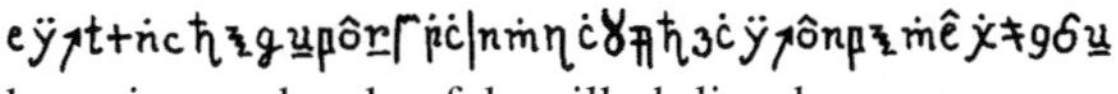

hyp: is mache ebenfals wilhuhrlise bewegunge
corr: **ich** mache ebenfals wil**kü**hrli**ch**e bewegunge**n**

hyp: dos mit der andern hand
corr: do**ch** mit der andern hand

hyp: dritlens einer n mlt tobach mit de daume
corr: drit**t**ens einer **? ???** tobach mit de**m** daum**en**

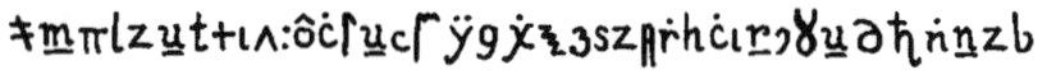

hyp: und de mitlelde finger der linche hand
corr: und de**m** mit**t**el**st**en finger der linche**n** hand

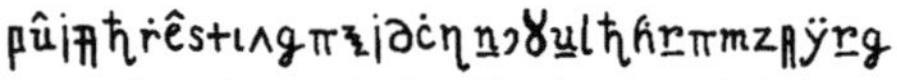

hyp: beruhre mit der linche hand dein
corr: ber**ü**hre mit der linche**n** hand dein

This allowed us to virtually complete our table of substitutions (Figure 6). Three cipher letters remained ambiguous:

- ▮ could represent either SS or S
- ɤ could represent either H or K
- u̲ could represent either EN or EM

However, these three symbols are ambiguous only with respect to deciphering into modern German, not into old German, which used different spelling conventions.

The only remaining undeciphered symbols were the large ones: ⅄, ⊙, ∆, ✗, ◇, ⚶, ⏛, and ∏. These appear to be logograms, standing for the names of (doubly secret) people and organizations, as we see in this section: "the ⅄ asks him whether he desires to be ◇".

6. Contents

The book describes the initiation of "DER CANDIDAT" into a secret society, some functions of which are encoded with logograms. Appendix A contains our decipherment of the beginning of the manuscript.

7. Conclusion

We described the Copiale cipher and its decipherment. It remains to transcribe the rest of the manuscript and to do a careful translation. The document may contain further encoded information, and given the amount of work it represents, we believe there may be other documents using the same or similar schemes.

Plaintext (German)	Ciphertext
A	ṗ ṅ ĥ ♀*
Ä	♀*
B	ꝑ
C	ɔ
D	π z
E	â ê î ô û ▯ ⱻ
F	ſ
G	6 ẋ
H	ħ ɤ*
I	ÿ η ι
J	ɟ
K	ɤ*
L	ċ
M	+
N	m̲ r̲ n̲ 9
O	Δ ȯ
Ö	⊠
P	d
R	ṙ ʒ į
S	| ▮*
T	ʌ
U	= ɟ
Ü	▯
V	ȣ
W	ṁ
X	ƒ
Y	∞
Z	ṡ
SCH	†
SS	▮*
ST	ſ
CH	↗
repeat previous consonant	:
EN / EM	u̲
space	a b c ∂ e ƒ ⱻ g h i x l m n o p q r s ſ t u v w x y z

Figure 6. Letter substitutions resulting from decipherment. Asterisks (*) indicate ambiguous cipher letters that appear twice in the chart. This table does not include the large characters: ⅄, ⊙, ∆, ✗, ◇, ⚶, ⏛, and ∏.

8. Acknowledgments

Thanks to Jonathan Graehl for plotting the cluster map of cipher letters. This work was supported in part by NSF grant 0904684.

9. References

K. Knight, A. Nair, N. Rathod, and K. Yamada, "Unsupervised Analysis for Decipherment Problems", Proc. ACL-COLING, 2006.

Appendix A

Ciphertext:

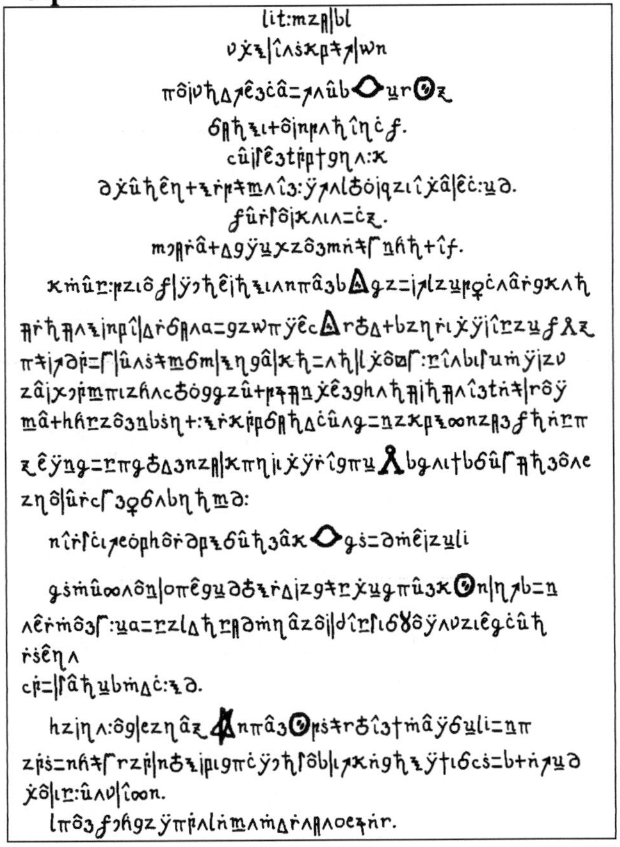

Plaintext, as deciphered:

gesetz buchs
der hocherleuchte e
geheimer theil.
erster abschnitt
geheimer unterricht vor die gesellen.
erster titul.
ceremonien der aufnahme.

wenn die sicherheit der durch den ältern thürheter besorget und die vom dirigirenden durch aufsetzung seines huths geöffnet ist wird der candidat von dem jüngern thürhüter aus einem andern zimmer abgeholet und bey der hand ein und vor des dirigirenden tisch geführet dieser frägt ihn:

erstlich ob er begehre zu werden

zweytens denen verordnungen der sich unterwerffen und ohne wiederspenstigkeit die lehrzeit ausstehen wolle.

drittens die der gu verschweigen und dazu auf das verbindlichste sich anheischig zu machen gesinnet sey.

der candidat antwortet ja.

Initial translation:

First lawbook
of the e
Secret part.
First section
Secret teachings for apprentices.
First title.
Initiation rite.

If the safety of the is guaranteed, and the is opened by the chief , by putting on his hat, the candidate is fetched from another room by the younger doorman and by the hand is led in and to the table of the chief , who asks him:

First, if he desires to become .

Secondly, if he submits to the rules of the and without rebelliousness suffer through the time of apprenticeship.

Thirdly, be silent about the of the and furthermore be willing to offer himself to volunteer in the most committed way.

The candidate answers yes.

Learning the Optimal use of Dependency-parsing Information for Finding Translations with Comparable Corpora

Daniel Andrade[†], **Takuya Matsuzaki**[†], **Jun'ichi Tsujii**[‡]
[†]Department of Computer Science, University of Tokyo
{daniel.andrade, matuzaki}@is.s.u-tokyo.ac.jp
[‡]Microsoft Research Asia, Beijing
jtsujii@microsoft.com

Abstract

Using comparable corpora to find new word translations is a promising approach for extending bilingual dictionaries (semi-) automatically. The basic idea is based on the assumption that similar words have similar contexts across languages. The context of a word is often summarized by using the bag-of-words in the sentence, or by using the words which are in a certain dependency position, e.g. the predecessors and successors. These different context positions are then combined into one context vector and compared across languages. However, previous research makes the (implicit) assumption that these different context positions should be weighted as equally important. Furthermore, only the same context positions are compared with each other, for example the successor position in Spanish is compared with the successor position in English. However, this is not necessarily always appropriate for languages like Japanese and English. To overcome these limitations, we suggest to perform a linear transformation of the context vectors, which is defined by a matrix. We define the optimal transformation matrix by using a Bayesian probabilistic model, and show that it is feasible to find an approximate solution using Markov chain Monte Carlo methods. Our experiments demonstrate that our proposed method constantly improves translation accuracy.

1 Introduction

Using comparable corpora to automatically extend bilingual dictionaries is becoming increasingly popular (Laroche and Langlais, 2010; Andrade et al., 2010; Ismail and Manandhar, 2010; Laws et al., 2010; Garera et al., 2009). The general idea is based on the assumption that similar words have similar contexts across languages. The context of a word can be described by the sentence in which it occurs (Laroche and Langlais, 2010) or a surrounding word-window (Rapp, 1999; Haghighi et al., 2008). A few previous studies, like (Garera et al., 2009), suggested to use the predecessor and successors from the dependency-parse tree, instead of a word window. In (Andrade et al., 2011), we showed that including dependency-parse tree context positions together with a sentence bag-of-words context can improve word translation accuracy. However previous works do not make an attempt to find an *optimal* combination of these different context positions.

Our study tries to find an optimal weighting and aggregation of these context positions by learning a linear transformation of the context vectors. The motivation is that different context positions might be of different importance, e.g. the direct predecessors and successors from the dependency tree might be more important than the larger context from the whole sentence. Another motivation is that dependency positions cannot be always compared across different languages, e.g. a word which tends to occur as a modifier in English, can tend to occur in Japanese in a different dependency position.

As a solution, we propose to learn the optimal combination of dependency and bag-of-words sentence information. Our approach uses a linear transformation of the context vectors, before comparing

Proceedings of the 4th Workshop on Building and Using Comparable Corpora, pages 10–18,
49th Annual Meeting of the Association for Computational Linguistics,
Portland, Oregon, 24 June 2011. ©*2011 Association for Computational Linguistics*

them using the cosine similarity. This can be considered as a generalization of the cosine similarity. We define the optimal transformation matrix by the maximum-a-posterior (MAP) solution of a Bayesian probabilistic model. The likelihood function for a translation matrix is defined by considering the expected achieved translation accuracy. As a prior, we use a Dirichlet distribution over the diagonal elements in the matrix and a uniform distribution over its non-diagonal elements. We show that it is feasible to find an approximation of the optimal solution using Markov chain Monte Carlo (MCMC) methods. In our experiments, we compare the proposed method, which uses this approximation, with the baseline method which uses the cosine similarity without any linear transformation. Our experiments show that the translation accuracy is constantly improved by the proposed method.

In the next section, we briefly summarize the most relevant previous work. In Section 3, we then explain the baseline method which is based on previous research. Section 4 explains in detail our proposed method, followed by Section 5 which provides an empirical comparison to the baseline, and analysis. We summarize our findings in Section 6.

2 Previous Work

Using comparable corpora to find new translations was pioneered in (Rapp, 1999; Fung, 1998). The basic idea for finding a translation for a word q (query), is to measure the context of q and then to compare the context with each possible translation candidate, using an existing dictionary. We will call words for which we have a translation in the given dictionary, *pivot* words. First, using the source corpus, they calculate the degree of association of a query word q with all pivot words. The degree of association is a measure which is based on the co-occurrence frequency of q and the pivot word in a certain context position. A context (position) can be a word-window (Rapp, 1999), sentence (Utsuro et al., 2003), or a certain position in the dependency-parse tree (Garera et al., 2009; Andrade et al., 2011). In this way, they get a context vector for q, which contains the degree of association to the pivot words in different context positions. Using the target corpus, they then calculate a context vector for each possible translation candidate x, in the same way. Finally, they compare the context vector of q with the context vector of each candidate x, and retrieve a ranked list of possible translation candidates. In the next section, we explain the baseline which is based on that previous research.

The general idea of *learning* an appropriate method to compare high-dimensional vectors is not new. Related research is often called "metric-learning", see for example (Xing et al., 2003; Basu et al., 2004). However, for our objective function it is difficult to find an analytic solution. To our knowledge, the idea of parameterizing the transformation matrix, in the way we suggest in Section 4, and to learn an approximate solution with a fast sampling strategy is new.

3 Baseline

Our baseline measures the degree of association between the query word q and each pivot word with respect to several context positions. As a context position we consider the predecessors, successors, siblings with respect to the dependency parse tree, and the whole sentence (bag-of-words). The dependency information which is used is also illustrated in Figure 1. As a measure of the degree of association we use the Log-odds-ratio as proposed in (Laroche and Langlais, 2010).

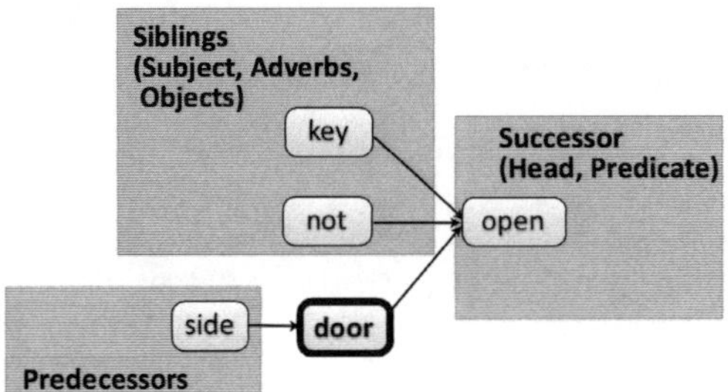

Figure 1: Example of the dependency information used by our approach. Here, from the perspective of "door".

Next, we define the context vector which contains the degree of association between the query and each pivot in several context positions. First, for each context position i we define a vector $\mathbf{q_i}$ which contains the degree of association with each pivot word in the context position i. If we number the pivot words from 1 to n, then this vector can be written as $\mathbf{q_i} = (q_i^1, \ldots, q_i^n)$. Note that in our case i ranges from 1 to 4, representing the context positions predecessors (1), successors (2), siblings (3), and the sentence bag-of-words (4). Finally, the complete context vector for the query q is a long vector $\mathbf{q}$ which appends each $\mathbf{q_i}$, i.e.: $\mathbf{q} = (\mathbf{q_1}, \ldots, \mathbf{q_4})$. Next, in the same way as before, we create a context vector $\mathbf{x}$ for each translation candidate x in the target language. For simplicity, we assume that each pivot word in the source language has only one corresponding translation in the target language. As a consequence, the dimensions of $\mathbf{q}$ and $\mathbf{x}$ are the same. Finally we can score each translation candidate by using the cosine similarity between $\mathbf{q}$ and $\mathbf{x}$.

We claim that all of the context positions (1 to 4) can contain information which is helpful to identify translation candidates. However, we do not know about their relative importance, neither do we know whether these dependency positions can be compared across language pairs as different as Japanese and English. The cosine similarity simply weights all dependency position equally important and ignores problems which might occur when comparing dependency positions across languages.

4 Proposed Method

Our proposed method tries to overcome the shortcomings of the cosine-similarity by using the following generalization:

$$sim(\mathbf{q}, \mathbf{x}) = \frac{\mathbf{q}\mathbf{A}\mathbf{x}^T}{\sqrt{\mathbf{q}\mathbf{A}\mathbf{q}^T}\sqrt{\mathbf{x}\mathbf{A}\mathbf{x}^T}}, \quad (1)$$

where A is a positive-definite matrix in $\mathbb{R}^{dn \times dn}$, and ^{T} is the transpose of a vector. This can also be considered as linear transformation of the vectors using $\sqrt{\mathbf{A}}$ before using the normal cosine similarity, see also (Basu et al., 2004).[1]

The challenge is to find an appropriate matrix A which is expected to take the correlations between the different dimensions into account, and which optimally weights the different dimensions. Note that, if we set A to the identity matrix, we recover the normal cosine similarity, which is our baseline.

Clearly, finding an optimal matrix in $\mathbb{R}^{dn \times dn}$ is infeasible due to the high dimensionality. We will therefore restrict the structure of A.

Let $\mathbf{I}$ be the identity matrix in $\mathbb{R}^{n \times n}$, then we define the matrix A, as follows:

$$\mathbf{A} = \begin{pmatrix} d_1\mathbf{I} & z_{1,2}\mathbf{I} & z_{1,3}\mathbf{I} & z_{1,4}\mathbf{I} \\ z_{1,2}\mathbf{I} & d_2\mathbf{I} & z_{2,3}\mathbf{I} & z_{2,4}\mathbf{I} \\ z_{1,3}\mathbf{I} & z_{2,3}\mathbf{I} & d_3\mathbf{I} & z_{3,4}\mathbf{I} \\ z_{1,4}\mathbf{I} & z_{2,4}\mathbf{I} & z_{3,4}\mathbf{I} & d_4\mathbf{I} \end{pmatrix}$$

It is clear from this definition that $d_1, \ldots, d_4$ weights the context positions 1 to 4. Furthermore, $z_{i,j}$ can be interpreted as a the confusion coefficient between context position i and j. For example, a high value for $z_{2,3}$ means that a pivot word which occurs in the sibling position in Japanese (source language), might not necessarily occur in the sibling position in English (target language), but instead in the successor position. However, in order to reduce the dimensionality of the parameter space further, we assume that each such $z_{i,j}$ has the same value z. Therefore, matrix A becomes

$$\mathbf{A} = \begin{pmatrix} d_1\mathbf{I} & z\mathbf{I} & z\mathbf{I} & z\mathbf{I} \\ z\mathbf{I} & d_2\mathbf{I} & z\mathbf{I} & z\mathbf{I} \\ z\mathbf{I} & z\mathbf{I} & d_3\mathbf{I} & z\mathbf{I} \\ z\mathbf{I} & z\mathbf{I} & z\mathbf{I} & d_4\mathbf{I} \end{pmatrix}.$$

In the next subsection we will explain how we define an optimal solution for A.

4.1 Optimal solution for A

We use a Bayesian probabilistic model in order to define the optimal solution for A. Formally we try to find the maximum-a-posterior (MAP) solution of A, i.e.:

$$\arg\max_A p(A|data, \alpha). \quad (2)$$

The posterior probability is defined by

$$p(A|data, \alpha) \propto f_{auc}(data|A) \cdot p(A|\alpha). \quad (3)$$

$f_{auc}(data|A)$ is the (unnormalized) likelihood function. $p(A|\alpha)$ is the prior that captures our prior beliefs about A, and which is parameterized by a hyperparameter α.

[1]Therefore, exactly speaking A is not the transformation matrix, however it defines uniquely the transformation matrix $\sqrt{\mathbf{A}}$.

4.1.1 The likelihood function $f_{auc}(data|A)$

As a likelihood function we use a modification of the area under the curve (AUC) of the accuracy-vs-rank graph. The accuracy-vs-rank graph shows the translation accuracy at different ranks. $data$ refers to the part of the gold-standard which is used for training. Our complete gold-standard contains 443 domain-specific Japanese nouns (query words). Each Japanese noun in the gold standard corresponds to one pair of the form <Japanese noun (query), English translations (answers)>. We denote the accuracy at rank r, by acc_r. The accuracy acc_r is determined by counting how often the correct answer is listed in the top r translation candidates suggested for a query, divided by the number of all queries in $data$. The likelihood function is now defined as follows:

$$f_{auc}(data|A) = \sum_{r=1}^{20} acc_r \cdot (21 - r)\,. \qquad (4)$$

That means $f_{auc}(data|A)$ accumulates the accuracies at the ranks from 1 to 20, where we weight accuracies at top ranks higher.

4.1.2 The prior $p(A|\alpha)$

The prior over the transformation matrix is factorized in the following manner:

$$p(A|\alpha) = p(z|d_1, \ldots, d_4) \cdot p(d_1, \ldots, d_4|\alpha)\,.$$

The prior over the diagonal is defined as a Dirichlet distribution:

$$p(d_1, \ldots, d_4|\alpha) = \frac{1}{B(\alpha)} \prod_{i=1}^{4} d_i^{\alpha-1}$$

where α is the concentration parameter of the symmetric Dirichlet, and $B(\alpha)$ is the normalization constant. The prior over the non-diagonal value a is defined as:

$$p(z|d_1, \ldots, d_4) = \frac{1}{\lambda} \cdot 1_{[0,\lambda]}(z) \qquad (5)$$

where $\lambda = min\{d_1, \ldots, d_4\}$.

First, note that our prior limits the possible matrices A to matrices which have diagonal entries which are between 0 and 1. This is not a restriction since the ranking of the translation candidates induced by the parameterized cosine similarity will not change if A is multiplied by a constant $c > 0$. To see this, note that

$$sim(\mathbf{q}, \mathbf{x}) = \frac{\mathbf{q}(c \cdot \mathbf{A})\mathbf{x}}{\sqrt{\mathbf{q}(c \cdot \mathbf{A})\mathbf{q}}\sqrt{\mathbf{x}(c \cdot \mathbf{A})\mathbf{x}}}$$
$$= \frac{\mathbf{qAx}}{\sqrt{\mathbf{qAq}}\sqrt{\mathbf{xAx}}}\,.$$

Second, note that our prior limits A further, by requiring, in Equation (5), that every non-diagonal element is smaller or equal than any diagonal element. That requirement is sensible since we do not expect that a optimal similarity measure between English and Japanese will prefer context which is similar in *different* dependency positions, over context which is similar in the *same* context positions. To see this, imagine the extreme case where for example d_1 is 0, and instead z_{12} is 1. In that case the similarity measure would ignore any similarity in the predecessor position, but would instead compare the predecessors in Japanese with the successors in English.

Finally, note that our prior puts probability mass over a subset of the *positive-definite* matrices in $\mathbb{R}^{4\times4}$, and puts no probability mass on matrices which are not positive-definite. As a consequence, the similarity measure in Equation (1) is ensured to be well-defined.

4.2 Training

In the following we explain how we use the training data in order to find a good solution for the matrix A.

4.2.1 Setting hyperparameter α

Recall, that α weights our prior belief about how strong we think that the different context positions should be weighted equally. From a practical point-of-view, we do not know how strong we should weight that prior belief. We therefore use empirical Bayes to estimate α, that is we use part of the training data to set α. First, using half of the training set, we find the A which maximizes $p(A|data, \alpha)$ for several α. Then, the remaining half of the training set is used to evaluate $f_{auc}(data|A)$ to find the best α. Note that the prior $p(A|\alpha)$ can also be considered as a regularization to prevent overfitting. In the next sub-section we will explain how to find an approximation of A which maximizes $p(A|data, \alpha)$.

4.2.2 Finding a MAP solution for A

Recall that matrix A is defined by using only five parameters. Since the problem is low-dimensional, we can therefore expect to find a reasonable solution using sampling methods. For finding an approximation of the maximum-a-posteriori (MAP) solution of $p(A|data, \alpha)$, we use the following Markov chain Monte Carlo procedure:

1. Initialize $d_1, \ldots, d_4$ and z.

2. Leave z constant, and run Simulated-Annealing to find the $d_1, \ldots, d_4$ which maximize $p(A|data, \alpha)$.

3. Given $d_1, \ldots, d_4$, sample from the uniform distribution $[1, \min(d_1, \ldots d_4)]$ in order to find the z which maximizes $p(A|data, \alpha)$.

The steps 2. and 3. are repeated till the convergence of the parameters.

Concerning step 2., we use Simulated-Annealing for finding a (local) maximum of $p(d_1, \ldots, d_4|data, \alpha)$ with the following settings: As a jumping distribution we use a Dirichlet distribution which we update every 1000 iterations. The cooling rate is set to $\frac{1}{iteration}$.

For step 2. and 3. it is of utmost importance to be able to evaluate $p(A|data, \alpha)$ fast. The computationally expensive part of $p(A|data, \alpha)$ is to evaluate $f_{auc}(data|A)$. In order to quickly evaluate $f_{auc}(data|A)$, we need to pre-calculate part of $sim(q, x)$ for all queries q and all translation candidates x. To illustrate the basic idea, consider $sim(q, x)$ without the normalization of $\mathbf{q}$ and $\mathbf{x}$ with respect to A, i.e.:

$$sim(q, x) = \mathbf{q}\mathbf{A}\mathbf{x}^T = (\mathbf{q}_1, \ldots, \mathbf{q}_4)\mathbf{A}(\mathbf{x}_1, \ldots, \mathbf{x}_4)^T .$$

Let us denote $\mathbf{I}_{dn}^-$ a block matrix in $\mathbb{R}^{dn \times dn}$ which contains in each $n \times n$ block the identity matrix except in its diagonal; the diagonal of $\mathbf{I}_{dn}^-$ contains the $n \times n$ matrix which is zero in all entries. We can now rewrite matrix A as:

$$A = \begin{pmatrix} d_1\mathbf{I} & \mathbf{0} & \mathbf{0} & \mathbf{0} \\ \mathbf{0} & d_2\mathbf{I} & \mathbf{0} & \mathbf{0} \\ \mathbf{0} & \mathbf{0} & d_3\mathbf{I} & \mathbf{0} \\ \mathbf{0} & \mathbf{0} & \mathbf{0} & d_4\mathbf{I} \end{pmatrix} + z \cdot \mathbf{I}_{dn}^- .$$

And finally we can factor out the parameters $(d_1, \ldots d_4)$ and z in the following way:

$$sim(q, x) = (d_1, \ldots, d_4) \cdot \begin{pmatrix} \mathbf{q}_1\mathbf{x}_1^T \\ \vdots \\ \mathbf{q}_4\mathbf{x}_4^T \end{pmatrix} + z \cdot (\mathbf{q}\mathbf{I}_{dn}^- \mathbf{x}^T)$$

By pre-calculating $\begin{pmatrix} \mathbf{q}_1\mathbf{x}_1^T \\ \vdots \\ \mathbf{q}_4\mathbf{x}_4^T \end{pmatrix}$ and $\mathbf{q}\mathbf{I}_{dn}^- \mathbf{x}^T$, we can make the evaluation of each sample, in steps 2. and 3., computationally feasible.

5 Experiments

In the experiments of the present study, we used a collection of complaints concerning automobiles compiled by the Japanese Ministry of Land, Infrastructure, Transport and Tourism (MLIT)[2] and another collection of complaints concerning automobiles compiled by the USA National Highway Traffic Safety Administration (NHTSA)[3]. Both corpora are publicly available. The corpora are non-parallel, but are comparable in terms of content. The part of MLIT and NHTSA which we used for our experiments, contains 24090 and 47613 sentences, respectively. The Japanese MLIT corpus was morphologically analyzed and dependency parsed using Juman and KNP[4]. The English corpus NHTSA was POS-tagged and stemmed with Stepp Tagger (Tsuruoka et al., 2005; Okazaki et al., 2008) and dependency parsed using the MST parser (McDonald et al., 2005). Using the Japanese-English dictionary JMDic[5], we found 1796 content words in Japanese which have a translation which is in the English corpus. These content words and their translations correspond to our pivot words in Japanese and English, respectively.[6]

[2]http://www.mlit.go.jp/jidosha/carinf/rcl/defects.html

[3]http://www-odi.nhtsa.dot.gov/downloads/index.cfm

[4]http://www-lab25.kuee.kyoto-u.ac.jp/nl-resource/juman.html and http://www-lab25.kuee.kyoto-u.ac.jp/nl-resource/knp.html

[5]http://www.csse.monash.edu.au/ jwb/edict_doc.html

[6]Recall that we assume a one-to-one correspondence between a pivot in Japanese and English. If a Japanese pivot word as more than one English translation, we select the translation for which the relative frequency in the target corpus is closest to the pivot in the source corpus.

5.1 Evaluation

For the evaluation we extract a gold-standard which contains Japanese and English noun pairs that actually occur in both corpora.[7] The gold-standard is created with the help of the JMDic dictionary, whereas we correct apparently inappropriate translations, and remove general nouns such as 可能性 (possibility) and ambiguous words such as 米 (rice, America). In this way, we obtain a final list of 443 domain-specific Japanese nouns.

Each Japanese noun in the gold-standard corresponds to one pair of the form <Japanese noun (query), English translations (answers)>. We divide the gold-standard into two halves. The first half is used for for learning the matrix A, the second part is used for the evaluation. In general, we expect that the optimal transformation matrix A depends mainly on the languages (Japanese and English) and on the corpora (MLIT and NHTSA). However, in practice, the optimal matrix can also vary depending on the part of the gold-standard which is used for training. These random variations are especially large, if the part of the gold-standard which is used for training or testing is small.

In order to take these random effects into account, we perform repeated subsampling of the gold-standard. In detail, we randomly split the gold-standard into equally-sized training and test set. This is repeated five times, leading to five training and five test sets. The performance on each test set is shown in Table 1. OPTIMIZED-ALL marks the result of our proposed method, where matrix A is optimized using the training set. The optimization of the diagonal elements $d_1, \ldots, d_4$, and the non-diagonal value z is as described in Section 4.2. Finally, the baseline method, as described in 3, corresponds to OPTIMIZED-ALL where $d_1, \ldots, d_4$ are set to 1, and z is set to 0. This baseline is denoted as NORMAL. We can see that the overall translation accuracy varies across the test sets. However, we see that in all test sets our proposed method OPTIMIZED-ALL performs better than the baseline NORMAL.

[7] Note that if the current query (Japanese noun) is a pivot word, then the word is not considered as a pivot word.

5.2 Analysis

In the previous section, we showed that the cosine-similarity is sub-optimal for comparing context vectors which contain information from different context positions. We showed that it is possible to find an approximation of a matrix A which optimally weights, and combines the different context positions. Recall, that the matrix A is described by the parameters $d_1 \ldots d_4$ and z, which can interpreted as context position weights and a confusion coefficient, respectively. Therefore, by looking at these parameters which we learned using each training set, we can get some interesting insights. Table 2 shows theses parameters learned for each training set.

We can see that the parameters, across the training sets, are not as stable as we wish. For example the weight for the predecessor position ranges from 0.27 to 0.44. As a consequence, the average values, shown in the last row of Table 2, have to be interpreted with care. We expect that the variance is due to the limited size of the training set, 220 <query, answers> pairs.

Nevertheless, we can draw some conclusions with confidence. For example, we see that the predecessor and successor positions are the most important contexts, since the weights for both are always higher than for the other context positions. Furthermore, we clearly see that the sibling and sentence (bag-of-words) contexts, although not as highly weighted as the former two, can be considered to be relevant, since each has a weight of around 0.20. Finally, we see that z, the confusion coefficient, is around 0.03, which is small.[8] Therefore, we verify z's usefulness with another experiment. We additionally define the method OPTIMIZED-DIAG which uses the same matrix as OPTIMIZED-ALL except that the confusion coefficient z is set to zero. In Table 1, we can see that the accuracy of OPTIMIZED-DIAG is constantly lower than OPTIMIZED-ALL.

Furthermore, we are interested in the role of the whole sentence (bag-of-words) information which is in the context vector (in position d_4 of the block vector). Therefore, we excluded the sentence informa-

[8] In other words, z is around 17% of its maximal possible value. The maximal possible value is around 0.18, since, recall that z is, by definition, smaller or equal to $\min\{d_1 \ldots d_4\}$.

Test Set	Method	Top-1 Accuracy	Top-5 Accuracy	Top-10 Accuracy	Top-15 Accuracy	Top-20 Accuracy
1	OPTIMIZED-ALL	**0.20**	**0.37**	**0.47**	**0.50**	**0.54**
	OPTIMIZED-DIAG	**0.20**	0.34	0.43	0.48	0.51
	NORMAL	0.18	0.32	0.43	0.47	0.50
2	OPTIMIZED-ALL	**0.20**	**0.35**	**0.43**	**0.48**	**0.52**
	OPTIMIZED-DIAG	0.19	0.33	0.42	0.46	**0.52**
	NORMAL	0.18	0.34	0.42	0.47	0.49
3	OPTIMIZED-ALL	**0.17**	**0.31**	**0.37**	**0.44**	**0.48**
	OPTIMIZED-DIAG	**0.17**	0.27	0.36	0.41	0.45
	NORMAL	0.16	0.27	0.36	0.41	0.44
4	OPTIMIZED-ALL	0.14	**0.30**	**0.38**	**0.43**	**0.46**
	OPTIMIZED-DIAG	0.14	0.26	0.34	0.4	0.43
	NORMAL	**0.15**	0.29	0.37	0.41	0.44
5	OPTIMIZED-ALL	0.18	**0.34**	**0.42**	**0.46**	**0.51**
	OPTIMIZED-DIAG	0.17	0.30	0.38	0.43	0.48
	NORMAL	**0.19**	0.31	0.40	0.44	0.48
average	OPTIMIZED-ALL	**0.18**	**0.33**	**0.41**	**0.46**	**0.50**
	OPTIMIZED-DIAG	0.17	0.30	0.39	0.44	0.48
	NORMAL	0.17	0.31	0.40	0.44	0.47

Table 1: Shows the accuracy at different ranks for all test sets, and, in the last column, the average over all test sets. The proposed method OPTIMIZED-ALL is compared to the baseline NORMAL. Furthermore, for analysis, the results when optimizing only the diagonal are marked as OPTIMIZED-DIAG.

Training Set	d_1 predecessor	d_2 successor	d_3 sibling	d_4 sentence	z confusion coefficient
1	0.35	0.26	0.19	0.20	0.03
2	0.27	0.29	0.21	0.23	0.03
3	0.35	0.31	0.16	0.18	0.02
4	0.44	0.24	0.17	0.16	0.04
5	0.39	0.28	0.20	0.13	0.03
average	0.36	0.28	0.19	0.18	0.03

Table 2: Shows the parameters which were learned using each training set. $d_1 \ldots d_4$ are the weights of the context positions, which sum up to 1. z marks the degree to which it is useful to compare context across different positions.

tion from the context vector. The accuracy results, averaged over the same test sets as before, are shown in Table 3. We can see that the accuracies are clearly lower than before (compare to Table 1). This clearly justifies to include additionally sentence information into the context vector. It is also interesting to note that the average z value is now 0.14.[9] This is considerable higher than before, and shows that a bag-of-words model can partly make the use of z redundant. However, note that the sentence bag-of-words model covers a broader context, beyond the direct predecessors, successor and siblings, which explains why a small z value is still relevant in the situation where we include sentence bag-of-words into the context vector.

Finally, to see why it can be helpful to compare *different* dependency positions from the context vectors of Japanese and English, we looked at concrete examples. We found, for example, that the translation accuracy of the query word ディスク (disc) improved when using OPTIMIZED-ALL instead of OPTIMIZED-DIAG. The pivot word 歪み (wrap) tends together with both the Japanese query ディスク (disc), and with the correct translation "disc" in English. However, that pivot word occurs in Japanese and English in different context positions. In the Japanese corpus 歪み (wrap) tends to occur

[9] That is 48% of its maximal possible value. Since for the dependency positions predecessor, successor and sibling we get the average weights 0.38, 0.33 and 0.29, respectively.

Method	Top-1	Top-5	Top-10	Top-15	Top-20
OPT-DEP	**0.13**	**0.25**	**0.34**	**0.38**	**0.41**
NOR-DEP	0.12	0.23	0.29	0.33	0.38

Table 3: The proposed method, but without the sentence information in the context vector, is denoted OPT-DEP. The baseline method, but without the sentence information in the context vector, is denoted NOR-DEP.

together with the query ディスク (disc) in sentences like for example the following:

"ブレーキ (break) **ディスク (disc)** に歪み (wrap) が生じた (occured)。"

That Japanese sentence can be literally translated as "A wrap occured in the brake disc.", where "wrap" is the sibling of "disc" in the dependency tree. However, in English, considered out of the perspective of "disc", the pivot word "wrap" tends to occur in a different dependency position. For example, the following sentence can be found in the English corpus:

"Front **disc wraps**."

In English "wrap" tends to occur as a successor of "disc". A non-zero confusion coefficient allows us to account some degree of similarity to situations where the query (here "ディスク"(disc)) and the translation candidate (here "disc") tend to occur with the same pivot word (here "wrap"), but in different dependency positions.

6 Conclusions

Finding new translations of single words using comparable corpora is a promising method, for example, to assist the creation and extension of bilingual dictionaries. The basic idea is to first create context vectors of the query word, and all the candidate translations, and then, in the second step, to compare these context vectors. Previous work (Laroche and Langlais, 2010; Fung, 1998; Garera et al., 2009) suggests that for this task the cosine-similarity is a good choice to compare context vectors. For example, Garera et al. (2009) include the information of various context positions from the dependency-parse tree in one context vector, and, afterwards, compares these context vectors using the cosine-similarity. However, this makes the implicit assumption that all context positions are equally important, and, furthermore, that context from *different* context positions does not need to be compared with each other. To overcome these limitations, we suggested to use a generalization of the cosine similarity which performs a linear transformation of the context vectors, before applying the cosine similarity. The linear transformation can be described by a positive-definite matrix A. We defined the optimal matrix A by using a Bayesian probabilistic model. We demonstrated that it is feasible to approximate the optimal matrix A by using MCMC-methods.

Our experimental results suggest that it is beneficial to weight context positions individually. For example, we found that predecessor and successor should be stronger weighted than sibling, and sentence information. Whereas, the latter two are also important, having a total weight of around 40%. Furthermore, we showed that for languages as different as Japanese and English it can be helpful to compare also *different* context positions across both languages. The proposed method constantly outperformed the baseline method. Top 1 accuracy increased by up to 2% percent points and Top 20 by up to 4% percent points.

For future work, we consider to use different parameterizations of the matrix A which could lead to even higher improvement in accuracy. Furthermore, we consider to include, and weight additional features like transliteration similarity.

Acknowledgment

We would like to thank the anonymous reviewers for their helpful comments. This work was partially supported by Grant-in-Aid for Specially Promoted Research (MEXT, Japan). The first author is supported by the MEXT Scholarship and by an IBM PhD Scholarship Award.

References

D. Andrade, T. Nasukawa, and J. Tsujii. 2010. Robust measurement and comparison of context similarity for finding translation pairs. In *Proceedings of the International Conference on Computational Linguistics*, pages 19–27.

D. Andrade, T. Matsuzaki, and J. Tsujii. 2011. Effective use of dependency structure for bilingual lexicon creation. In *Proceedings of the International Conference on Computational Linguistics and Intelligent Text Processing*, Lecture Notes in Computer Science, pages 80–92. Springer Verlag.

S. Basu, M. Bilenko, and R.J. Mooney. 2004. A probabilistic framework for semi-supervised clustering. In *Proceedings of the ACM SIGKDD International Conference on Knowledge Discovery and Data Mining*, pages 59–68.

P. Fung. 1998. A statistical view on bilingual lexicon extraction: from parallel corpora to non-parallel corpora. *Lecture Notes in Computer Science*, 1529:1–17.

N. Garera, C. Callison-Burch, and D. Yarowsky. 2009. Improving translation lexicon induction from monolingual corpora via dependency contexts and part-of-speech equivalences. In *Proceedings of the Conference on Computational Natural Language Learning*, pages 129–137. Association for Computational Linguistics.

A. Haghighi, P. Liang, T. Berg-Kirkpatrick, and D. Klein. 2008. Learning bilingual lexicons from monolingual corpora. In *Proceedings of the Annual Meeting of the Association for Computational Linguistics*, pages 771–779. Association for Computational Linguistics.

A. Ismail and S. Manandhar. 2010. Bilingual lexicon extraction from comparable corpora using in-domain terms. In *Proceedings of the International Conference on Computational Linguistics*, pages 481 – 489.

A. Laroche and P. Langlais. 2010. Revisiting context-based projection methods for term-translation spotting in comparable corpora. In *Proceedings of the International Conference on Computational Linguistics*, pages 617 – 625.

F. Laws, L. Michelbacher, B. Dorow, C. Scheible, U. Heid, and H. Schütze. 2010. A linguistically grounded graph model for bilingual lexicon extraction. In *Proceedings of the International Conference on Computational Linguistics*, pages 614–622. International Committee on Computational Linguistics.

R. McDonald, K. Crammer, and F. Pereira. 2005. Online large-margin training of dependency parsers. In *Proceedings of the Annual Meeting of the Association for Computational Linguistics*, pages 91–98. Association for Computational Linguistics.

N. Okazaki, Y. Tsuruoka, S. Ananiadou, and J. Tsujii. 2008. A discriminative candidate generator for string transformations. In *Proceedings of the Conference on Empirical Methods in Natural Language Processing*, pages 447–456. Association for Computational Linguistics.

R. Rapp. 1999. Automatic identification of word translations from unrelated English and German corpora. In *Proceedings of the Annual Meeting of the Association for Computational Linguistics*, pages 519–526. Association for Computational Linguistics.

Y. Tsuruoka, Y. Tateishi, J. Kim, T. Ohta, J. McNaught, S. Ananiadou, and J. Tsujii. 2005. Developing a robust part-of-speech tagger for biomedical text. *Lecture Notes in Computer Science*, 3746:382–392.

T. Utsuro, T. Horiuchi, K. Hino, T. Hamamoto, and T. Nakayama. 2003. Effect of cross-language IR in bilingual lexicon acquisition from comparable corpora. In *Proceedings of the conference on European chapter of the Association for Computational Linguistics*, pages 355–362. Association for Computational Linguistics.

E.P. Xing, A.Y. Ng, M.I. Jordan, and S. Russell. 2003. Distance metric learning with application to clustering with side-information. *Advances in Neural Information Processing Systems*, pages 521–528.

Building and using comparable corpora for domain-specific bilingual lexicon extraction

Darja Fišer
University of Ljubljana, Faculty of Arts,
Deparment of Translation
Aškerčeva 2
Ljubljana, Slovenia
darja.fiser@ff.uni-lj.si

Nikola Ljubešić
University of Zagreb, Faculty of Humanities
and Social Sciences
Ivana Lučića 3
Zagreb, Croatia
nikola.ljubesic@ffzg.hr

Špela Vintar
University of Ljubljana, Faculty of Arts,
Deparment of Translation
Aškerčeva 2
Ljubljana, Slovenia
spela.vintar@ff.uni-lj.si

Senja Pollak
University of Ljubljana, Faculty of Arts,
Deparment of Translation
Aškerčeva 2
Ljubljana, Slovenia
senja.pollak@ff.uni-lj.si

Abstract

This paper presents a series of experiments aimed at inducing and evaluating domain-specific bilingual lexica from comparable corpora. First, a small English-Slovene comparable corpus from health magazines was manually constructed and then used to compile a large comparable corpus on health-related topics from web corpora. Next, a bilingual lexicon for the domain was extracted from the corpus by comparing context vectors in the two languages. Evaluation of the results shows that a 2-way translation of context vectors significantly improves precision of the extracted translation equivalents. We also show that it is sufficient to increase the corpus for one language in order to obtain a higher recall, and that the increase of the number of new words is linear in the size of the corpus. Finally, we demonstrate that by lowering the frequency threshold for context vectors, the drop in precision is much slower than the increase of recall.

1 Introduction

Research into using comparable corpora in NLP has gained momentum in the past decade largely due to limited availability of parallel data for many language pairs and domains. As an alternative to already established parallel approaches (e.g. Och 2000, Tiedemann 2005) the comparable corpus-based approach relies on texts in two or more languages which are not parallel but nevertheless share several parameters, such as topic, time of publication and communicative goal (Fung 1998, Rapp 1999). The main advantage of this approach is the simpler, faster and more time efficient compilation of comparable corpora, especially from the rich web data (Xiao & McEnery 2006).

In this paper we describe the compilation process of a large comparable corpus of texts on health-related topics for Slovene and English that were published on the web. Then we report on a set of experiments we conducted in order to automatically extract translation equivalents for terms from the health domain. The parameters we tested and analysed are: 1- and 2-way translations of context vectors with a seed lexicon, the size of the corpus used for bilingual lexicon extraction, and the word frequency threshold for vector construction. The main contribution of this paper is a much-desired language- and domain-independent approach to bootstrapping bilingual lexica with minimal manual intervention as well as minimal reliance on the existing linguistic resources.

The paper is structured as follows: in the next section we give an overview of previous work relevant for our research. In Section 3 we present the construction of the corpus. Section 4 describes

Proceedings of the 4th Workshop on Building and Using Comparable Corpora, pages 19–26,
49th Annual Meeting of the Association for Computational Linguistics,
Portland, Oregon, 24 June 2011.

the experiments for bilingual lexicon extraction the results of which are reported, evaluated and discussed in Section 5. We conclude the paper with final remarks and ideas for future work.

2 Related work

Bilingual lexica are the key component of all cross-lingual NLP applications and their compilation remains a major bottleneck in computational linguistics. In this paper we follow the line of research that was inspired by Fung (1998) and Rapp (1999) who showed that texts do not need to be parallel in order to extract translation equivalents from them. Instead, their main assumption is that the term and its translation appear in similar contexts anyhow. The task of finding the appropriate translation equivalent of a term is therefore reduced to finding the word in the target language whose context vector is most similar to the source term's context vector based on their occurrence in a comparable corpus. This is basically a three-step procedure:

(1) Building context vectors. When representing a word's context, some approaches look at a simple co-occurrence window of a certain size while others include some syntactic information as well. For example, Otero (2007) proposes binary dependences previously extracted from a parallel corpus, while Yu and Tsujii (2009) use dependency parsers and Marsi and Krahmer (2010) use syntactic trees. Instead of context windows, Shao and Ng (2004) use language models. Next, words in co-occurrence vectors can be represented as binary features, by term frequency or weighted by different association measures, such as TF-IDF (Fung, 1998), PMI (Shezaf and Rappoport, 2010) or, one of the most popular, the log likelihood score. Approaches also exist that weigh co-occurrence terms differently if they appear closer to or further from the nucleus word in the context (e.g. Saralegi et al., 2008).
(2) Translating context vectors. Finding the most similar context vectors in the source and target language is not straightforward because a direct comparison of vectors in two different languages is not possible. This is why most researchers first translate features of source context vectors with machine-readable dictionaries and compute similarity measures on those. Koehn and Knight (2002) construct the seed dictionary automatically based on identical spelled words in the two languages. Similarly, cognate detection is used by Saralegi et al. (2008) by computing the longest common subsequence ratio. Déjean et al. (2005), on the other hand, use a bilingual thesaurus instead of a bilingual dictionary.
(3) Selecting translation candidates. After source context vectors have been translated, they are ready to be compared to the target context vectors. A number of different vector similarity measures have been investigated. Rapp (1999) applies city-block metric, while Fung (1998) works with cosine similarity. Recent work often uses Jaccard index or Dice coefficient (Saralegi et al., 2008). In addition, some approaches include a subsequent re-ranking of translation candidates based on cognates detection (e.g. Shao and Ng, 2004).

3 Corpus construction

A common scenario in the NLP community is a project on a specific language pair in a new domain for which no ready-made resources are available. This is why we propose an approach that takes advantage of the existing general resources, which are then fine-tuned and enriched to be better suited for the task at hand. In this section we describe the construction of a domain-specific corpus that we use for extraction of translation equivalents in the second part of the paper.

3.1 Initial corpus

We start with a small part of the Slovene PoS tagged and lemmatized reference corpus FidaPLUS (Arhar et al., 2007) that contains collections of articles from the monthly health and lifestyle magazine called *Zdravje*[1], which were published between 2003 and 2005 and contain 1 million words.
We collected the same amount of text from the most recent issues of the Health Magazine, which is a similar magazine for the English-speaking readers. We PoS-tagged and lemmatized the English part of the corpus with the TreeTagger (Schmid, 1994).

[1] http://www.zdravje.si/category/revija-zdravje [1.4.2010]

3.2 Corpus extension

We then extended the initial corpus automatically from the 2 billion-word ukWaC (Ferraresi et al., 2008) and the 380 million-word slWaC (Ljubešić and Erjavec, 2011), very large corpora that were constructed from the web by crawling the .uk and .si domain respectively.
We took into account all the documents from these two corpora that best fit the initial corpora by computing a similarity measure between models of each document and the initial corpus in the corresponding language. The models were built with content words lemmas as their parameters and TF-IDF values as the corresponding parameter values. The inverse document frequency was computed for every language on a newspaper domain of 20 million words. The similarity measure used for calculating the similarity between a document model and a corpus model was cosine with a similarity threshold of 0.2. This way, we were able to extend the Slovene part of the corpus from 1 to 6 million words and the English part to as much as 50 million words. We are aware of more complex methods for building comparable corpora, such as (Li and Gaussier, 2010), but the focus of this paper is on using comparable corpora collected from the web on the bilingual lexicon extraction task, and not the corpus extension method itself. Bilingual lexicon extraction from the extended corpus is described in the following section.

4 Bilingual lexicon extraction

In this section we describe the experiments we conducted in order to extract translation equivalents of key terms in the health domain. We ran a series of experiments in which we adjusted the following parameters:

(1) 1- and 2-way translation of context vectors with a seed dictionary;
(2) corpus size of the texts between the languages;
(3) the word frequency threshold for vector construction.

Although several parameters change in each run of the experiment, the basic algorithm for finding translation equivalents in comparable corpora is always the same:

(1) build context vectors for all unknown words in the source language that satisfy the minimum frequency criterion and translate the vectors with a seed dictionary;
(2) build context vectors for all candidate translations satisfying the frequency criterion in the target language;
(3) compute the similarity of all translated source vectors with the target vectors and rank translation candidates according to this score.

Previous research (Ljubešić et al., 2011) has shown that best results are achieved by using content words as features in context vectors and a context window of 7 with encoded position. The highest-scoring combination of vector association and similarity measures turned out to be Log Likelihood (Dunning, 1993) and Jensen-Shannon divergence (Lin, 1991), so we are using those throughout the experiments presented in this paper.

4.1 Translation of context vectors

In order to be able to compare two vectors in different languages, a seed dictionary to translate features in context vectors of source words is needed. We tested our approach with a 1-way translation of context features of English vectors into Slovene and a 2-way translation of the vectors from English into Slovene and vice versa where we then take the harmonic mean of the context similarity in both directions for every word pair.
A similar 2-way approach is described in (Chiao et al, 2004) with the difference that they average on rank values, not on similarity measures. An empirical comparison with their method is given in the automatic evaluation section.
A traditional general large-sized English-Slovene dictionary was used for the 1-way translation, which was then complemented with another general large-sized Slovene-English dictionary by the same author in the 2-way translation setting. Our technique relies on the assumption that additional linguistic knowledge is encoded in the independent dictionary in the opposite direction and was indirectly inspired by a common approach to filter out the noise in bilingual lexicon extraction from parallel corpora with source-to-target and target-to-source word-alignment.

Only content-word dictionary entries were taken into account. No multi-word entries were considered either. And, since we do not yet deal with polysemy at this stage of our research, we only extracted the first sense for each dictionary entry. The seed dictionaries we obtained in this way contained 41.405 entries (Eng-Slo) and 30.955 entries (Slo-Eng).

4.2 Corpus size

Next, we tested the impact of the extended corpus on the quality and quantity of the extracted translation equivalents by gradually increasing the size of the corpus from 1 to 6 million words.
Not only did we increase corpus size for each language equally, we also tested a much more realistic setting in which the amount of data available for one language is much higher than for the other, in our case English for which we were able to compile a 50 million word corpus, which is more than eight times more than for Slovene.

4.3 Word frequency threshold

Finally, we tested the precision and recall of the extracted lexica based on the minimum frequency of the words in the corpus from as high as 150 and down to 25 occurrences. This is an important parameter that shows the proportion of the corpus lexical inventory our method can capture and with which quality.

5 Evaluation of the results

At this stage of our research we have limited the experiments to nouns. This speeds up and simplifies our task but we believe it still gives an adequate insight into the usefulness of the approach for a particular domain since nouns carry the highest domain-specific terminological load.

5.1 Automatic evaluation

Automatic evaluation of the results was performed against a gold standard lexicon of health-related terms that was obtained from the top-ranking nouns in the English health domain model of the initial corpus and that at the same time appeared in the comprehensive dictionary of medical terms mediLexicon[2] and were missing from the general bilingual seed dictionary. The gold standard contains 360 English single-word terms with their translations into Slovene. If more than one translation variant is possible for a single English term, all variants appear in the gold standard and any of these translations suggested by the algorithm is considered as correct.
Below we present the results of three experiments that best demonstrate the performance and impact of the key parameters for bilingual lexicon extraction from comparable corpora that we were testing in this research. The evaluation measure for precision used throughout this research is mean reciprocal rank (Vorhees, 2001) on first ten translation candidates. Recall is calculated as the percentage of goldstandard entries we were able to calculate translation candidates for. Additionally, a global recall impact of our methods is shown as the overall number of entries for which we were able to calculate translation candidates. Unless stated otherwise, the frequency threshold for the generation of context vectors in the experiments was set to 50.
We begin with the results of 1- and 2-way context vector translations that we tested on the initial 1-million-word corpus we constructed from health magazines as well as on a corpus of the same size we extracted from the web. We compared the results of our method with that proposed in (Chiao et al, 2004) strengthening our claim that it is the additional information in the reverse dictionary that makes the significant impact, not the reversing itself.
As Table 1 shows, using two general dictionaries (2-way two dict) significantly improves the results as a new dictionary brings additional information. That it is the dictionary improving the results is proven by using just one, inverted dictionary in the 2-way manner, which produced worse results than the 1-way approach (2-way inverse dict). The approach of Chiao et al (2004) is also based on new dictionary knowledge since using only one inverted dictionary with their 2-way method yielded results that were almost identical to the 1-way computation. Using rank, not similarity score in averaging results proved to be a good approach (2-way Chiao two dict), but not as efficient as our approach which uses similarity scores (2-way two dict). Our approach yields higher precision and is also easier to compute. Namely, for every candidate pair only the reverse similarity score has

[2] http://www.medilexicon.com [1.4.2010]

to be computed, and not all similarity scores for every inverse pair to obtain a rank value.

Therefore, only the 2-way translation setting averaging on similarity scores is used in the rest of the experiments. It is interesting that the results on the web corpus have a higher precision but a lower recall (0.355 on the initial corpus and 0.198 on the web corpus). Higher precision can be explained with the domain modelling technique that was used to extract web data, which may have contributed to a terminologically more homogenous collection of documents in the health domain. On the other hand, the lower recall can be explained with the extracted web documents being less terminologically loaded than the initial corpus.

Corpus	1-way	2-way inverse dict	2-way Chiao two dict	2-way two dict
1 M initial	0.591	0.566	0.628	0.641
1 M web	0.626	0.610	0.705	0.710

Table 1: Precision regarding the corpus source and the translation method

The second parameter we tested in our experiments was the impact of corpus size on the quality and amount of the extracted translation equivalents. For the first 6 million words the Slovene and English parts of the corpus were enlarged in equal proportions and after that only the English part of the corpus was increased up to 18 million words.

Corpus size	P	R	No. of translated words	Not already in dict
1	0.718	0.198	1246	244
6	0.668	0.565	4535	1546
18	0.691	0.716	9122	4184

Table 2: Precision, recall, number of translated words and number of new words (not found in the dictionary) obtained with different corpus sizes

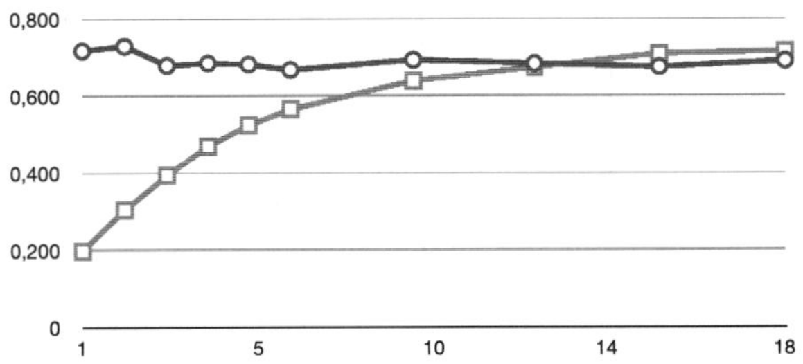

Figure 1: Precision and recall as a function of corpus size

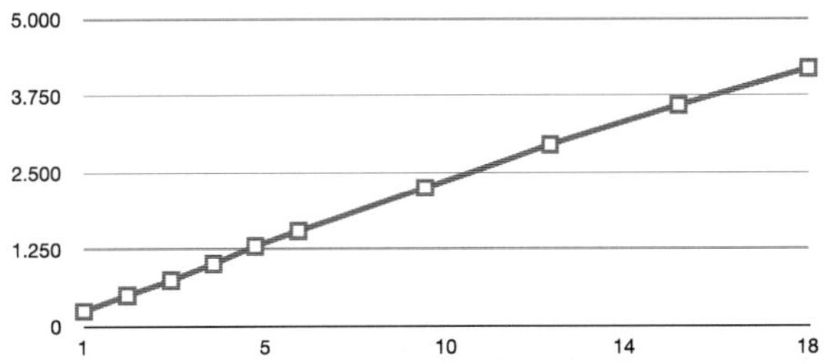

Figure 2: The number of new words (not found in the seed dictionary) as a function of corpus size

Figure 1 shows that precision with regard to the gold standard is more or less constant with an average of 0.68 if we disregard the first two measurements that are probably bad estimates since the intersection with the gold standard is small (as shown in Table 1) and evens out as the size of the corpus increases.

When analyzing recall against the gold standard we see the typical logarithmic recall behavior when depicted as a function of corpus size. On the other hand, when we consider the number of new translation equivalents (i.e. the number of source words that do not appear in the seed dictionary), the function behaves almost linearly (see Figure 2). This can be explained with the fact that in the dictionary the most frequent words are best represented. Because of that we can observe a steady increase in the number of words not present in the seed lexicon that pass the frequency threshold with the increasing corpus size.

Finally, we study the impact of the word frequency threshold for context vector generation on the quality and amount of the extracted translation equivalents on the six million corpora in both languages.

Frequency	P	No. of translated words	F1
25	0.561	7203	0.719
50	0.668	4535	0.648
75	0.711	3435	0.571
100	0.752	2803	0.513
125	0.785	2374	0.464
150	0.815	2062	0.424

Table 3: Precision, number of new words and F1 obtained with different frequency thresholds

As can be seen in Table 3, by lowering the frequency criterion, the F1 measure increases showing greater gain in recall than loss in precision. For calculating recall, the number of new words passing the frequency criterion is normalized with the assumed number of obtainable lexicon entries set to 7.203 (the number of new words obtained with the lowest frequency criterion).

This is a valuable insight since the threshold can be set according to different project scenarios. If, for example, lexicographers can be used in order to check the translation candidates and choose the best ones among them, the threshold may well be left low and they will still be able to identify the correct translation very quickly. If, on the other hand, the results will be used directly by another application, the threshold will be raised in order to reduce the amount of noise introduced by the lexicon for the following processing stages.

5.2 Manual evaluation

For a more qualitative inspection of the results we performed manual evaluation on a random sample of 100 translation equivalents that are not in the general seed dictionary or present in our gold standard. We were interested in finding out to what extent these translation equivalents belong to the health domain and if their quality is comparable to the results of the automatic evaluation.

Manual evaluation was performed on translation equivalents extracted from the comparable corpus containing 18 million English words and 6 million Slovene words, where the frequency threshold was set to 50. 51% of the manually evaluated words belonged to the health domain, 23% were part of general vocabulary, 10% were proper names and the rest were acronyms and errors arising from PoS-tagging and lemmatization in the ukWaC corpus. Overall, in 45% the first translation equivalent was correct and additional 11% contained the correct translation among the ten best-ranked candidates.

For 44 % of the extracted translation equivalents no appropriate translation was suggested. Among the evaluated health-domain terms, 61% were translated correctly with the first candidate and for the additional 20% the correct translation appeared among the first 10 candidates.

Of the 19% health-domain terms with no appropriate translation suggestion, 4 terms, that is 21% of the wrongly translated terms, were translated as direct hypernyms and could loosely be considered as correct (e.g. the English term *bacillus* was translated as *mikroorganizem* into Slovene, which means microorganism). Even most other translation candidates were semantically closely related, in fact, there was only one case in the manually inspected sample that provided completely wrong translations.

Manual evaluation shows that the quality of translations for out-of-goldstandard terms is consistent with the results of automatic evaluation. A closer look revealed that we were able to obtain translation equivalents not only for the general vocabulary but especially terms relevant for the health domain, and furthermore, that their quality is also considerably higher than for the general vocabulary which is not of our primary interest in this research.

The results could be further improved by filtering out the noise obtained from errors in PoS-tagging and lemmatization and, more importantly, by identifying proper names. Multi-word expressions should also be tackled as they present problems, especially in cases of 1:many mappings, such as the English single-word term *immunodeficiency* that is translated with a multi-word expression in Slovene (*imunska pomanjkljivost*).

6 Conclusions

In this paper we described the compilation process of a domain-specific comparable corpus from already existing general resources. The corpus compiled from general web corpora was used in a set of experiments to extract translation equivalents for the domain vocabulary by comparing contexts in which terms appear in the two languages.

The results show that a 2-way translation of context vectors consistently improves the quality of the extracted translation equivalents by using additional information given from the reverse dictionary. Next, increasing the size of only one part of the comparable corpus brings a slight increase in precision but a very substantial increase in recall.

If we are able to translate less than 20% of the gold standard with a 1 million word corpus, the recall is exceeds 70% when we extend the English part of the corpus to 15 million words. Moreover, the increase of the number of new words we obtain in this way keeps being linear for even large corpus sizes. We can also expect the amount of available text to keep rising in the future.

This is a valuable finding because a scenario in which much more data is available for one of the two languages in question is a very common one.

Finally, we have established that the word frequency threshold for building context vectors can be lowered in order to obtain more translation equivalents without a big sacrifice in their quality. For example, a 10% drop in precision yields almost twice as many translation equivalents.

Manual evaluation has shown that the quality of health-related terms that were at the center of our research is considerably higher than the rest of the vocabulary but has also revealed some noise in POS-tagging and lemmatization of the ukWaC corpus that consequently lowers the results of our method and should be dealt with in the future.

A straightforward extension of this research is to tackle other parts of speech in addition to nouns. Other shortcomings of our method that will have to be addressed in our future work are multi-word expressions and multiple senses of polysemous words and their translations. We also see potential in using cognates for re-ranking translation candidates as they are very common in the health domain.

Acknowledgments

Research reported in this paper has been supported by the ACCURAT project within the EU 7th Framework Programme (FP7/2007-2013), grant agreement no. 248347, and by the Slovenian Research Agency, grant no. Z6-3668.

References

Arhar, Š., Gorjanc, V., and Krek, S. (2007). FidaPLUS corpus of Slovenian - The New Generation of the Slovenian Reference Corpus: Its Design and Tools. In *Proceedings of the Corpus Linguistics Conference* (CL2007), Birmingham, pp. 95-110.

Déjean, H., Gaussier, E., Renders, J.-M. and Sadat, F. (2005). Automatic processing of multilingual medical terminology: Applications to thesaurus enrichment and cross-language information retrieval. *Artificial Intelligence in Medicine*, 33(2): 111–124.

Doe, J. (2011): *Bilingual lexicon extraction from comparable corpora: A comparative study.*

Doe, J. (2011): *Compiling web corpora for Croatian and Slovene.*

Dunning, T. (1993). Accurate methods for the statistics of surprise and coincidence. *Computational Linguistics - Special issue on using large corpora,* 19(1).

Fung, P. (1998). A statistical view on bilingual lexicon extraction: From parallel corpora to nonparallel corpora. In *Proc. of the 3rd Conference of the Association for Machine Translation in the Americas*, pp. 1–17.

Fung, P., Prochasson, E. and Shi, S. (2010). Trillions of Comparable Documents. In *Proc. of the 3rd workshop on Building and Using Comparable Corpora* (BUCC'10), Language Resource and Evaluation Conference (LREC2010), Malta, May 2010, pp. 26–34.

Grefenstette, G. (1994). *Explorations in Automatic Thesaurus Discovery*. Kluwer Academic Publishers, Norwell, MA.

Koehn, P. and Knight, K. (2002). Learning a translation lexicon from monolingual corpora. In *Proc. of the workshop on Unsupervised lexical acquisition* (ULA '02) at ACL 2002, Philadelphia, USA, pp. 9–16.

Lin, J. (1991). Divergence measures based on the Shannon entropy. *IEEE Transactions on Information Theory*, 37(1): 145-151.

Ljubešić, N. and Erjavec, T. (2011). hrWaC and slWaC: Compiling Web Corpora for Croatian and Slovene. (submitted to International Workshop on Balto-Slavonic Natural Language Processing).

Ljubešić, N., Fišer D., Vintar Š. and Pollak S. Bilingual Lexicon Extraction from Comparable Corpora: A Comparative Study. (accepted for WoLeR 2011 at ESSLLI International Workshop on Lexical Resources).

Marsi, E. and Krahmer, E. (2010). Automatic analysis of semantic similarity in comparable text through syntactic tree matching. In *Proc. of the 23rd International Conference on Computational Linguistics* (Coling 2010), pages 752–760.

Och, F. J. and Ney, H. (2000). Improved Statistical Alignment Models. In *Proc. of the 38th Annual Meeting of the Association for Computational Linguistics*, Hongkong, China, pp. 440–447.

Otero, P. G. (2007). Learning Bilingual Lexicons from Comparable English and Spanish Corpora. In *Proc. of the Machine Translation Summit* (MTS 2007), pp. 191–198.

Rapp, R. (1999). Automatic identification of word translations from unrelated English and German corpora. In *Proc. of the 37th annual meeting of the Association for Computational Linguistics* (ACL '99), pp. 519–526.

Schmid, H. (1994): Probabilistic Part-of-Speech Tagging Using Decision Trees. In *Proc. of International Conference on New Methods in Language Processing*.

Saralegi, X., San Vicente, I. and Gurrutxaga, A. (2008). Automatic Extraction of Bilingual Terms from Comparable Corpora in a Popular Science Domain. In *Proc. of the 1st Workshop on Building and Using Comparable Corpora* (BUCC) at LREC 2008.

Shao, L. and Ng, H. T. (2004). Mining New Word Translations from Comparable Corpora. *In Proc. of the 20th International Conference on Computational Linguistics* (COLING '04), Geneva, Switzerland.

Shezaf, D. and Rappoport, A. (2010). Bilingual Lexicon Generation Using Non-Aligned Signatures. In *Proc.of the 48th Annual Meeting of the Association for Computational Linguistics* (ACL 2010), Uppsala, Sweden, pp. 98–107.

Steinberger, R., Pouliquen, B., Widiger, A., Ignat, C., Erjavec, T., Tufiş, D. and Varga, D. (2006). The JRC-Acquis: A multilingual aligned parallel corpus with 20+ languages. In *Proc. of the 5th International Conference on Language Resources and Evaluation* (LREC 2006), pp. 2142–2147.

Tiedemann, J. (2005). Optimisation of Word Alignment Clues. *Natural Language Engineering*, 11(03): 279–293.

Vorhees, E. M. (2001). *Overview of the TREC-9 Question Answering Track*. In Proceedings of the Ninth Text REtrieval Conference (TREC-9), 2001.

Xiao, Z., McEnery, A. (2006). Collocation, semantic prosody and near synonymy: a cross-linguistic perspective. *Applied Linguistics* 27(1): 103–129.

Yu, K. and Tsujii, J. (2009). *Bilingual dictionary extraction from Wikipedia*. In *Proc. of the 12th Machine Translation Summit* (MTS 2009), Ottawa, Ontario, Canada.

Bilingual Lexicon Extraction from Comparable Corpora Enhanced with Parallel Corpora

Emmanuel Morin and **Emmanuel Prochasson**
Université de Nantes, LINA - UMR CNRS 6241
2 rue de la Houssinière, BP 92208
44322 Nantes Cedex 03
{emmanuel.morin,emmanuel.prochasson}@univ-nantes.fr

Abstract

In this article, we present a simple and effective approach for extracting bilingual lexicon from comparable corpora enhanced with parallel corpora. We make use of structural characteristics of the documents comprising the comparable corpus to extract parallel sentences with a high degree of quality. We then use state-of-the-art techniques to build a specialized bilingual lexicon from these sentences and evaluate the contribution of this lexicon when added to the comparable corpus-based alignment technique. Finally, the value of this approach is demonstrated by the improvement of translation accuracy for medical words.

1 Introduction

Bilingual lexicons are important resources of many applications of natural language processing such as cross-language information retrieval or machine translation. These lexicons are traditionally extracted from bilingual corpora.

In this area, the main work involves parallel corpora, i.e. a corpus that contains source texts and their translations. From sentence-to-sentence aligned corpora, symbolic (Carl and Langlais, 2002), statistical (Daille et al., 1994), or hybrid techniques (Gaussier and Langé, 1995) are used for word and expression alignments. However, despite good results in the compilation of bilingual lexicons, parallel corpora are rather scarce resources, especially for technical domains and for language pairs not involving English. For instance, current resources of parallel corpora are built from the proceedings of international institutions such as the European Union (11 languages) or the United Nations (6 languages), bilingual countries such as Canada (English and French languages), or bilingual regions such as Hong Kong (Chinese and English languages).

For these reasons, research in bilingual lexicon extraction is focused on another kind of bilingual corpora. These corpora, known as comparable corpora, are comprised of texts sharing common features such as domain, genre, register, sampling period, etc. without having a source text-target text relationship. Although the building of comparable corpora is easier than the building of parallel corpora, the results obtained thus far on comparable corpora are contrasted. For instance, good results are obtained from large corpora — several million words — for which the accuracy of the proposed translation is between 76% (Fung, 1998) and 89% (Rapp, 1999) for the first 20 candidates. (Cao and Li, 2002) have achieved 91% accuracy for the top three candidates using the Web as a comparable corpus. But for technical domains, for which large corpora are not available, the results obtained, even though encouraging, are not completely satisfactory yet. For instance, (Déjean et al., 2002) obtained a precision of 44% and 57% for the first 10 and 20 candidates in a 100,000-word medical corpus, and 35% and 42% in a multi-domain 8 million-word corpus. For French/English single words, (Chiao and Zweigenbaum, 2002) using a medical corpus of 1.2 million words, obtained a precision of about 50% and 60% for the top 10 and top 20 candidates. (Morin et al., 2007) obtained a precision of 51% and 60% for the top 10 and 20 candidates in a 1.5

Proceedings of the 4th Workshop on Building and Using Comparable Corpora, pages 27–34,
49th Annual Meeting of the Association for Computational Linguistics,
Portland, Oregon, 24 June 2011. ©*2011 Association for Computational Linguistics*

million-word French-Japanese diabetes corpus.

The above work in bilingual lexicon extraction from comparable corpora relies on the assumption that words which have the same meaning in different languages tend to appear in the same lexical contexts (Fung, 1998; Rapp, 1999). Based on this assumption, a standard approach consists of building context vectors for each word of the source and target languages. The candidate translations for a particular word are obtained by comparing the translated source context vector with all target context vectors. In this approach, the translation of the words of the source context vectors depends on the coverage of the bilingual dictionary vis-à-vis the corpus. This aspect can be a potential problem if too few corpus words are found in the bilingual dictionary (Chiao and Zweigenbaum, 2003; Déjean et al., 2002).

In this article, we want to show how this problem can be partially circumvented by combining a general bilingual dictionary with a specialized bilingual dictionary based on a parallel corpus extracted through mining of the comparable corpus. In the same way that recent works in Statistical Machine Translation (SMT) mines comparable corpora to discover parallel sentences (Resnik and Smith, 2003; Yang and Li, 2003; Munteanu and Marcu, 2005; Abdul-Rauf and Schwenk, 2009, among others), this work contributes to the bridging of the gap between comparable and parallel corpora by offering a framework for bilingual lexicon extraction from comparable corpus with the help of parallel corpus-based pairs of terms.

The remainder of this article is organized as follows. In Section 2, we first present the method for bilingual lexicon extraction from comparable corpora enhanced with parallel corpora and the associated system architecture. We then quantify and analyse in Section 3 the performance improvement of our method on a medical comparable corpora when used to extract specialized bilingual lexicon. Finally, in Section 4, we discuss the present study and present our conclusions.

2 System Architecture

The overall architecture of the system for lexical alignment is shown in Figure 1 and comprises parallel corpus- and comparable corpus-based alignments. Starting from a comparable corpus harvested from the web, we first propose to extract parallel sentences based on the structural characteristics of the documents harvested. These parallel sentences are then used to build a bilingual lexicon through a tool dedicated to bilingual lexicon extraction. Finally, this bilingual lexicon is used to perform the comparable corpus-based alignment. For a word to be translated, the output of the system is a ranked list of candidate translations.

2.1 Extracting Parallel Sentences from Comparable Corpora

Parallel sentence extraction from comparable corpora has been studied by a number of researchers (Ma and Liberman, 1999; Chen and Nie, 2000; Resnik and Smith, 2003; Yang and Li, 2003; Fung and Cheung, 2004; Munteanu and Marcu, 2005; Abdul-Rauf and Schwenk, 2009, among others) and several systems have been developed such as BITS (Bilingual Internet Test Search) (Ma and Liberman, 1999), PTMiner (Parallel Text Miner) (Chen and Nie, 2000), and STRAND (Structural Translation Recognition for Acquiring Natural Data) (Resnik and Smith, 2003). Their work relies on the observation that a collection of texts in different languages composed independently and based on sharing common features such as content, domain, genre, register, sampling period, etc. contains probably some sentences with a source text-target text relationship. Based on this observation, dynamic programming (Yang and Li, 2003), similarity measures such as Cosine (Fung and Cheung, 2004) or word and translation error ratios (Abdul-Rauf and Schwenk, 2009), or maximum entropy classifier (Munteanu and Marcu, 2005) are used for discovering parallel sentences.

Although our purpose is similar to these works, the amount of data required by these techniques makes them ineffective when applied to specialized comparable corpora used to discover parallel sentences. In addition, the focus of this paper is not to propose a new technique for this task but to study how parallel sentences extracted from a comparable corpus can improve the quality of the candidate translations. For theses reasons, we propose to make use of structural characteristics of the documents comprising the comparable corpus to extract auto-

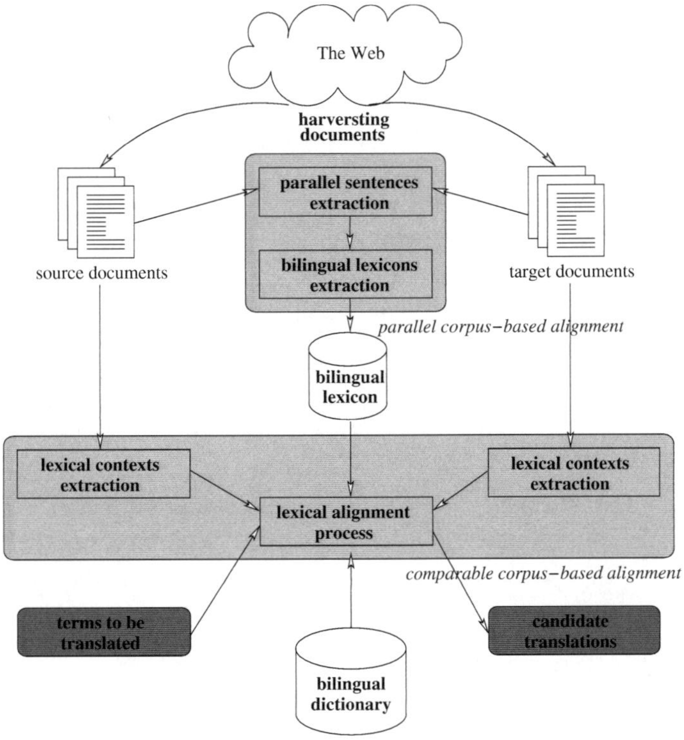

Figure 1: Overview of the system for lexical alignment

matically parallel sentences.

In fact, specialized comparable corpora are generally constructed via the consultation of specialized Web portals. For instance, (Chiao and Zweigenbaum, 2002) use CISMeF[1] for building the French part of their comparable corpora and CliniWeb[2] for the English part, and (Déjean and Gaussier, 2002) use documents extracted from MEDLINE[3] to build a German/English comparable corpus. Consequently, the documents collected through these portals are often scientific papers. Moreover, when the language of these papers is not the English, the paper usually comprises an abstract, keywords and title in the native language and their translations in the English language. These characteristics of scientific paper is useful for the efficient extraction of parallel sentences or word translations from the documents forming a specialized comparable corpus for which one part will inevitably be in English.

In this study, the documents comprising the French/English specialized comparable corpus were taken from the medical domain within the subdomain of 'breast cancer'. These documents have been automatically selected from the Elsevier website[4] among the articles published between 2001 and 2008 for which the title or the keywords of the articles contain the multi-word term 'cancer du sein' in French and 'breast cancer' in English. We thus collected 130 documents in French and 118 in English and about 530,000 words for each language. Since the 130 French documents previously collected are scientific papers, each document contains a French abstract which is accompanied by its English translation. We exploit this structural characteristic of the French documents in order to build a small specialized parallel corpus directly correlated to the subdomain of 'breast cancer' involved in the comparable corpus.

2.2 Parallel Corpus-Based Alignment

We use the *Uplug*[5] collection of tools for alignment (Tiedemann, 2003) to extract translations from our

[1] `http://www.chu-rouen.fr/cismef/`
[2] `http://www.ohsu.edu/cliniweb/`
[3] `http://www.ncbi.nlm.nih.gov/PubMed`
[4] `http://www.elsevier.com`
[5] `http://stp.ling.uu.se/cgi-bin/joerg/Uplug`

specialized parallel corpus. The output of such a tool is a list of aligned *parts of sentences*, that has to be post-process and filtered in our case. We clean the alignment with a simple yet efficient method in order to obtain only word translations. We associate every source word from a source sequence with every target word from the target sequence. As an example, *uplug* efficiently aligns the English word *breast cancer* with the French word *cancer du sein* (the data are described in Section 3.1). We obtain the following lexical alignment:

- cancer (fr) $\rightarrow$ (en) breast, cancer
- du (fr) $\rightarrow$ (en) breast, cancer
- sein (fr) $\rightarrow$ (en) breast, cancer

With more occurrences of the French word *cancer*, we are able to align it with the English words {breast, cancer, cancer, cancer, the, of, breast, cancer}. We can then filter such a list by counting the translation candidates. In the previous example, we obtain: cancer (fr) $\rightarrow$ breast/2, the /1, of/1, cancer/4. The English word *cancer* is here the best match for the French word *cancer*. In many cases, only one alignment is obtained. For example, there is only one occurrence of the French word *chromosome*, aligned with the English word *chromosome*.

In order to filter translation candidates, we keep 1:1 candidates if their frequencies are comparable in the original corpus. We keep the most frequent translation candidates (in the previous example, *cancer*) if their frequencies in the corpus are also comparable. This in-corpus frequency constraint is useful for discarding candidates that appear in many alignments (such as functional words). The criterion for frequency acceptability is:

$$min(f_1, f_2)/max(f_1, f_2) > 2/3$$

with f_1 and f_2 the frequency of words to be aligned in the parallel corpus.

By this way, we build a French/English specialized bilingual lexicon from the parallel corpus. This lexicon, called breast cancer dictionary (BC dictionary) in the remainder of this article, is composed of 549 French/English single words.

2.3 Comparable Corpus-Based Alignment

The comparable corpus-based alignment relies on the simple observation that a word and its translation tend to appear in the same lexical contexts. Based on this observation, the alignment method, known as the *standard approach*, builds context vectors in the source and the target languages where each vector element represents a word which occurs within the window of the word to be translated (for instance a seven-word window approximates syntactic dependencies). In order to emphasize significant words in the context vector and to reduce word-frequency effects, the context vectors are normalized according to association measures. Then, the translation is obtained by comparing the source context vector to each translation candidate vector after having translated each element of the source vector with a general dictionary.

The implementation of this approach can be carried out by applying the four following steps (Fung, 1998; Rapp, 1999):

1. We collect all the lexical units in the context of each lexical unit i and count their occurrence frequency in a window of n words around i. For each lexical unit i of the source and the target languages, we obtain a context vector v_i which gathers the set of co-occurrence units j associated with the number of times that j and i occur together $occ(i, j)$. In order to identify specific words in the lexical context and to reduce word-frequency effects, we normalize context vectors using an association score such as Mutual Information (MI) or Log-likelihood, as shown in equations 1 and 2 and in Table 1 (where $N = a + b + c + d$).

2. Using a bilingual dictionary, we translate the lexical units of the source context vector. If the bilingual dictionary provides several translations for a lexical unit, we consider all of them but weight the different translations according to their frequency in the target language.

3. For a lexical unit to be translated, we compute the similarity between the translated context vector and all target vectors through vector distance measures such as Cosine or Weighted

Jaccard (WJ) (see equations 3 and 4 where $assoc^i_j$ stands for "association score").

4. The candidate translations of a lexical unit are the target lexical units ranked following the similarity score.

	j	$\neg j$
i	$a = occ(i, j)$	$b = occ(i, \neg j)$
$\neg i$	$c = occ(\neg i, j)$	$d = occ(\neg i, \neg j)$

Table 1: Contingency table

$$MI(i, j) = log \frac{a}{(a + b)(a + c)} \quad (1)$$

$$\begin{aligned} \lambda(i, j) = \quad & a \log(a) + b \log(b) + c \log(c) \\ & + d \log(d) + (N) \log(N) \\ & - (a + b) \log(a + b) \\ & - (a + c) \log(a + c) \\ & - (b + d) \log(b + d) \\ & - (c + d) \log(c + d) \end{aligned} \quad (2)$$

$$Cosine^{v_k}_{v_l} = \frac{\sum_t assoc^l_t \, assoc^k_t}{\sqrt{\sum_t {assoc^l_t}^2} \sqrt{\sum_t {assoc^k_t}^2}} \quad (3)$$

$$WJ^{v_k}_{v_l} = \frac{\sum_t min(assoc^l_t, assoc^k_t)}{\sum_t max(assoc^l_t, assoc^k_t)} \quad (4)$$

This approach is sensitive to the choice of parameters such as the size of the context, the choice of the association and similarity measures. The most complete study about the influence of these parameters on the quality of bilingual alignment has been carried out by Laroche and Langlais (2010).

3 Experiments and Results

In the previous section, we have introduced our comparable corpus and described the method dedicated to bilingual lexicon extraction from comparable corpora enhanced with parallel corpora. In this section, we then quantify and analyse the performance improvement of our method on a medical comparable corpus when used to extract specialized bilingual lexicon.

3.1 Experimental Test bed

The documents comprising the French/English specialized comparable corpus have been normalised through the following linguistic pre-processing steps: tokenisation, part-of-speech tagging, and lemmatisation. Next, the function words were removed and the words occurring less than twice in the French and the English parts were discarded. Finally, the comparable corpus comprised about 7,400 distinct words in French and 8,200 in English.

In this study, we used four types of bilingual dictionary: i) the Wiktionary[6] free-content multilingual dictionary, ii) the ELRA-M0033[7] professional French/English bilingual dictionary, iii) the MeSH[8] metha-thesaurus, and iv) the BC dictionary (see Section 2.2). Table 2 shows the main features of the dictionaries, namely: the number of distinct French single words in the dictionary (# SWs dico.), the number of distinct French single words in the dictionary after projection on the French part of the comparable corpus (# SWs corpus), and the number of translations per entry in the dictionary (# TPE). For instance, 42% of the French context vectors could be translated with the Wiktionary (3,099/7,400).

Table 2: Main features of the French/English dictionaries

Name	# SWs dict.	# SWs corpus	# TPE
Wiktionary	20,317	3,099	1.8
ELRA	50,330	4,567	2.8
MeSH	18,972	833	1.6
BC	549	549	1.0

In bilingual terminology extraction from specialized comparable corpora, the terminology reference list required to evaluate the performance of the alignment programs are often composed of 100 single-word terms (SWTs) (180 SWTs in (Déjean and Gaussier, 2002), 95 SWTs in (Chiao and Zweigenbaum, 2002), and 100 SWTs in (Daille and Morin, 2005)). To build our reference list, we selected 400 French/English SWTs from the UMLS[9]

[6] http://www.wiktionary.org/

[7] http://www.elra.info/

[8] http://www.ncbi.nlm.nih.gov/mesh

[9] http://www.nlm.nih.gov/research/umls

meta-thesaurus and the *Grand dictionnaire terminologique*[10]. We kept only the French/English pair of SWTs which occur more than five times in each part of the comparable corpus. As a result of filtering, 122 French/English SWTs were extracted.

3.2 Experimental Results

In order to evaluate the influence of the parallel corpus-based bilingual lexicon induced from the comparable corpus on the quality of comparable corpus based-bilingual terminology extraction, four experiments were carried out. For each experiment, we change the bilingual dictionary required for the translation phase of the standard approach (see Section 2.3):

1. The first experiment uses only the Wiktionary. Since the coverage of the Wiktionary from the comparable corpus is small (see Table 2), the results obtained with this dictionary yield a lower boundary.

2. The second experiment uses the Wiktionary added to the BC dictionary. This experiment attempts to verify the hypothesis of this study.

3. The third experiment uses the Wiktionary added to the MeSH thesaurus. This experiment attempts to determine whether a specialised dictionary (in this case the MeSH) would be more suitable than a specialized bilingual dictionary (in this case the BC dictionary) directly extracted from the corpus.

4. The last experiment uses only the ELRA dictionary. Since the coverage of the ELRA dictionary from the comparable corpus is the best (see Table 2), the results obtained with this one yield a higher boundary.

Table 3 shows the coverage of the four bilingual lexical resources involved in the previous experiments in the comparable corpus. The first column indicates the number of single words belonging to a dictionary found in the comparable corpus (# SWs corpus). The other column indicates the coverage of each dictionary in the ELRA dictionary (Coverage ELRA). Here, 98.9% of the single words belonging to the Wiktionary are included in the ELRA dictionary whereas less than 95% of the single words belonging to the Wiktionary+BC and Wiktionary+MeSH dictionaries are included in the ELRA dictionary. Moreover, the MeSH and BC dictionaries are two rather distinct specialized resources since they have only 117 single words in common.

[10] http://www.granddictionnaire.com/

Table 3: Coverage of the bilingual lexical resources in the comparable corpus

Name	# SWs corpus	Coverage ELRA
Wiktionary	3,099	98.8%
Wiktionary + BC	3,326	94.8%
Wiktionary + MeSH	3,465	94.9%
ELRA	4,567	100%

In the experiments reported here, the size of the context window n was set to 3 (i.e. a seven-word window), the association measure was the Mutual Information and the distance measure the Cosine (see Section 2.3). Other combinations of parameters were assessed but the previous parameters turned out to give the best performance.

Figure 2 summarises the results obtained for the four experiments for the terms belonging to the reference list according to the French to English direction. As one could expect, the precision of the result obtained with the ELRA dictionary is the best and the precision obtained with the Wiktionary is the lowest. For instance, the ELRA dictionary improves the precision of the Wiktionary by about 14 points for the Top 10 and 9 points for the top 20. These results confirm that the coverage of the dictionary is an important factor in the quality of the results obtained. Now, when you add the BC dictionary to the Wiktionary, the results obtained are also much better than those obtained with the Wiktionary alone and very similar to those obtained with the ELRA dictionary alone (without taking into account the top 5). This result suggests that a standard general language dictionary enriched with a small specialized dictionary can replace a large general language dictionary.

Furthermore, this combination is more interesting than the combination of the MeSH dictionary with the Wiktionary. Since the BC dictionary is induced from the corpus, this dictionary is directly correlated to the theme of breast cancer involved in the corpus. Consequently the BC dictionary is more suitable than the MeSH dictionary i) even if the MeSH dictionary specializes in the medical domain and ii) even if more words in the comparable corpus are found in the MeSH dictionary than in the BC dictionary.

This last observation should make us relativize the claim: the greater the number of context vector elements that are translated, the more discriminating the context vector will be for selecting translations in the target language. We must also take into account the specificity of the context vector elements in accordance with the thematic of the documents making up the corpus studied in order to improve bilingual lexicon extraction from specialized comparable corpora.

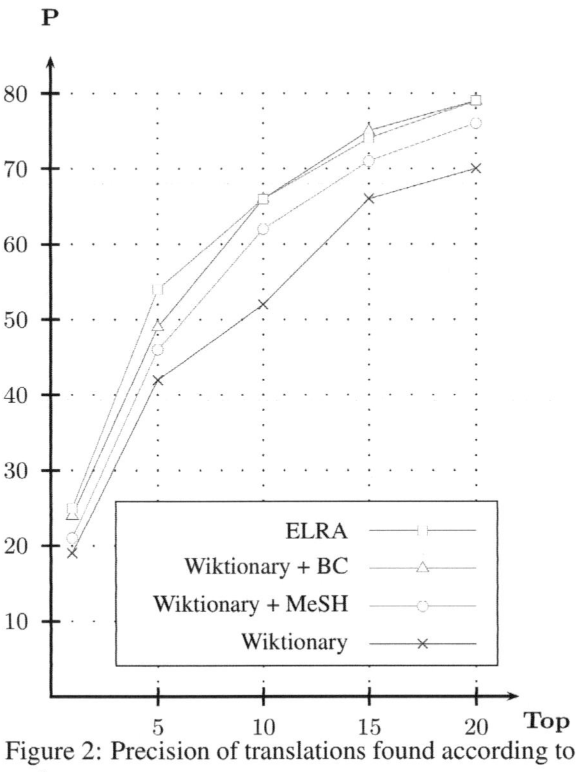

Figure 2: Precision of translations found according to the rank

4 Conclusion and Discussion

In this article, we have shown how the quality of bilingual lexicon extraction from comparable corpora could be improved with a small specialized bilingual lexicon induced through parallel sentences included in the comparable corpus. We have evaluated the performance improvement of our method on a French/English comparable corpus within the sub-domain of breast cancer in the medical domain. Our experimental results show that this simple bilingual lexicon, when combined with a general dictionary, helps improve the accuracy of single word alignments by about 14 points for the Top 10 and 9 points for the top 20. Even though we focus here on one structural characteristic (i.e. the abstracts) of the documents comprising the comparable corpus to discover parallel sentences and induced bilingual lexicon, the method could be easily applied to other comparable corpora for which a bilingual dictionary can be extracted by using other characteristics such as the presence of parallel segments or paraphrases in the documents making up the comparable corpus.

Acknowledgments

The research leading to these results has received funding from the European Communitys Seventh Framework Programme (FP7/2007-2013) under Grant Agreement no 248005.

References

Sadaf Abdul-Rauf and Holger Schwenk. 2009. On the use of comparable corpora to improve SMT performance. In *Proceedings of the 12th Conference of the European Chapter of the Association for Computational Linguistics (EACL'09)*, pages 16–23, Athens, Greece.

Yunbo Cao and Hang Li. 2002. Base Noun Phrase Translation Using Web Data and the EM Algorithm. In *Proceedings of the 19th International Conference on Computational Linguistics (COLING'02)*, pages 127–133, Tapei, Taiwan.

Michael Carl and Philippe Langlais. 2002. An Intelligent Terminology Database as a Pre-processor for Statistical Machine Translation. In L.-F. Chien, B. Daille, K. Kageura, and H. Nakagawa, editors, *Proceedings of the 2nd International Workshop on Computational Terminology (COMPUTERM'02)*, pages 15–21, Tapei, Taiwan.

Jiang Chen and Jian-Yun Nie. 2000. Parallel Web Text Mining for Cross-Language Information Retrieval. In *Proceedings of Recherche d'Information Assistée par Ordinateur (RIAO'00)*, pages 62–77, Paris, France.

Yun-Chuang Chiao and Pierre Zweigenbaum. 2002. Looking for candidate translational equivalents in specialized, comparable corpora. In *Proceedings of the 19th International Conference on Computational Linguistics (COLING'02)*, pages 1208–1212, Tapei, Taiwan.

Yun-Chuang Chiao and Pierre Zweigenbaum. 2003. The effect of a general lexicon in corpus-based identification of French-English medical word translations. In R. Baud, M. Fieschi, P. Le Beux, and P. Ruch, editors, *The New Navigators: from Professionals to Patients, Actes Medical Informatics Europe*, volume 95 of *Studies in Health Technology and Informatics*, pages 397–402.

Béatrice Daille and Emmanuel Morin. 2005. French-English Terminology Extraction from Comparable Corpora. In *Proceedings of the 2nd International Joint Conference on Natural Language Processing (IJCLNP'05)*, pages 707–718, Jeju Island, Korea.

Béatrice Daille, Éric Gaussier, and Jean-Marc Langé. 1994. Towards Automatic Extraction of Monolingual and Bilingual Terminology. In *Proceedings of the 15th International Conference on Computational Linguistics (COLING'94)*, volume I, pages 515–521, Kyoto, Japan.

Hervé Déjean and Éric Gaussier. 2002. Une nouvelle approche à l'extraction de lexiques bilingues à partir de corpus comparables. *Lexicometrica, Alignement lexical dans les corpus multilingues*, pages 1–22.

Hervé Déjean, Fatia Sadat, and Éric Gaussier. 2002. An approach based on multilingual thesauri and model combination for bilingual lexicon extraction. In *Proceedings of the 19th International Conference on Computational Linguistics (COLING'02)*, pages 218–224, Tapei, Taiwan.

Pascale Fung and Percy Cheung. 2004. Mining Very-Non-Parallel Corpora: Parallel Sentence and Lexicon Extraction via Bootstrapping and EM. In D. Lin and D. Wu, editors, *Proceedings of Empirical Methods on Natural Language Processing (EMNLP'04)*, pages 57–63, Barcelona, Spain.

Pascale Fung. 1998. A Statistical View on Bilingual Lexicon Extraction: From Parallel Corpora to Non-parallel Corpora. In D. Farwell, L. Gerber, and E. Hovy, editors, *Proceedings of the 3rd Conference of the Association for Machine Translation in the Americas (AMTA'98)*, pages 1–16, Langhorne, PA, USA.

Éric Gaussier and Jean-Marc Langé. 1995. Modèles statistiques pour l'extraction de lexiques bilingues. *Traitement Automatique des Langues (TAL)*, 36(1–2):133–155.

Audrey Laroche and Philippe Langlais. 2010. Revisiting Context-based Projection Methods for Term-Translation Spotting in Comparable Corpora. In *Proceedings of the 23rd International Conference on Computational Linguistics (COLING'10)*, pages 617–625, Beijing, China.

Xiaoyi Ma and Mark Y. Liberman. 1999. Bits: A Method for Bilingual Text Search over the Web. In *Proceedings of Machine Translation Summit VII*, Kent Ridge Digital Labs, National University of Singapore.

Emmanuel Morin, Béatrice Daille, Koichi Takeuchi, and Kyo Kageura. 2007. Bilingual Terminology Mining – Using Brain, not brawn comparable corpora. In *Proceedings of the 45th Annual Meeting of the Association for Computational Linguistics (ACL'07)*, pages 664–671, Prague, Czech Republic.

Dragos Stefan Munteanu and Daniel Marcu. 2005. Improving Machine Translation Performance by Exploiting Non-Parallel Corpora. *Computational Linguistics*, 31(4):477–504.

Reinhard Rapp. 1999. Automatic Identification of Word Translations from Unrelated English and German Corpora. In *Proceedings of the 37th Annual Meeting of the Association for Computational Linguistics (ACL'99)*, pages 519–526, College Park, MD, USA.

Philip Resnik and Noah A. Smith. 2003. The Web as a parallel corpus. *Computational Linguistics*, 29(3):349–380.

J. Tiedemann. 2003. *Recycling Translations - Extraction of Lexical Data from Parallel Corpora and their Application in Natural Language Processing*. Ph.D. thesis, Studia Linguistica Upsaliensia 1.

Christopher C. Yang and Kar Wing Li. 2003. Automatic construction of English/Chinese parallel corpora. *Journal of the American Society for Information Science and Technology*, 54(8):730–742.

Bilingual Lexicon Extraction from Comparable Corpora as Metasearch

Amir Hazem and Emmanuel Morin
Université de Nantes,
LINA - UMR CNRS 6241
2 rue de la Houssinière,
BP 92208 44322 Nantes Cedex 03
amir.hazem@univ-nantes.fr
emmanuel.morin@univ-nantes.fr

Sebastian Peña Saldarriaga
1100 rue Notre-Dame Ouest,
Montréal, Québec,
Canada H3C 1K3
spena@synchromedia.ca

Abstract

In this article we present a novel way of looking at the problem of automatic acquisition of pairs of translationally equivalent words from comparable corpora. We first present the standard and extended approaches traditionally dedicated to this task. We then reinterpret the extended method, and motivate a novel model to reformulate this approach inspired by the metasearch engines in information retrieval. The empirical results show that performances of our model are always better than the baseline obtained with the extended approach and also competitive with the standard approach.

1 Introduction

Bilingual lexicon extraction from comparable corpora has received considerable attention since the 1990s (Rapp, 1995; Fung, 1998; Fung and Lo, 1998; Peters and Picchi, 1998; Rapp, 1999; Chiao and Zweigenbaum, 2002a; Déjean et al., 2002; Gaussier et al., 2004; Morin et al., 2007; Laroche and Langlais, 2010, among others). This attention has been motivated by the scarcity of parallel corpora, especially for countries with only one official language and for language pairs not involving English. Furthermore, as a parallel corpus is comprised of a pair of texts (a source text and a translated text), the vocabulary appearing in the translated text is highly influenced by the source text, especially in technical domains. Consequently, comparable corpora are considered by human translators to be more trustworthy than parallel corpora (Bowker and Pearson, 2002). Comparable corpora are clearly of use in the enrichment of bilingual dictionaries and thesauri (Chiao and Zweigenbaum, 2002b; Déjean et al., 2002), and in the improvement of cross-language information retrieval (Peters and Picchi, 1998).

According to (Fung, 1998), bilingual lexicon extraction from comparable corpora can be approached as a problem of information retrieval (IR). In this representation, the query would be the word to be translated, and the documents to be found would be the candidate translations of this word. In the same way that as documents found, the candidate translations are ranked according to their relevance (i.e. a document that best matches the query). More precisely, in the *standard approach* dedicated to bilingual lexicon extraction from comparable corpora, a word to be translated is represented by a vector context composed of the words that appear in its lexical context. The candidate translations for a word are obtained by comparing the translated source context vector with the target context vectors through a general bilingual dictionary. Using this approach, good results on single word terms (SWTs) can be obtained from large corpora of several million words, with an accuracy of about 80% for the top 10-20 proposed candidates (Fung and McKeown, 1997; Rapp, 1999). Cao and Li (2002) have achieved 91% accuracy for the top three candidates using the Web as a comparable corpus. Results drop to 60% for SWTs using specialized small size language corpora (Chiao and Zweigenbaum, 2002a; Déjean and Gaussier, 2002; Morin et al., 2007).

In order to avoid the insufficient coverage of the bilingual dictionary required for the translation of source context vectors, an *extended approach* has

Proceedings of the 4th Workshop on Building and Using Comparable Corpora, pages 35–43,
49th Annual Meeting of the Association for Computational Linguistics,
Portland, Oregon, 24 June 2011. ©*2011 Association for Computational Linguistics*

been proposed (Déjean et al., 2002; Daille and Morin, 2005). This approach can be seen as a query reformulation process in IR for which similar words are substituted for the word to be translated. These similar words share the same lexical environments as the word to be translated without appearing with it. With the extended approach, (Déjean et al., 2002) obtained for single French-English words 43% and 51% precision out of the ten and twenty first candidates applied to a medical corpus of 100 000 words (respectively 44% and 57% with the standard approach) and 79% and 84% precision on the ten and twenty first candidates applied to a social science corpus of 8 million words (respectively 35% and 42% with the standard approach). Within this context, we want to show how metasearch engines can be used for bilingual lexicon extraction from specialized comparable corpora. In particular, we will focus on the use of different strategies to take full advantage of similar words.

The remainder of this paper is organized as follows. Section 2 presents the standard and extended approaches based on lexical context vectors dedicated to word alignment from comparable corpora. Section 3 describes our metasearch approach that can be viewed as the combination of different search engines. Section 4 describes the different linguistic resources used in our experiments and evaluates the contribution of the metasearch approach on the quality of bilingual terminology extraction through different experiments. Finally, Section 5 presents our conclusions.

2 Related Work

In this section, we first describe the standard approach dedicated to word alignment from comparable corpora. We then present an extension of this approach.

2.1 Standard Approach

The main work in bilingual lexicon extraction from comparable corpora is based on lexical context analysis and relies on the simple observation that a word and its translation tend to appear in the same lexical contexts. The basis of this observation consists in the identification of first-order affinities for each source and target language: *First-order affinities describe what other words are likely to be found in the immediate vicinity of a given word* (Grefenstette, 1994a, p. 279). These affinities can be represented by context vectors, and each vector element represents a word which occurs within the window of the word to be translated (for instance a seven-word window approximates syntactical dependencies).

The implementation of this approach can be carried out by applying the following four steps (Rapp, 1995; Fung and McKeown, 1997):

Context characterization

All the lexical units in the context of each lexical unit i are collected, and their frequency in a window of n words around i extracted. For each lexical unit i of the source and the target languages, we obtain a context vector $\mathbf{i}$ where each entry, $\mathbf{i}_j$, of the vector is given by a function of the co-occurrences of units j and i. Usually, association measures such as the mutual information (Fano, 1961) or the log-likelihood (Dunning, 1993) are used to define vector entries.

Vector transfer

The lexical units of the context vector $\mathbf{i}$ are translated using a bilingual dictionary. Whenever the bilingual dictionary provides several translations for a lexical unit, all the entries are considered but weighted according to their frequency in the target language. Lexical units with no entry in the dictionary are discarded.

Target language vector matching

A similarity measure, $\mathrm{sim}(\bar{\mathbf{i}}, \mathbf{t})$, is used to score each lexical unit, t, in the target language with respect to the translated context vector, $\bar{\mathbf{i}}$. Usual measures of vector similarity include the cosine similarity (Salton and Lesk, 1968) or the weighted jaccard index (WJ) (Grefenstette, 1994b) for instance.

Candidate translation

The candidate translations of a lexical unit are the target lexical units ranked following the similarity score.

2.2 Extended Approach

The main shortcoming of the standard approach is that its performance greatly relies on the coverage of the bilingual dictionary. When the context vectors

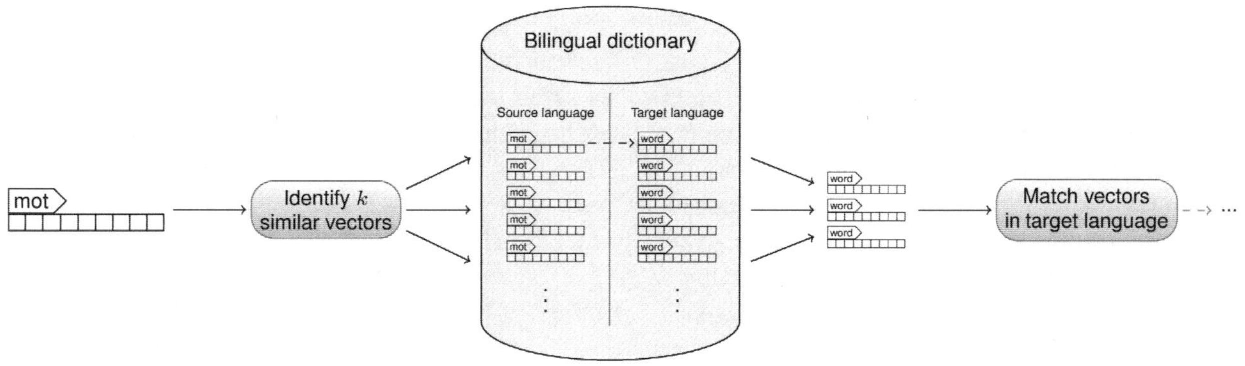

Figure 1: Illustration of the extended approach.

are well translated, the translation retrieval rate in the target language improves.

Although, the coverage of the bilingual dictionary can be extended by using specialized dictionaries or multilingual thesauri (Chiao and Zweigenbaum, 2003; Déjean et al., 2002), translation of context vectors remains the core of the approach.

In order to be less dependent on the coverage of the bilingual dictionary, Déjean and Gaussier (2002) have proposed an extension to the standard approach. The basic intuition of this approach is that words sharing the same meaning will share the same environments. The approach is based on the identification of second-order affinities in the source language: *Second-order affinities show which words share the same environments. Words sharing second-order affinities need never appear together themselves, but their environments are similar* (Grefenstette, 1994a, p. 280).

Generally speaking, a bilingual dictionary is a bridge between two languages established by its entries. The extended approach is based on this observation and avoids explicit translation of vectors as shown in Figure 1. The implementation of this extended approach can be carried out in four steps where the first and last steps are identical to the standard approach (Déjean and Gaussier, 2002; Daille and Morin, 2005):

Reformulation in the target language

For a lexical unit i to be translated, we identify the k-nearest lexical units (k nlu), among the dictionary entries corresponding to words in the source language, according to $\mathrm{sim}(\mathbf{i}, \mathbf{s})$. Each nlu is translated via the bilingual dictionary, and the vector in the target language, $\overline{\mathbf{s}}$, corresponding to the translation is selected. If the bilingual dictionary provides several translations for a given unit, $\overline{\mathbf{s}}$ is given by the union of the vectors corresponding to the translations. It is worth noting that the context vectors are not translated directly, thus reducing the influence of the dictionary.

Vector matching against reformulations

The similarity measure, $\mathrm{sim}(\overline{\mathbf{s}}, \mathbf{t})$, is used to score each lexical unit, t, in the target language with respect to the k nlu. The final score assigned to each unit, t, in the target language is given by:

$$\mathrm{sim}(\mathbf{i}, \mathbf{t}) = \sum_{s \in k\mathrm{NLU}} \mathrm{sim}(\mathbf{i}, \mathbf{s}) \times \mathrm{sim}(\overline{\mathbf{s}}, \mathbf{t}) \qquad (1)$$

An alternate scoring function has been proposed by Daille and Morin (2005). The authors computed the centroid vector of the k nlu, then scored target units with respect to the centroid.

3 The Metasearch Approach

3.1 Motivations

The approach proposed by Déjean and Gaussier (2002) implicitly introduces the problem of selecting a good k. Generally, the best choice of k depends on the data. Although several heuristic techniques, like cross-validation, can be used to select a good value of k, it is usually defined empirically.

The application of the extended approach (EA) to our data showed that the method is unstable with respect to k. In fact, for values of k over 20, the precision drops significantly. Furthermore, we cannot ensure result stability within particular ranges of values. Therefore, the value of k should be carefully tuned.

Starting from the intuition that each nearest lexical unit (nlu) contributes to the characterization of a lexical unit to be translated, our proposition aims at providing an algorithm that gives a better precision while ensuring higher stability with respect to the number of nlu. Pushing the analogy of IR style approaches (Fung and Lo, 1998) a step further, we propose a novel way of looking at the problem of word translation from comparable corpora that is conceptually simple: a metasearch problem.

In information retrieval, metasearch is the problem of combining different ranked lists, returned by multiple search engines in response to a given query, in such a way as to optimize the performance of the combined ranking (Aslam and Montague, 2001). Since the k nlu result in k distinct rankings, metasearch provides an appropriate framework for exploiting information conveyed by the rankings.

In our model, we consider each list of a given nlu as a response of a search engine independently from the others. After collecting all the lists of the selected nlu's, we combine them to obtain the final similarity score. It is worth noting that all the lists are normalized to maximize in such a way the contribution of each nlu. A good candidate is the one that obtains the highest similarity score which is calculated with respect to the selected k. If a given candidate has a high frequency in the corpus, it may be similar not only to the selected nearest lexical units (k), but also to other lexical units of the dictionary. If the candidate is close to the selected nlu's and also close to other lexical units, we consider it as a potential noise (the more neighbours a candidate has, the more it's likely to be considered as noise). We thus weight the similarity score of a candidate by taking into account this information. We compare the distribution of the candidate with the k nlu and also with all its neighbours. This leads us to suppose that a good candidate should be closer to the selected nlu's than the rest of its neighbours, if it's not the case there is more chances for this candidate to be a wrong translation.

3.2 Proposed Approach

In the following we will describe our extension to the method proposed by Déjean and Gaussier (2002). The notational conventions adopted are reviewed in Table 1. Elaborations of definitions will be given when the notation is introduced. In all our experiments both terms and lexical units are single words.

Symbol	Definition
l	a list of a given lexical unit.
k	the number of selected nearest lexical units (lists).
$freq(w, k)$	the number of lists (k) in which a term appears.
n	all the neighbours of a given term.
u	all the lexical units of the dictionary.
w_l	a term of a given list l.
$s(w_l)$	the score of the term w in the list l.
$\max_l$	the maximum score of a given list l.
$\max_{All}$	the maximum score of all the lists.
$s_{norm}(w_l)$	the normalized score of term w in the list l.
$s(w)$	the final score of a term w.
θ_w	the regulation parameter of the term w.

Table 1: Notational conventions.

The first step of our method is to collect each list of each nlu. The size of the list has its importance because it determines how many candidates are close to a given nlu. We noticed from our experiments that, if we choose lists with small sizes, we should lose information and if we choose lists with large sizes, we could keep more information than necessary and this should be a potential noise, so we consider that a good size of each list should be between 100 and 200 terms according to our experiments.

After collecting the lists, the second step is to normalize the scores. Let us consider the equation 2 :

$$s_{norm}(w_l) = s(w_l) \times \frac{\max_l}{\max_{All}} \tag{2}$$

We justify this by a rationale derived from two observations. First, scores in different rankings are compatible since they are based on the same similarity measure (i.e., on the same scale). The second observations follows from the first: if $\max(l) \gg$

max (m), then the system is more confident about the scores of the list l than m.

Using scores as fusion criteria, we compute the similarity score of a candidate by summing its scores from each list of the selected nlu's :

$$\mathrm{s}(w) = \theta_w \times \frac{\sum_{l=1}^{k} \mathrm{s}_{norm}(w_l)}{\sum_{l=1}^{n} \mathrm{s}_{norm}(w_l)} \quad (3)$$

the weight θ is given by :

$$\theta_w = freq(w,k) \times \frac{(u - (k - freq(w,k)))}{(u - freq(w,n))} \quad (4)$$

The aim of this parameter is to give more confidence to a term that occurs more often with the selected nearest neighbours (k) than the rest of its neighbours. We can not affirm that the best candidate is the one that follows this idea, but we can nevertheless suppose that candidates that appear with a high number of lexical units are less confident and have higher chances to be wrong candidates (we can consider those candidates as noise). So, θ allows us to regulate the similarity score, it is used as a confident weight or a regulation parameter. We will refer to this model as the multiple source (MS) model. We also use our model without using θ and refer to it by (LC), this allows us to show the impact of θ in our results.

4 Experiments and Results

4.1 Linguistic Resources

We have selected the documents from the Elsevier website[1] in order to obtain a French-English specialized comparable corpus. The documents were taken from the medical domain within the subdomain of 'breast cancer'. We have automatically selected the documents published between 2001 and 2008 where the title or the keywords contain the term 'cancer du sein' in French and 'breast cancer' in English. We thus collected 130 documents in French and 118 in English and about 530,000 words for each language. The documents comprising the French/English specialized comparable corpus have been normalized through the following linguistic pre-processing steps: tokenisation, part-of-speech tagging, and lemmatisation. Next, the function words were removed and the words occurring less than twice (i.e. hapax) in the French and the English parts were discarded. Finally, the comparable corpus comprised about 7,400 distinct words in French and 8,200 in English.

The French-English bilingual dictionary required for the translation phase was composed of dictionaries that are freely available on the Web. It contains, after linguistic pre-processing steps, 22,300 French single words belonging to the general language with an average of 1.6 translations per entry.

In bilingual terminology extraction from specialized comparable corpora, the terminology reference list required to evaluate the performance of the alignment programs are often composed of 100 single-word terms (SWTs) (180 SWTs in (Déjean and Gaussier, 2002), 95 SWTs in (Chiao and Zweigenbaum, 2002a), and 100 SWTs in (Daille and Morin, 2005)). To build our reference list, we selected 400 French/English SWTs from the UMLS[2] meta-thesaurus and the *Grand dictionnaire terminologique*[3]. We kept only the French/English pair of SWTs which occur more than five times in each part of the comparable corpus. As a result of filtering, 122 French/English SWTs were extracted.

4.2 Experimental Setup

Three major parameters need to be set to the extended approach, namely the similarity measure, the association measure defining the entry vectors and the size of the window used to build the context vectors. Laroche and Langlais (2010) carried out a complete study about the influence of these parameters on the quality of bilingual alignment.

As similarity measure, we chose to use the weighted jaccard index:

$$\mathrm{sim}(\mathbf{i},\mathbf{j}) = \frac{\sum_t \min(\mathbf{i}_t, \mathbf{j}_t)}{\sum_t \max(\mathbf{i}_t, \mathbf{j}_t)} \quad (5)$$

The entries of the context vectors were determined by the log-likelihood (Dunning, 1993), and we used a seven-word window since it approximates syntactic dependencies. Other combinations of parameters were assessed but the previous parameters turned out to give the best performance.

[1] www.elsevier.com

[2] http://www.nlm.nih.gov/research/umls

[3] http://www.granddictionnaire.com/

4.3 Results

To evaluate the performance of our method, we use as a baseline, the extended approach (EA) proposed by Déjean and Gaussier (2002). We compare this baseline to the two metasearch strategies defined in Section 3: the metasearch model without the regulation parameter θ (LC); and the one which is weighted by $theta$ (MS). We also provide results obtained with the standard approach (SA).

We first investigate the stability of the metasearch strategies with respect to the number of nlu considered. Figure 2 show the precision at Top 20 as a function of k.

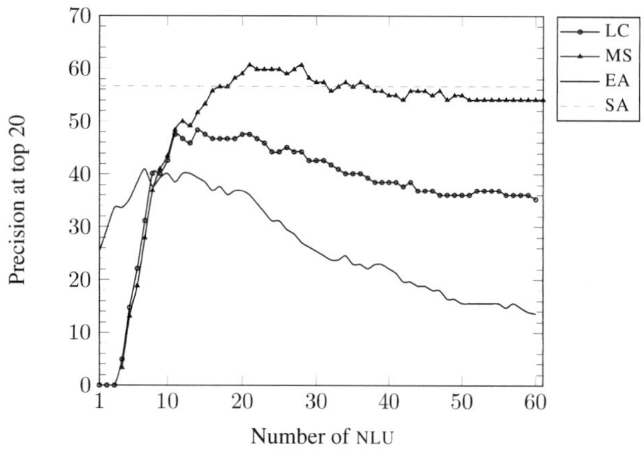

Figure 2: Precision at top 20 as a function of the number of nlu.

In order to evaluate the contribution of the parameter θ, we chose to evaluate the metasearch method starting from $k = 4$, this explains why the precision is extremely low for low values of k. We further considered that less than four occurrences of a term in the whole lexical units lists can be considered as noise. On the other side, we started from $k = 1$ for the extended approach since it makes no use of the parameter θ. Figure 2 shows that extended approach reaches its best performance at $k = 7$ with a precision of 40.98%. Then, after $k = 15$ the precision starts steadily decreasing as the value of k increases.

The metasearch strategy based only on similarity scores shows better results than the baseline. For every value of $k \geq 10$, the LC model outperform the extended approach. The best precision (48.36%) is obtained at $k = 14$, and the curve corresponding to the LC model remains above the baseline regardless of the increasing value of the parameter k. The curve corresponding to the MS model is always above the (EA) for every value of $k \geq 10$. The MS model consistently improves the precision, and achieves its best performance (60.65%) at $k = 21$.

We can notice from Figure 2 that the LC and MS models outperform the baseline (EA). More importantly, these models exhibit a better stability of the precision with respect to the k-nearest lexical units. Although the performance decrease as the value of k increases, it does not decrease as fast as in the baseline approach.

For the sake of comparability, we also provide results obtained with the standard approach (SA) (56.55%) represented by a straight line as it is not dependent on k. As we can see, the metasearch approach (MS) outperforms the standard approach for values of k bertween 20 and 30 and for greater values of k the precision remains more or less almost the same as the standard approach (SA). Thus, the metasearch model (MS) can be considered as a competitive approach regarding to its results as it is shown in the figure 2.

Finally, Figure 3 shows the contribution of each nlu taken independently from the others. This confirms our intuition that each nlu contribute to the characterization of a lexical unit to be translated, and supports our idea that their combination can improve the performances.

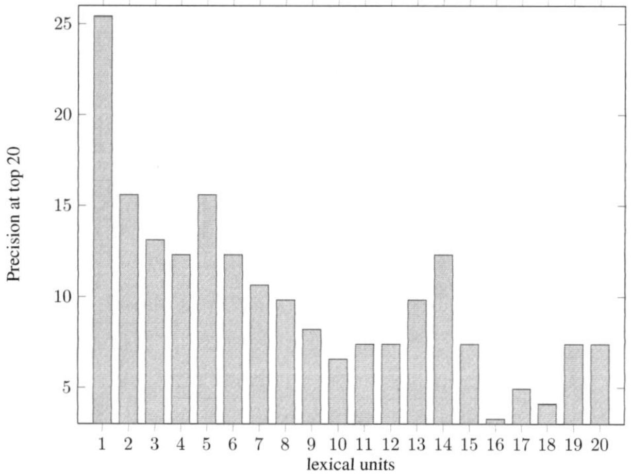

Figure 3: Precision at top 20 for each of the 20 nlu. The precision is computed by taking the each nlu independently from the others.

Figure 3 shows the top 20 of each nlu. Notice

that the nlu are ordered from the most similar to the lexical unit to be translated to the less similar, and that each one of the nearest lexical units contains information that it is worth taking into account.

Although each nlu can only translate few terms, by using the metasearch idea we are able to improve the retrieval of translation equivalents. The main idea of the metasearch paradigm is to take into account the information conveyed by all the k nlu, using either similarity scores, their behaviour with all the neighbours, in order to improve the performance of the alignment process.

Although significant improvements can be obtained with the metasearch models (comparatively to the EA and SA approach), especially concerning precision stability with respect to the k nlu, we believe that we need to address the estimation of k beforehand. Rather than fixing the same k for all the units to be translated, there is the possibility to adapt an optimal value of k to each lexical unit, according to some criteria which have to be determined.

Approachs	Top 5	Top 10	Top 15	Top 20
SA	37.70	45.08	52.45	56.55
EA	21.31	31.14	36.88	40.98
MS	**40.98**	**54.91**	**56.55**	**60.65**

Table 2: Precision(%) at top 5, 10, 15, 20 for SA, EA and MS.

Finally, we present in table 2 a comparison between SA, EA and MS for the top 5, 10, 15 and 20. By choosing the best configuration of each method, we can note that our method outperforms the others in each top. In addition, for the top 10 our precision is very close to the precision of the standard approach (SA) at the top 20. we consider these results as encouraging for future work.

4.4 Discussion

Our experiments show that the parameter k remains the core of both EA and MS approaches. A good selection of the nearest lexical units of a term guarantee to find the good translation. It is important to say that EA and MS which are based on the k nlu's depends on the coverage of the terms to be translated. Indeed, these approaches face three cases : firstly, if the frequency of the word to be translated is high and the frequency of the good translation in the target language is low, this means that the nearest lexical units of the candidate word and its translation are unbalanced. This leads us to face a lot of noise because of the high frequency of the source word that is over-represented by its nlu's comparing to the target word which is under-represented. Secondly, we consider the inverse situation, which is: low frequency of the source word and high frequency of the target translation, here as well, we have both the source and the target words that are unbalanced regarding to the selected nearest lexical units. The third case, represents more or less the same distribution of the frequencies of source candidate and target good translation. This can be considered as the most appropriate case to find the good translation by applying the approaches based on the nlu's (EA or MS). Our experiments show that our method works well in all the cases by using the parameter θ which regulate the similarity score by taken into account the distribution of the candidate according to both : selected nlu's and all its neighbours. In resume, words to be translated as represented in case one and two give more difficulties to be translated because of their unbalanced distribution which leads to an unbalanced nlu's. Future works should confirm the possibility to adapt an optimal value of k to each candidate to be translated, according to its distribution with respect to its neighbours.

5 Conclusion

We have presented a novel way of looking at the problem of bilingual lexical extraction from comparable corpora based on the idea of metasearch engines. We believe that our model is simple and sound. Regarding the empirical results of our proposition, performances of the multiple source model on our dataset was better than the baseline proposed by Déjean and Gaussier (2002), and also outperforms the standard approach for a certain range of k. We believe that the most significant result is that a new approach to finding single word translations has been shown to be competitive. We hope that this new paradigm can lead to insights that would be unclear in other models. Preliminary tests in this perspective show that using an appropriate value of k for each word can improve the performance of the lexical extraction process. Dealing with this problem is an interesting line for future research.

6 Acknowledgments

The research leading to these results has received funding from the French National Research Agency under grant ANR-08-CORD-013.

References

Javed A. Aslam and Mark Montague. 2001. Models for Metasearch. In *SIGIR '01, proceedings of the 24th Annual SIGIR Conference*, pages 276–284.

Lynne Bowker and Jennifer Pearson. 2002. *Working with Specialized Language: A Practical Guide to Using Corpora*. Routledge, London/New York.

Yunbo Cao and Hang Li. 2002. Base Noun Phrase Translation Using Web Data and the EM Algorithm. In *Proceedings of the 19th International Conference on Computational Linguistics (COLING'02)*, pages 127–133, Tapei, Taiwan.

Yun-Chuang Chiao and Pierre Zweigenbaum. 2002a. Looking for candidate translational equivalents in specialized, comparable corpora. In *Proceedings of the 19th International Conference on Computational Linguistics (COLING'02)*, pages 1208–1212, Tapei, Taiwan.

Yun-Chuang Chiao and Pierre Zweigenbaum. 2002b. Looking for French-English Translations in Comparable Medical Corpora. *Journal of the American Society for Information Science*, 8:150–154.

Yun-Chuang Chiao and Pierre Zweigenbaum. 2003. The Effect of a General Lexicon in Corpus-Based Identification of French-English Medical Word Translations. In Robert Baud, Marius Fieschi, Pierre Le Beux, and Patrick Ruch, editors, *The New Navigators: from Professionals to Patients, Actes Medical Informatics Europe*, volume 95 of *Studies in Health Technology and Informatics*, pages 397–402, Amsterdam. IOS Press.

Béatrice Daille and Emmanuel Morin. 2005. French-English Terminology Extraction from Comparable Corpora. In *Proceedings of the 2nd International Joint Conference on Natural Language Processing (IJ-CLNP'05)*, pages 707–718, Jeju Island, Korea.

Hervé Déjean and Éric Gaussier. 2002. Une nouvelle approche à l'extraction de lexiques bilingues à partir de corpus comparables. *Lexicometrica, Alignement lexical dans les corpus multilingues*, pages 1–22.

Hervé Déjean, Fatia Sadat, and Éric Gaussier. 2002. An approach based on multilingual thesauri and model combination for bilingual lexicon extraction. In *Proceedings of the 19th International Conference on Computational Linguistics (COLING'02)*, pages 218–224, Tapei, Taiwan.

Ted Dunning. 1993. Accurate Methods for the Statistics of Surprise and Coincidence. *Computational Linguistics*, 19(1):61–74.

Robert M. Fano. 1961. *Transmission of Information: A Statistical Theory of Communications*. MIT Press, Cambridge, MA, USA.

Pascale Fung and Yuen Yee Lo. 1998. An ir approach for translating new words from nonparallel, comparable texts. In *Proceedings of the 17th international conference on Computational linguistics (COLING'98)*, pages 414–420.

Pascale Fung and Kathleen McKeown. 1997. Finding Terminology Translations from Non-parallel Corpora. In *Proceedings of the 5th Annual Workshop on Very Large Corpora (VLC'97)*, pages 192–202, Hong Kong.

Pascale Fung. 1998. A Statistical View on Bilingual Lexicon Extraction: From ParallelCorpora to Non-parallel Corpora. In David Farwell, Laurie Gerber, and Eduard Hovy, editors, *Proceedings of the 3rd Conference of the Association for Machine Translation in the Americas (AMTA'98)*, pages 1–16, Langhorne, PA, USA.

Éric Gaussier, Jean-Michel Renders, Irena Matveeva, Cyril Goutte, and Hervé Déjean. 2004. A Geometric View on Bilingual Lexicon Extraction from Comparable Corpora. In *Proceedings of the 42nd Annual Meeting of the Association for Computational Linguistics (ACL'04)*, pages 526–533, Barcelona, Spain.

Gregory Grefenstette. 1994a. Corpus-Derived First, Second and Third-Order Word Affinities. In *Proceedings of the 6th Congress of the European Association for Lexicography (EURALEX'94)*, pages 279–290, Amsterdam, The Netherlands.

Gregory Grefenstette. 1994b. *Explorations in Automatic Thesaurus Discovery*. Kluwer Academic Publisher, Boston, MA, USA.

Audrey Laroche and Philippe Langlais. 2010. Revisiting Context-based Projection Methods for Term-Translation Spotting in Comparable Corpora. In *Proceedings of the 23rd International Conference on Computational Linguistics (COLING'10)*, pages 617–625, Beijing, China.

Emmanuel Morin, Béatrice Daille, Koichi Takeuchi, and Kyo Kageura. 2007. Bilingual Terminology Mining – Using Brain, not brawn comparable corpora. In *Proceedings of the 45th Annual Meeting of the Association for Computational Linguistics (ACL'07)*, pages 664–671, Prague, Czech Republic.

Carol Peters and Eugenio Picchi. 1998. Cross-language information retrieval: A system for comparable corpus querying. In Gregory Grefenstette, editor, *Cross-language information retrieval*, chapter 7, pages 81–90. Kluwer Academic Publishers.

Reinhard Rapp. 1995. Identify Word Translations in Non-Parallel Texts. In *Proceedings of the 35th Annual Meeting of the Association for Computational Linguistics (ACL'95)*, pages 320–322, Boston, MA, USA.

Reinhard Rapp. 1999. Automatic Identification of Word Translations from Unrelated English and German Corpora. In *Proceedings of the 37th Annual Meeting of the Association for Computational Linguistics (ACL'99)*, pages 519–526, College Park, MD, USA.

Gerard Salton and Michael E. Lesk. 1968. Computer evaluation of indexing and text processing. *Journal of the Association for Computational Machinery*, 15(1):8–36.

Two Ways to Use a Noisy Parallel News corpus for improving Statistical Machine Translation

Souhir Gahbiche-Braham **Hélène Bonneau-Maynard** **François Yvon**

Université Paris-Sud 11
LIMSI-CNRS
91403 Orsay, France
{souhir,hbm,yvon}@limsi.fr

Abstract

In this paper, we present two methods to use a noisy parallel news corpus to improve statistical machine translation (SMT) systems. Taking full advantage of the characteristics of our corpus and of existing resources, we use a bootstrapping strategy, whereby an existing SMT engine is used both to detect parallel sentences in comparable data and to provide an adaptation corpus for translation models. MT experiments demonstrate the benefits of various combinations of these strategies.

1 Introduction

In Statistical Machine Translation (SMT), systems are created from *parallel corpora* consisting of a set of source language texts aligned with its translation in the target language. Such corpora however only exist (at least are publicly documented and available) for a limited number of domains, genres, registers, and language pairs. In fact, there are a few language pairs for which parallel corpora can be accessed, except for very narrow domains such as political debates or international regulatory texts. Another very valuable resource for SMT studies, especially for under-resource languages, are *comparable corpora*, made of pairs of monolingual corpora that contain texts of similar genres, from similar periods, and/or about similar topics.

The potential of comparable corpora has long been established as a useful source from which to extract bilingual word dictionaries (see eg. (Rapp, 1995; Fung and Yee, 1998)) or to learn multilingual terms (see e.g. (Langé, 1995; Smadja et al., 1996)).

More recently, the relative corpus has caused the usefulness of comparable corpora be reevaluated as a potential source of parallel fragments, be they paragraphs, sentences, phrases, terms, chunks, or isolated words. This tendency is illustrated by the work of e.g. (Resnik and Smith, 2003; Munteanu and Marcu, 2005), which combines Information Retrieval techniques (to identify parallel documents) and sentence similarity detection to detect parallel sentences.

There are many other ways to improve SMT models with comparable or monolingual data. For instance, the work reported in (Schwenk, 2008) draws inspiration from recent advances in unsupervised training of acoustic models for speech recognition and proposes to use self-training on in-domain data to adapt and improve a baseline system trained mostly with out-of-domain data.

As discussed e.g. in (Fung and Cheung, 2004), comparable corpora are of various nature: there exists a continuum between truly parallel and completely unrelated texts. Algorithms for exploiting comparable corpora should thus be tailored to the peculiarities of the data on which they are applied.

In this paper, we report on experiments aimed at using a noisy parallel corpus made out of news stories in French and Arabic in two different ways: first, to extract new, in-domain, parallel sentences; second, to adapt our translation and language models. This approach is made possible due to the specificities of our corpus. In fact, our work is part of a project aiming at developing a platform for processing multimedia news documents (texts, interviews, images and videos) in Arabic, so as to streamline the

Proceedings of the 4th Workshop on Building and Using Comparable Corpora, pages 44–51,
49th Annual Meeting of the Association for Computational Linguistics,
Portland, Oregon, 24 June 2011. ©*2011 Association for Computational Linguistics*

work of a major international news agency. As part as the standard daily work flow, a significant portion of the French news are translated (or adapted) in Arabic by journalists. Having access to one full year of the French and Arabic corpus (consisting, to date, of approximately one million stories (150 million words)), we have in our hands an ideal comparable resource to perform large scale experiments.

These experiments aim at comparing various ways to build an accurate machine translation system for the news domain using (i) a baseline system trained mostly with out-of-domain data (ii) the comparable dataset. As will be discussed, given the very large number of parallel news in the data, our best option seems to reconstruct an in-domain training corpus of automatically detected parallel sentences.

The rest of this paper is organized as follows. In Section 2, we relate our work to some existing approaches for using comparable corpora. Section 3 presents our methodology for extracting parallel sentences, while our phrase-table adaptation strategies are described in Section 4. In Section 5, we describe our experiments and contrast the results obtained with several adaptation strategies. Finally, Section 6 concludes the paper.

2 Related work

From a bird's eye view, attempts to use comparable corpora in SMT fall into two main categories: first, approaches aimed at extracting parallel fragments; second, approaches aimed at adapting existing resources to a new domain.

2.1 Extracting parallel fragments

Most attempts at automatically extracting parallel fragments use a two step process (see (Tillmann and Xu, 2009) for a counter-example): a set of candidate parallel texts is first identified; within this short list of possibly paired texts, parallel sentences are then identified based on some similarity score.

The work reported in (Zhao and Vogel, 2002) concentrates on finding parallel sentences in a set of comparable stories pairs in Chinese/English. Sentence similarity derives from a probabilistic alignment model for documents, which enables to recognize parallel sentences based on their length ratio, as well as on the IBM 1 model score of their word-to-word alignment. To account for various levels of parallelism, the model allows some sentences in the source or target language to remain unaligned.

The work of (Resnik and Smith, 2003) considers mining a much larger "corpora" consisting of documents collected on the Internet. Matched documents and sentences are primarily detected based on surface and/or formal similarity of the web addresses or of the page internal structure.

This line of work is developed notably in (Munteanu and Marcu, 2005): candidate parallel texts are found using Cross-Lingual Information Retrieval (CLIR) techniques; sentence similarity is indirectly computed using a logistic regression model aimed at detecting parallel sentences. This formalism allows to enrich baseline features such as the length ratio, the word-to-word (IBM 1) alignment scores with supplementary scores aimed at rewarding sentences containing identical words, etc. More recently, (Smith et al., 2010) reported significant improvements mining parallel Wikipedia articles using more sophisticated indicators of sentence parallelism, incorporating a richer set of features and cross-sentence dependencies within a Conditional Random Fields (CRFs) model. For lack of find enough parallel sentences, (Munteanu and Marcu, 2006; Kumano and Tokunaga, 2007) consider the more difficult issue of mining parallel *phrases*.

In (Abdul-Rauf and Schwenk, 2009), the authors, rather than computing a similarity score between a source and a target sentence, propose to use an existing translation engine to process the source side of the corpus, thus enabling sentence comparison to be performed in the target language, using the edit distance or variants thereof (WER or TER). This approach is generalized to much larger collections in (Uszkoreit et al., 2010), which draw advantage of working in one language to adopt efficient parallelism detection techniques (Broder, 2000).

2.2 Comparable corpora for adaptation

Another very productive use of comparable corpora is to *adapt* or *specialize* existing resources (dictionaries, translation models, language models) to specific domains and/or genres. We will only focus here on adapting the translation model; a review of the literature on language model adaptation is in (Bellagarda, 2001) and the references cited therein.

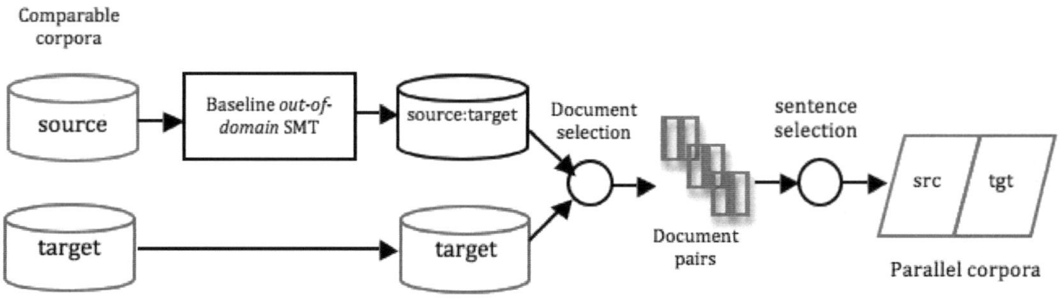

Figure 1: Extraction of parallel corpora

The work in (Snover et al., 2008) is a first step towards augmenting the translation model with new translation rules: these rules associate, with a tiny probability, every phrase in a source document with the most frequent target phrases found in a comparable corpus specifically built for this document.

The study in (Schwenk, 2008) considers *self-training*, which allows to adapt an existing system to new domains using monolingual (source) data. The idea is to automatically translate the source side of an in-domain corpus using a reference translation system. Then, according to some confidence score, the best translations are selected to form an *adaptation corpus*, which can serve to retrain the translation model. The authors of (Cettolo et al., 2010) follow similar goals with different means: here, the baseline translation model is used to obtain a phrase alignment between source and target sentences in a comparable corpus. These phrase alignments are further refined, before new phrases *not in the original phrase-table*, can be collected.

The approaches developed below borrow from both traditions: given (i) the supposed high degree of parallelism in our data and (ii) the size of the available comparable data, we are in a position to apply any of the above described technique. This is all the easier to do as all stories are timestamped, which enables to easily spot candidate parallel texts. In both cases, we will apply a bootstrapping strategy using as baseline a system trained with out-of-domain data.

3 Extracting Parallel Corpora

This section presents our approach for extracting a parallel corpus from a comparable in-domain corpora so as to adapt a SMT system to a specific domain. Our methodology assumes that both a baseline *out-of-domain* translation system and a comparable *in-domain* corpus are available, two requirements that are often met in practice.

As shown in Figure 1, our approach for extracting an *in-domain* parallel corpus from the *in-domain* comparable corpus consists in 3 steps and closely follows (Abdul-Rauf and Schwenk, 2009):

translation: translating the source side of the comparable corpora;

document pairs selection : selecting, in the comparable corpus, documents that are similar to the translated output;

sentence pairs selection : selecting parallel sentences among the selected documents.

The main intuition is that computing document similarities in one language enables to use simple and effective comparison procedures, instead of having to define *ad hoc* similarities measures based on complex underlying alignment models.

The **translation** step consists here in translating the source (Arabic) side of the comparable corpus using a baseline *out-of-domain* system, which has been trained on parallel *out-of-domain* data.

The **document selection** step consists in trying to match the automatic translations (source:target) with the original documents in the target language. For each (source:target) document, a similarity score with all the target documents is computed. We contend here with a simple association score, namely the Dice coefficient, computed as the number of words in common in both documents, normalized by the length of the (source:target) document.

A priori knowledge, such as the publication dates

of the documents, are used to limit the number of document pairs to be compared. For each source document, the target document that has the best score is then selected as a potential parallel document. The resulting pairs of documents are then filtered depending on a threshold T_d, so as to avoid false matches (in the experiments described below, the threshold has been set so as to favor precision over recall).

At the end of this step, a set of similar source and target document pairs has been selected. These pairs may consist in documents that are exact translations of each other. In most cases, the documents are noisy translation and only a subset of their sentences are mutual translation.

The **sentence selection** step then consists in performing a sentence level alignment of each pair of documents to select a set of parallel sentences. Sentence alignment is then performed with the hunalign sentence alignment tool (Varga et al., 2005), which also provides alignment confidence measures. As for the document selection step, only sentence pairs that obtain an alignment score greater than a predefined threshold T_s are selected, where T_s is again chosen to favor prevision of alignments of recall. From these, $1:1$ alignments are retained, yielding a small, adapted, parallel corpus. This method is quite different from (Munteanu and Marcu, 2005)'s work where the sentence selection step is done by a Maximum Entropy classifier.

4 Domain Adaptation

In the course of mining our comparable corpus, we have produced a translation into French for all the source language news stories. This means that we have three parallel corpora at our disposal:

- The **baseline training corpus**, which is large (a hundred million words), delivering a reasonable translation performance quality of translation, but *out-of-domain*;
- The **extracted *in-domain* corpus**, which is much smaller, and potentially noisy;
- The **translated *in-domain* corpus**, which is of medium-size, and much worse in quality than the others.

Considering these three corpora, different adaptation methods of the translation models are explored. The first approach is to concatenate the **baseline** and **in-domain** training data (either **extracted** or **translated**) to train a new translation model. Given the difference in size between the two corpus, this approach may introduce a bias in the translation model in favor of *out-of-domain*.

The second approach is to train separate translation models with **baseline** on the one hand, and with *in-domain* on the other data and to weight their combination with MERT (Och, 2003). This alleviates the former problem but increases the number of features that need to be trained, running the risk to make MERT less stable.

A last approach is also considered, which consists in using only the **in-domain** data to train the translation model. In that case, the question is the small size of the *in-domain* data.

The comparative experiments on the three approaches, using the three corpora are described in next section.

5 Experiments and results

5.1 Context and data

The experiments have been carried out in the context of the Cap Digital SAMAR[1] project which aims at developping a platform for processing multimedia news in Arabic. Every day, about 250 news in Arabic, 800 in French and in English[2] are produced and accumulated on our disks. News collected from December 2009 to December 2010 constitute the comparable corpora, containing a set of 75,975 news for the Arabic part and 288,934 news for the French part (about 1M sentences for Arabic and 5M sentences for French).

The specificity of this comparable corpus is that many Arabic stories are known to be translation of news that were first written in French. The translations may not be entirely faithful: when translating a story, the journalist is in fact free to rearrange the structure, and to some extend, the content of a document (see example Figure 2).

In our experiments, the *in-domain* comparable corpus then consists in a set of Arabic and French

[1] http://www.samar.fr

[2] The English news have not been used in this study.

Arabic:
واضاف نحن في حماس لا مانع لدينا من استئناف المفاوضات غير المباشرة حول الصفقة من النقطة التي انتهت اليها والتي حاول ان يفشلها نتانياهو.
And he added, we in Hamas don't have a problem to resume indirect negotiations about the deal from the point at which it ended and at which Netanyahu tried to fail.

French: Le porte-parole a réaffirmé que le Hamas était prêt à reprendre les tractations au point où elles s'étaient arrêtées.
The spokesman reaffirmed that Hamas was ready to resume negotiations at the point where they stopped.

Figure 2: An example of incorrect/inexact translation in a pair of similar documents.

documents which are parallel, partly parallel, or not parallel at all, with no explicit link between Arabic and French parts.

5.2 Baseline translation system

The baseline *out-of-domain* translation system was trained on a corpus of 7.6 million of parallel sentences (see Table 1), that was harvested from publicly available sources on the web: the United Nations (UN) document database, the website of the World Health Organization (WHO) and the Project Syndicate Web site. The "UN" data constitutes by far the largest portion of this corpus, from which only the Project Syndicate documents can be considered as appropriate for the task at hand.

A 4-gram backoff French language model was built on 2.4 billion words of running texts, taken from the parallel data, as well as notably the Gigaword French corpus.

	ar		fr	
Corpus	**#tokens**	**voc**	**#tokens**	**voc**
baseline	162M	369K	186M	307K
extracted	3.6M	72K	4.0M	74K
translated	20.8M	217 K	22.1M	181K

Table 1: Corpus statistics: total number of tokens in the French and Arabic sides, Arabic and French vocabulary size. Numbers are given on the preprocessed data.

Arabic is a rich and morphologically complex language, and therefore data preprocessing is necessary to deal with data scarcity. All Arabic data were preprocessed by first transliterating the Arabic text with the BAMA (Buckwalter, 2002) transliteration tool. Then, the Arabic data are segmented into sentences. A CRF-based sentence segmenter for Arabic was built with the Wapiti[3] (Lavergne et al., 2010) package. A morphological analysis of the Arabic text is then done using the Arabic morphological analyzer and disambiguation tool MADA (Nizar Habash and Roth, 2009), with the MADA-D2 since it seems to be the most efficient scheme for large data (Habash and Sadat, 2006).

The preprocessed Arabic and French data were aligned using MGiza++[4] (Gao and Vogel, 2008). The Moses toolkit (Koehn et al., 2007) is then used to make the alignments symmetric using the *grow-diag-final-and* heuristic and to extract phrases with maximum length of 7 words. A distortion model lexically conditioned on both the Arabic phrases and French phrases is then trained. Feature weights were set by running MERT (Och, 2003) on the development set.

5.3 Extraction of the *in-domain* parallel corpus

We follow the method described in Section 3: Arabic documents are first translated into French using the baseline SMT system. For the document selection step each translated (ar:fr) document is compared only to the French documents of the same day. The thresholds for document selection and sentence selection were respectively set to 0.5 and 0.7. For a pair of similar documents, the average percentage of selected sentences is about 43%.

The document selection step allows to select documents containing around 35% of the total number of sentences from the initial Arabic part of the comparable corpus, a percentage that goes down to 15% after the sentence alignment step. The resulting *in-domain* parallel corpus thus consists in a set of 156K pairs of parallel sentences. Data collected during the last month of the period was isolated from the resulting corpus, and was used to randomly extract a development and a test set of approximately 1,000

[3]`http://wapiti.limsi.fr`

[4]`http://geek.kyloo.net/software/doku.php/mgiza:overview`

Reference:	Le ministre russe des Affaires étrangères, Sergueï Lavrov *a prévenu* mercredi [...]
Baseline:	*Pronostiquait* Ministre des affaires étrangères russe, Sergei Lavrov mercredi [...]
Extracted:	Le ministre russe des Affaires étrangères, Sergueï Lavrov *a averti* mercredi [...]
Reference:	Le porte-parole de Mme Clinton, *Philip Crowley*, a toutefois reconnu [...]
Baseline:	Pour *ukun FILIP Cruau* porte-parole de Clinton a reconnu ...
Extracted:	Mais *Philip Crowley*, le porte-parole de Mme Clinton a reconnu [...]

Figure 3: Comparative translations using the **baseline** translation and the **extracted** translation systems of two sentences: *"Russian Minister of Foreign Affairs, Sergueï Lavrov, informed Wednesday [...]"* and *"The spokesman for Mrs. Clinton, Philip Crowley, however, acknowledged [...]"*.

lines each. These 2,160 sentences were manually checked to evaluate the precision of the approach, and we found that 97.2% of the sentences were correctly paired. Table 1 compares the main characteristics of the three corpora used for training.

5.4 Translation Results

Translation results obtained on the test set are reported in terms of BLEU scores in Table 2, along with the corresponding phrase table sizes. The different adaptation approaches described in Section 4 were experimented with both **extracted** and **translated** corpora as adaptation corpus (see Section 3). As expected, adapting the translation model to the

SMT System	#Phrase pairs	BLEU
baseline	312.4M	24.0
extracted	10.9M	29.2
baseline+extracted (1 table)	321.6M	29.0
baseline+extracted (2 tables)	312.4M + 9.9M	**30.1**
translated	39M	26.7
extracted+translated (2 tables)	9.9M + 39M	28.2

Table 2: Arabic to French translation BLEU scores on a test set of 1000 sentences

news domain is very effective. Compared to the baseline system, all adapted systems obtain much better results (from 2 to 6 BLEU points). The **extracted** system outperforms the baseline system by 5 BLEU points, even though the training set is much smaller (3.6M compared to 162M tokens). This result indirectly validates the precision of our methodology.

Concatenating the baseline and extracted data to train a single translation model does not improve the smaller **extracted** system, thus maybe reflecting the fact that the large *out-of-domain* corpus overwhelms the contribution of the *in-domain* data. However, a log-linear combination of the corresponding phrase tables brings a small improvement (0.8 BLEU point).

Another interesting result comes from the performance of the system trained only on the **translated** corpus. *Without using any filtering of the automatic translations*, this artificial dataset enables to build another system which outperforms the baseline system by 2.5 BLEU points. This is another illustration of the greater importance of having matched domain data, even of a poorer quality, than good parallel *out-of-domain* sentences (Cettolo et al., 2010).

In the last experiment, all the available *in-domain* data (**extracted** and **translated**) are used in conjunction, with a separate phrase-table trained on each corpus. However, this did not enable to match the results of the **extracted** system, a paradoxical result that remains to be analyzed more carefully. Filtering automatic translations may be an issue.

A rapid observation of the translations provided by both the baseline system and the **extracted** system shows that the produced output are quite different. Figure 3 displays two typical examples: the first one illustrates the different styles in Arabic ("News" style often put subject *"Le ministre russe des affaires étrangères"* before verb *" a prévenu"* or *"a averti"* — which are semantically equivalent — whereas "UN" style is more classical, with the verb *"Pronostiquait"* followed by the subject *"ministre russe des Affaires étrangères"*). The second one shows how adaptation fixes the translation of words (here *"Philip Crowley"*) that were not (correctly) translated by the baseline system (*"ukun FILIP Cruau"*).

6 Conclusion

We have presented an empirical study of various methodologies for (i) extracting a parallel corpus from a comparable corpus (the so-called "Noisy Corpus") and (ii) using in-domain data to adapt a baseline SMT system. Experimental results, obtained using a large 150 million word Arabic/French comparable corpus, allow to jointly validate the extraction of the in-domain parallel corpus and the proposed adaptation methods. The best adapted system, trained on a combination of the baseline and the extracted data, improves the baseline by 6 BLEU points. Preliminary experiments with self-training also demonstrate the potential of this technique.

As a follow-up, we intend to investigate the evolution of the translation results as a function of the precision/recall quality of the extracted corpus, and of the quality of the automatically translated data. We have also only focused here on the adaptation of the translation model. We expect to achieve further gains when combining these techniques with LM adaptation techniques.

This work was partly supported by the FUI/SAMAR project funded by the *Cap Digital* competitivity cluster.

References

Sadaf Abdul-Rauf and Holger Schwenk. 2009. On the use of comparable corpora to improve smt performance. In *Proceedings of the 12th Conference of the European Chapter of the Association for Computational Linguistics*, EACL '09, pages 16–23, Morristown, NJ, USA. Association for Computational Linguistics.

Jérôme R. Bellagarda. 2001. An overview of statistical language model adaptation. In *Proceedings of the ISCA Tutorial and Research Workshop (ITRW) on Adaptation Methods for Speech Recognition*, pages 165–174, Sophia Antipolis, France.

Andrei Z. Broder. 2000. Identifying and filtering near-duplicate documents. In *Proceedings of the 11th Annual Symposium on Combinatorial Pattern Matching*, COM '00, pages 1–10, London, UK. Springer-Verlag.

Tim Buckwalter. 2002. *Buckwalter Arabic Morphological Analyzer.* Linguistic Data Consortium. (LDC2002L49).

Mauro Cettolo, Marcello Federico, and Nicola Bertoldi. 2010. Mining Parallel Fragments from Comparable Texts. In Marcello Federico, Ian Lane, Michael Paul, and François Yvon, editors, *Proceedings of the seventh International Workshop on Spoken Language Translation (IWSLT)*, pages 227–234.

Pascale Fung and Percy Cheung. 2004. Multilevel bootstrapping for extracting parallel sentences from a quasi parallel corpus. In *Proceedings of the conference on Empirical Methods in Natural Language Processing (EMNLP 04)*, pages 1051–1057.

Pascale Fung and Lo Yuen Yee. 1998. An IR approach for translating new words from nonparallel, comparable texts. In *Proceedings of the 36th Annual Meeting of the Association for Computational Linguistics and 17th International Conference on Computational Linguistics-Volume 1*, pages 414–420. Association for Computational Linguistics.

Qin Gao and Stephan Vogel. 2008. Parallel implementations of word alignment tool. In *Software Engineering, Testing, and Quality Assurance for Natural Language Processing*, SETQA-NLP '08, pages 49–57.

Nizar Habash and Fatiha Sadat. 2006. Arabic preprocessing schemes for statistical machine translation. In *Proceedings of the Human Language Technology Conference of the NAACL, Companion Volume: Short Papers*, NAACL-Short '06, pages 49–52, Morristown, NJ, USA. Association for Computational Linguistics.

Philipp Koehn, Hieu Hoang, Alexandra Birch, Chris Callison-Burch, Marcello Federico, Nicola Bertoldi, Brooke Cowan, Wade Shen, Christine Moran, Richard Zens, Chris Dyer, Ondřej Bojar, Alexandra Constantin, and Evan Herbst. 2007. Moses: open source toolkit for statistical machine translation. In *Proceedings of the 45th Annual Meeting of the ACL on Interactive Poster and Demonstration Sessions*, ACL '07, pages 177–180, Morristown, NJ, USA. Association for Computational Linguistics.

Tadashi Kumano and Hideki Tanaka Takenobu Tokunaga. 2007. Extracting phrasal alignments from comparable corpora by using joint probability smt model. In Andy Way and Barbara Gawronska, editors, *Proceedings of the 11th International Conference on Theoretical and Methodological Issues in Machine Translation (TMI'07)*, Skövde, Sweden.

Jean-Marc Langé. 1995. Modèles statistiques pour l'extraction de lexiques bilingues. *Traitement Automatique des Langues*, 36(1-2):133–155.

Thomas Lavergne, Olivier Cappé, and François Yvon. 2010. Practical very large scale crfs. In *Proceedings of the 48th Annual Meeting of the Association for*

Computational Linguistics, pages 504–513, Uppsala, Sweden.

Dragos Stefan Munteanu and Daniel Marcu. 2005. Improving machine translation performance by exploiting non-parallel corpora. *Computational Linguistics*, 31(4):477–504.

Dragos Stefan Munteanu and Daniel Marcu. 2006. Extracting parallel sub-sentential fragments from non-parallel corpora. In *Proceedings of the 21st International Conference on Computational Linguistics and the 44th annual meeting of the Association for Computational Linguistics*, ACL-44, pages 81–88, Stroudsburg, PA, USA. Association for Computational Linguistics.

Owen Rambow Nizar Habash and Ryan Roth. 2009. Mada+tokan: A toolkit for arabic tokenization, diacritization, morphological disambiguation, pos tagging, stemming and lemmatization. In Khalid Choukri and Bente Maegaard, editors, *Proceedings of the Second International Conference on Arabic Language Resources and Tools*, Cairo, Egypt, April. The MEDAR Consortium.

Franz Josef Och. 2003. Minimum error rate training in statistical machine translation. In *Proceedings of the 41st Annual Meeting of the Association for Computational Linguistics*, pages 160–167, Sapporo, Japan.

Reinhard Rapp. 1995. Identifying word translations in non-parallel texts. In *Proceedings of the 33rd annual meeting on Association for Computational Linguistics*, ACL '95, pages 320–322, Stroudsburg, PA, USA. Association for Computational Linguistics.

Philip Resnik and Noah A. Smith. 2003. The Web as a parallel corpus. *Computational Linguistics*, 29:349–380.

Holger Schwenk. 2008. Investigations on large-scale lightly-supervised training for statistical machine translation. In *Proceedings of the International Workshop on Spoken Language Translation*, pages 182–189, Hawaii, USA.

Frank Smadja, Kathleen R. McKeown, and Vasileios Hatzivassiloglou. 1996. Translating collocations for bilingual lexicons: a statistical approach. *Computational Linguistics*, 22:1–38, March.

Jason R. Smith, Chris Quirk, and Kristina Toutanova. 2010. Extracting parallel sentences from comparable corpora using document level alignment. In *Human Language Technologies: The 2010 Annual Conference of the North American Chapter of the Association for Computational Linguistics*, HLT '10, pages 403–411, Stroudsburg, PA, USA. Association for Computational Linguistics.

Matthew Snover, Bonnie Dorr, and Richard Schwartz. 2008. Language and translation model adaptation using comparable corpora. In *Proceedings of the Conference on Empirical Methods in Natural Language Processing*, EMNLP '08, pages 857–866, Stroudsburg, PA, USA. Association for Computational Linguistics.

Christoph Tillmann and Jian-ming Xu. 2009. A simple sentence-level extraction algorithm for comparable data. In *Proceedings of Human Language Technologies: The 2009 Annual Conference of the North American Chapter of the Association for Computational Linguistics, Companion Volume: Short Papers*, NAACL-Short '09, pages 93–96, Stroudsburg, PA, USA. Association for Computational Linguistics.

Jakob Uszkoreit, Jay M. Ponte, Ashok C. Popat, and Moshe Dubiner. 2010. Large scale parallel document mining for machine translation. In *Proceedings of the 23rd International Conference on Computational Linguistics*, COLING '10, pages 1101–1109, Stroudsburg, PA, USA. Association for Computational Linguistics.

Dániel Varga, László Németh, Péter Halácsy, András Kornai, Viktor Trón, and Viktor Nagy. 2005. Parallel corpora for medium density languages. In *Proceedings of the RANLP*, pages 590–596.

Bing Zhao and Stephan Vogel. 2002. Adaptive parallel sentence mining from Web bilingual news collection. In *Proceedings of the International Conference on Data Mining*, pages 745–748. IEEE Computer Society.

Paraphrase Fragment Extraction from Monolingual Comparable Corpora

Rui Wang
Language Technology Lab
DFKI GmbH
Stuhlsatzenhausweg 3 / Building D3 2
Saarbruecken, 66123 Germany
rwang@coli.uni-sb.de

Chris Callison-Burch
Computer Science Department
Johns Hopkins University
3400 N. Charles Street (CSEB 226-B)
Baltimore, MD 21218, USA
ccb@cs.jhu.edu

Abstract

We present a novel paraphrase fragment pair extraction method that uses a monolingual comparable corpus containing different articles about the same topics or events. The procedure consists of document pair extraction, sentence pair extraction, and fragment pair extraction. At each stage, we evaluate the intermediate results manually, and tune the later stages accordingly. With this minimally supervised approach, we achieve 62% of accuracy on the paraphrase fragment pairs we collected and 67% extracted from the MSR corpus. The results look promising, given the minimal supervision of the approach, which can be further scaled up.

1 Introduction

Paraphrase is an important linguistic phenomenon which occurs widely in human languages. Since paraphrases capture the variations of linguistic expressions while preserving the meaning, they are very useful in many applications, such as machine translation (Marton et al., 2009), document summarization (Barzilay et al., 1999), and recognizing textual entailment (RTE) (Dagan et al., 2005).

However, such resources are not trivial to obtain. If we make a comparison between paraphrase and MT, the latter has large parallel bilingual/multilingual corpora to acquire translation pairs in different granularity; while it is difficult to find a "naturally" occurred paraphrase "parallel" corpora. Furthermore, in MT, certain words can be translated into a (rather) small set of candidate words in the target language; while in principle, each paraphrase can have infinite number of "target" expressions, which reflects the variety of each human language.

A variety of paraphrase extraction approaches have been proposed recently, and they require different types of training data. Some require bilingual parallel corpora (Callison-Burch, 2008; Zhao et al., 2008), others require monolingual parallel corpora (Barzilay and McKeown, 2001; Ibrahim et al., 2003) or monolingual comparable corpora (Dolan et al., 2004).

In this paper, we focus on extracting paraphrase fragments from monolingual corpora, because this is the most abundant source of data. Additionally, this would potentially allow us to extract paraphrases for a variety of languages that have monolingual corpora, but which do not have easily accessible parallel corpora.

This paper makes the following contributions:

1. We adapt a translation fragment pair extraction method to paraphrase extraction, i.e., from bilingual corpora to monolingual corpora.

2. We construct a large collection of paraphrase fragments from monolingual comparable corpora and achieve similar quality from a manually-checked paraphrase corpus.

3. We evaluate both intermediate and final results of the paraphrase collection, using the crowdsourcing technique, which is effective, fast, and cheap.

Proceedings of the 4th Workshop on Building and Using Comparable Corpora, pages 52–60,
49th Annual Meeting of the Association for Computational Linguistics,
Portland, Oregon, 24 June 2011. ©*2011 Association for Computational Linguistics*

Corpora		Sentence level	Sub-sentential level
Paraphrase acquisition			
Monolingual	Parallel	e.g., Barzilay and McKeown (2001)	This paper
	Comparable	e.g., Quirk et al. (2004)	e.g., Shinyama et al. (2002) & This paper
Bilingual	Parallel	N/A	e.g., Bannard and Callison-Burch (2005)
Statistical machine translation			
Bilingual	Parallel	Most SMT systems	SMT phrase tables
	Comparable	e.g., Fung and Lo (1998)	e.g., Munteanu and Marcu (2006)

Table 1: Previous work in paraphrase acquisition and machine translation.

2 Related Work

Roughly speaking, there are three dimensions to characterize the previous work in paraphrase acquisition and machine translation, whether the data comes from monolingual or bilingual corpora, whether the corpora are parallel or comparable, and whether the output is at the sentence level or at the sub-sentential level. Table 1 gives one example in each category.

Paraphrase acquisition is mostly done at the sentence-level, e.g., (Barzilay and McKeown, 2001; Barzilay and Lee, 2003; Dolan et al., 2004), which is not straightforward to be used as a resource for other NLP applications. Quirk et al. (2004) adopted the MT approach to "translate" one sentence into a paraphrased one. As for the corpora, Barzilay and McKeown (2001) took different English translations of the same novels (i.e., monolingual parallel corpora), while the others experimented on multiple sources of the same news/events, i.e., monolingual comparable corpora.

At the sub-sentential level, interchangeable patterns (Shinyama et al., 2002; Shinyama and Sekine, 2003) or inference rules (Lin and Pantel, 2001) are extracted, which are quite successful in named-entity-centered tasks, like information extraction, while they are not generalized enough to be applied to other tasks or they have a rather small coverage, e.g. RTE (Dinu and Wang, 2009). To our best knowledge, there is few focused study on *general* paraphrase fragments extraction at the sub-sentential level, from comparable corpora. A recent study by Belz and Kow (2010) mainly aimed at natural language generation, which they performed a small scale experiment on a specific topic, i.e., British hills.

Given the available parallel corpora from the MT community, there are studies focusing on extracting paraphrases from bilingual corpora (Bannard and Callison-Burch, 2005; Callison-Burch, 2008; Zhao et al., 2008). The way they do is to treat one language as an pivot and equate two phrases in the other languages as paraphrases if they share a common pivot phrase. Paraphrase extraction draws on phrase pair extraction from the translation literature. Since parallel corpora have many alternative ways of expressing the same foreign language concept, large quantities of paraphrase pairs can be extracted.

As for the MT research, the standard statistical MT systems require large size of parallel corpora for training and then extract sub-sentential translation phrases. Apart from the limited parallel corpora, comparable corpora are non-parallel bilingual corpora whose documents convey the similar information are also widely considered by many researchers, e.g., (Fung and Lo, 1998; Koehn and Knight, 2000; Vogel, 2003; Fung and Cheung, 2004a; Fung and Cheung, 2004b; Munteanu and Marcu, 2005; Wu and Fung, 2005). A recent study by Smith et al. (2010) extracted parallel sentences from comparable corpora to extend the existing resources.

At the sub-sentential level, Munteanu and Marcu (2006) extracted sub-sentential translation pairs from comparable corpora based on the log-likelihood-ratio of word translation probability. They exploit the possibility of making use of reports within a limited time window, which are about the same event or having overlapping contents, but in different languages. Quirk et al. (2007) extracted fragments using a generative model of noisy translations. They show that even in non-parallel corpora, useful parallel words or phrases can still be found and the size of such data is much larger than that of

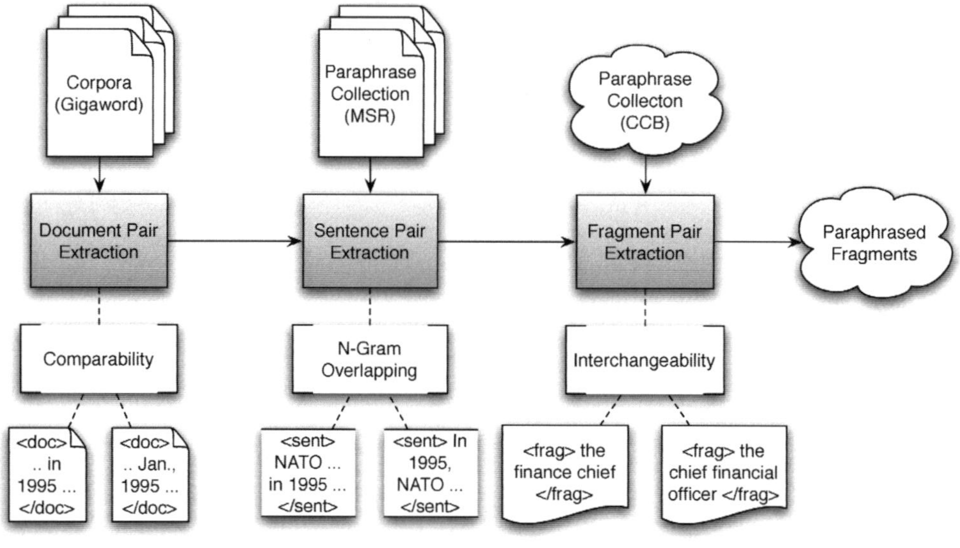

Figure 1: A three stage pipeline is used to extract paraphrases from monolingual texts

parallel corpora. In this paper, we adapt ideas from the MT research on extracting sub-sentential translation fragments from bilingual comparable corpora (Munteanu and Marcu, 2006), and use the techniques to extract paraphrases from monolingual parallel and comparable corpora.

Evaluation is another challenge for resource collection, which usually requires tremendous labor resources. Both Munteanu and Marcu (2006) and Quirk et al. (2007) evaluated their resources indirectly in MT systems, while in this paper, we make use of the crowd-sourcing technique to manually evaluate the quality of the paraphrase collection. In parcitular, Amazon's Mechanical Turk[1] (MTurk) provides a way to pay people small amounts of money to perform tasks that are simple for humans but difficult for computers. Examples of these Human Intelligence Tasks (or HITs) range from labeling images to moderating blog comments to providing feedback on relevance of results for a search query. Using MTurk for NLP task evaluation has been shown to be significantly cheaper and faster, and there is a high agreement between aggregate non-expert annotations and gold-standard annotations provided by the experts (Snow et al., 2008).

[1] `http://www.mturk.com/`

3 Fragment Pair Acquisition

Figure 1 shows the pipeline of our paraphrase acquisition method. We evaluate quality at each stage using Amazon's Mechanical Turk. In order to ensure that the non-expert annotators complete the task accurately, we used both positive and negative controls. If annotators answered either control incorrectly, we excluded their answers. For all the experiments we describe in this paper, we obtain the answers within a couple of hours or an overnight. Our focus in this paper is on fragment extraction, but we briefly describe document and sentence pair extraction first.

3.1 Document Pair Extraction

Monolingual comparable corpora contain texts about the same events or subjects, written in one language by different authors (Barzilay and Elhadad, 2003). We extract pairs of newswire articles written by different news agencies from the GIGAWORD corpus, which contains articles from six different agencies. Although the comparable documents are not in parallel, at the sentential or sub-sentential level, the paraphrased fragments may still exist.

To quantify the comparability between two documents, we calculate the number of overlapping words and give them different weights based on TF-IDF (Salton and McGill, 1983) using the *More-*

LikeThis[2] function provided by *Lucene*.

After collecting the document pairs, we asked annotators, "Are these two documents about the same topic?", and allowing them to answer "Yes", "No", and "Not sure". Each set of six document pairs contained, four to be evaluated, one positive control (a pair of identical documents) and one negative control (a pair of random documents). We sampled 400 document pairs with the comparability score between 0.8 and 0.9, and another 400 pairs greater than 0.9. We presented them in a random order and each was labeled by three annotations. After excluding the annotations containing incorrect answers for either control, we took a majority vote for every document pair, and if three annotations are different from each other.

We found document pairs with >0.9 were classified by annotators to be related more than half the time, and a higher threshold would greatly decrease the number of document pairs extracted. We performed subsequent steps on the 3896 document pairs that belonged to this category.

3.2 Sentence Pair Extraction

After extracting pairs of related documents, we next selected pairs of related sentences from within paired documents. The motivation behind is that the standard word alignment algorithms can be easily applied to the paired sentences instead of documents. To do so we selected sentences with overlapping n-grams up to length n=4. Obviously for paraphrasing, we want some of the n-grams to differ, so we varied the amount of overlap and evaluated sentence pairs with a variety of threshold bands[3].

We evaluated 10 pairs of sentences at a time, including one positive control and two negative controls. A random pair of sentential paraphrases from the RTE task acted as the positive control. The negative controls included one random pair of non-paraphrased, but highly relevant sentences, and a random pair of sentences. Annotators classified the sentence pairs as: paraphrases, related sentences,

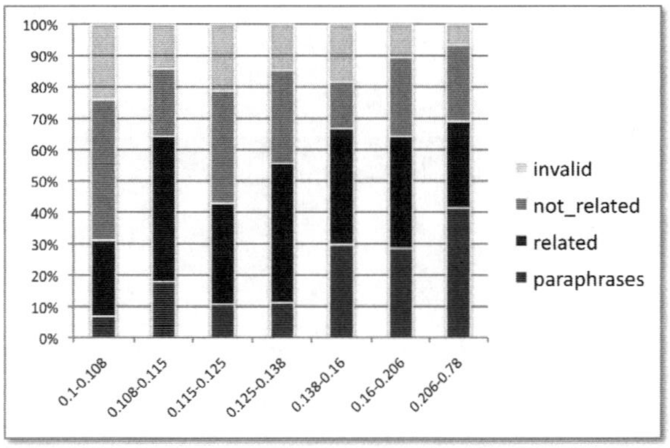

Figure 2: Results of the sentence pair extraction. The x-axis is the threshold for the comparability scores; and the y-axis is the distribution of the annotations.

and non-related sentences.

We uniformly sampled 200 sentence pairs from each band. They are randomly shuffled into more than 100 HITs and each HIT got three annotations. Figure 2 shows the distribution of annotations across different groups, after excluding answers that failed the controls.

Our best scoring threshold band was 0.2-0.8. Sentence pairs with this overlap were judged to be paraphrases 45% of the time, to be related 30% of the time, and to be unrelated 25% of the time. Although the F2 heuristic proposed by Dolan et al. (2004), which takes the first two sentences of each document pair, obtains higher relatedness score (we evaluated F2 sentences as 50% paraphrases, 37% related, and 13% unrelated), our n-gram overlap method extracted much more sentence pairs per document pair.

One interesting observation other than the general increasing tendency is that the portion of the related sentence pairs is not monotonic, which exactly reflects our intuition about a good comparability value (neither too high nor too low). However, some errors are difficult to exclude. For instance, one sentence says "The airstrikes were halted for 72 hours last Thursday..." and the other says "NATO and UN officials extended the suspension of airstrikes for a further 72 hours from late Sunday...". Without fine-grained analysis of the temporal expressions, it is difficult to know whether they are talking about the same event. The F2 method does provide us a fairly good way to exclude some unrelated sentence pairs, but note that the pairs collected by this method are

[2] http://lucene.apache.org/java/2_9_1/api/contrib-queries/org/apache/lucene/search/similar/MoreLikeThis.html

[3] In the experiment setting, the thresholds (maximum comparability and minimum comparability) for the 4 groups are, {0.78,0.206}, {0.206,0.138}, {0.138,0.115}, {0.115,0.1}.

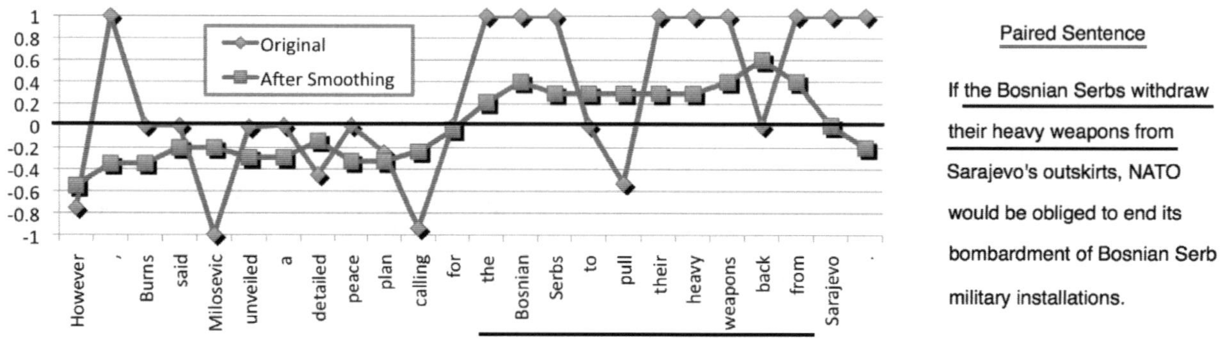

Figure 3: An example of fragment pair extraction. Stop words are all set to 1 initially. Zero is the threshold, and the underscored phrases are the outputs.

only about 0.5% of using the comparability scores.

We show in Figure 1 that we also use an additional sentence-level paraphrase corpus as the input of this module. We take all the positive instances (i.e. the two sentences in a pair are paraphrase to each other) and pass them to the later stage as well, as for comparison with our paraphrase collection extracted from the comparable sentence pairs. In all, we used 276,120 sentence pairs to feed our fragment extraction method.

3.3 Fragment Pair Extraction

The basic procedure is to 1) establish alignments between words or n-grams and 2) extract target paraphrase fragments. For the first step, we use two approaches. One is to change the common substring alignment problem from string to word sequence and we extend the longest common substring (LCS) extraction algorithm to multiple common n-grams. An alternative way is to use a normal word aligner (widely used as the first step in MT systems) to accomplish the job. For our experiments, we use the BerkeleyAligner[4] (Liang et al., 2006) by feeding it a dictionary of pairs of identical words along with the paired sentences. We can also combine these two methods by performing the LCS alignment first and adding additional word alignments from the aligner. These form the three configurations of our system (Table 2).

Following Munteanu and Marcu (2006), we use both positive and negative lexical associations for the alignment. The positive association measures how likely one word will be aligned to another (value from 0 to 1); and the negative associations indicates how *unlikely* an alignment exists between a word pair (from -1 to 0). The basic idea to have both is that when a word cannot be aligned with any other words, it will choose the *least unlikely* one. If the positive association of w_1 being aligned with w_2 is defined as the conditional probability $p(w_1|w_2)$, the negative associations will simply be $p(w_1|\neg w_2)$. Since we obtain a distribution of all the possible words aligned with w_1 from the word aligner, both $p(w_1|w_2)$ and $p(w_1|\neg w_2)$ can be calculated; for the LCS alignment, we simply set $p(w_1|w_2)$ as 1 and $p(w_1|\neg w_2)$ as -1, if w_1 and w_2 are aligned; and vice versa, if not.

After the initialization of all the word alignments using the two associations, each word takes the average of the neighboring four words and itself. The intuition of this smoothing is to tolerate a few unaligned parts (if they are surrounded by aligned parts). Finally, all the word alignments having a positive score will be selected as the candidate fragment elements. Figure 3 shows an example of this process.

The second step, fragment extraction, is a bit tricky, since a *fragment* is not clearly defined like a *document* or a *sentence*. One option is to follow the MT definition of a *phrase*, which means a sub-sentential n-gram string (usually n is less than 10). Munteanu and Marcu (2006) adopted this, and considered all the possible sub-sentential translation fragments as their targets, i.e. the adjacent n-grams. For instance, in Figure 3, all the adjacent words above the threshold (i.e. zero) will form the target

[4] `http://code.google.com/p/berkeleyaligner/`

Configurations			
Aligner+ Phrase Extraction	LCS+ Chunk	Word+ N-Gram	LCS+Word+ Chunk
Our Corpus			
PARAPHRASE	15%	36%	32%
RELATED	21%	26%	21%
SUM	36%	**62%**	53%
The MSR Corpus			
PARAPHRASE	38%	44%	49%
RELATED	20%	19%	18%
SUM	58%	63%	**67%**

Table 2: Distribution of the Extracted Fragment Pairs of our Corpus and MSR Corpus. We manually evaluated 1051 sentence pairs in all. We use LCS or word aligner as the initialization and apply n-gram-based or chunk-based phrase extraction. The first column serves as the baseline.

paraphrase, "the Bosnian Serbs to pull their heavy weapons back from" and those aligned words in the other sentence "the Bosnian Serbs withdraw their heavy weapons from" will be the source paraphrase. The disadvantage of this definition is that the extracted fragment pairs might not be easy for human beings to interpret or they are even ungrammatical (cf. the fourth example in Table 5). An alternative way is to follow the linguistic definition of a *phrase*, e.g. noun phrase (NP), verb phrase (VP), etc. In this case, we need to use (at least) a chunker to preprocess the text and obtain the proper boundary of each fragment and we used the OpenNLP chunker.

We finalize our paraphrase collection by filtering out identical fragment pairs, subsumed fragment pairs (one fragment is fully contained in the other), and fragment having only one word. Apart from sentence pairs collected from the comparable corpora, we also did experiments on the existing MSR paraphrase corpus (Dolan and Brockett, 2005), which is a collection of manually annotated sentential paraphrases.

The evaluation on both collections is done by the MTurk. Each task contains 8 pairs of fragments to be evaluated, plus one positive control using identical fragment pairs, and one negative control using a pair of random fragments. All the fragments are shown with the corresponding sentences from where they are extracted[5]. The question being asked is "How are the two highlighted phrases related?", and the possible answers are, "These phrases refer to the same thing as each other" (PARAPHRASE), "These phrases are overlap but contain different information" (RELATED), and "The phrases are unrelated or invalid" (INVALID). Table 2 shows the results (excluding invalid sentence pairs) and Table 5 shows some examples.

In general, the results on MSR is better than those on our corpus[6]. Comparing the different settings, for our corpus, word alignment with n-gram fragment extraction works better; and for corpora with higher comparability (e.g. the MSR corpus), the configuration of using both LCS and word alignments and the chunk-based fragment extraction outperforms the others. In fact, PARAPHRASE and RELATED are not quite comparable[7], since the boundary mismatch of the fragments may not be obvious to the Turkers. Nevertheless, we would assume a cleaner output from the chunk-based method, and both approaches achieve similar levels of quality.

Zhao et al. (2008) extracted paraphrase fragment pairs from bilingual parallel corpora, and their log-liner model outperforms Bannard and Callison-Burch (2005)'s maximum likelihood estimation method with 67% to 60%. Notice that, our starting corpora are (noisy) comparable corpora instead of parallel ones (for our corpus), and the approach is almost unsupervised[8], so that it can be easily scaled up to other larger corpora, e.g. the news websites. Furthermore, we compared our fragment pair collection with Callison-Burch (2008)'s approach on the same MSR corpus, only about 21% of the extracted paraphrases appear on both sides, which shows the potential to combine different resources.

4 Analysis of the Collections

In this section, we present some analysis on the fragment pair collection. We show the basic statistics of the corpora and then some examples of the output.

[5]We thought about evaluating pairs of isolated fragments, but later found out it was difficult to make the judgement.

[6]A sample of the corpus can be downloaded here: http://www.coli.uni-saarland.de/~rwang/resources/paraphrases.

[7]Thanks to the anonymous reviewer who pointed this out.

[8]The MTurk annotations can be roughly viewed as a guide for parameter tuning instead of *training* the system

As for comparison, we choose two other paraphrase collections, one is acquired from parallel bilingual corpora (Callison-Burch, 2008) and the other is using the same fragment extraction algorithm on the MSR corpus.

4.1 Statistics of the Corpora

Stage	Collection Size	%
GIGAWORD (1995)	600,000	10%
Documents Retrieved	150,000	2.5%
Document Pairs Selected	10,000	0.25%
Sentence Pairs Extracted	270,000	0.1%
Fragment Pairs Extracted	90,000	0.01%

Table 3: The size of our corpus. We only used ca. 10% of the GIGAWORD corpus in the experiments and the size of the collection at each stage are shown in the table.

Table 3 roughly shows the percentage of the extracted data compared with the original GIGAWORD corpus at each stage[9]. In the experiments reported here, we only use a subset of the news articles in 1995. If we scale to the full GIGAWORD corpus (19 Gigabytes, news from 1994 to 2006), we expect an order of magnitude more fragment pairs to be collected.

Apart from the size of the corpus, we are also interested in the composition of the corpus. Table 4 shows the proportions of some n-grams contained in the corpus. Here CCB denotes the paraphrase collection acquired from parallel bilingual corpora reported in (Callison-Burch, 2008), and MSR' denotes the collection using the same algorithm on the MSR corpus.

In Table 4, the four columns from the left are about the fragments (one part of each fragment pair), and the six columns from the right are about paraphrases. For example, 1 & 2 indicates the paraphrase contains one single word on one side and a 2-gram on the other side. Since we deliberately exclude single words, the n-gram distributions of OUR and MSR are "flatter" than the other two corpora, but still, 2-grams fragments occupy more than 40% in all cases. The n-gram distributions of the paraphrases are even more diverse for the OUR and MSR corpora. The sum of the listed proportions are only around 45%, while for CCB and MSR', the sums are about 95%.

[9] All the numbers in the table are roughly estimated, due to the variations of different settings. This just gives us an impression of the space for improvement.

4.2 Examples

Table 5 shows some examples from the best two settings. From our corpus, both simple paraphrases ("Governor ... said" and "Gov. ... announced") and more varied ones ("rose to fame as" and "the highlight of his career") can be extracted. It's clear that the smoothing and extraction algorithms do help with finding non-trivial paraphrases (shown in Figure 3). The extracted phrase "campaign was" shows the disadvantage of n-gram-based phrase extraction method, since the boundary of the fragment could be improper. Using a chunker can effectively exclude such problems, as shown in the lower part of the table, where all the extracted paraphrases are grammatical phrases. Even from a parallel paraphrase corpus at the sentence level, the acquired fragment pairs (w/o context) could be non-paraphrases. For instance, the second pair from the MSR corpus shows that one news agency gives more detailed information about the launching site than the other, and the last example is also debatable, whether it's "under $200" or "around $200" depending on the reliability of the information source.

5 Summary and Future Work

In this paper, we present our work on paraphrase fragment pair extraction from monolingual comparable corpora, inspired by Munteanu and Marcu (2006)'s bilingual method. We evaluate our intermediate results at each of the stages using MTurk. Both the quality and the quantity of the collected paraphrase fragment pairs are promising given the minimal supervision. As for the ongoing work, we are currently expanding our extraction process to the whole GIGAWORD corpus, and we plan to apply it to other comparable corpora as well. For the future work, we consider incorporating more linguistic constraints, e.g. using a syntactic parser (Callison-Burch, 2008), to further improve the quality of the collection. More importantly, applying the collected paraphrase fragment pairs to other NLP applications (e.g. MT, RTE, etc.) will give us a better view of the utility of this resource.

N-grams	Phrases				Para-phrases					
	1	2	3	4	1 & 1	1 & 2	2 & 2	1 & 3	2 & 3	3 & 3
OUR	N/A	**43.4%**	30.5%	16.4%	N/A	N/A	**20.0%**	N/A	16.7%	8.8%
MSR	N/A	**41.7%**	30.5%	16.0%	N/A	N/A	**20.1%**	N/A	16.6%	9.4%
CCB	10.7%	**42.7%**	32.0%	10.9%	**34.7%**	16.3%	24.0%	2.5%	9.4%	6.9%
MSR'	8.1%	**41.4%**	37.2%	10.0%	**29.0%**	16.6%	26.8%	2.8%	10.7%	9.6%

Table 4: The (partial) distribution of N-grams (N=1-4) in different paraphrase collections.

From Our Corpus: using word aligner and n-gram-based phrase extraction	
... unveiled a detailed peace plan calling for the Bosnian Serbs **to pull their heavy weapons back from** Sarajevo. If the Bosnian Serbs **withdraw their heavy weapons from** Sarajevo's outskirts, ...	Paraphrase
In San Juan, **Puerto Rico, Governor Pedro Rosello said** the the storm could hit the US territory by Friday, ... In **Puerto Rico, Gov. Pedro Rossello announced** that banks will be open only until 11 a.m. Friday and ...	Paraphrase
Kunstler **rose to fame as** the lead attorney for the "Chicago Seven," ... **The highlight of his career** came when he defended the Chicago Seven ...	Paraphrase
... initiated **the air attacks** in response to Serb shelling of Sarajevo that killed 38 people Monday. The **campaign was** to respond to a shelling of Sarajevo Monday that killed 38 people.	Invalid
From MSR Corpus: using both LCS and word aligner and chunk-based phrase extraction	
O'Brien's attorney, Jordan Green, **declined to comment**. Jordan Green, the prelate's private lawyer, said he **had no comment**.	Paraphrase
Iraq's nuclear program had been dismantled, and there "was no convincing evidence **of its reconstitution**." Iraq's nuclear program had been dismantled and there was no convincing evidence **it was being revived**, ...	Paraphrase
... to blast off between next Wednesday and Friday **from a launching site** in the Gobi Desert. ... to blast off as early as tomorrow or as late as Friday **from the Jiuquan launching site** in the Gobi Desert.	Related
... Super Wireless Media Router, which will be available in the first quarter of 2004, **at under $200**. The router will be available in the first quarter of 2004 and will cost **around $200**, the company said.	Related

Table 5: Some examples of the extracted paraphrase fragment pairs.

Acknowledgments

The first author would like to thank the EuroMatrix-Plus project (IST-231720) which is funded by the European Commission under the Seventh Framework Programme. The second author is supported by the EuroMatrixPlusProject, by the DARPA GALE program under Contract No. HR0011-06-2-0001, and by the NSF under grant IIS-0713448. The authors would like to thank Mirella Lapata and Delip Rao for the useful discussions as well as the anonymous Turkers who helped us to accomplish the tasks.

References

Colin Bannard and Chris Callison-Burch. 2005. Paraphrasing with bilingual parallel corpora. In *Proceedings of ACL*.

R. Barzilay and N. Elhadad. 2003. Sentence alignment for monolingual comparable corpora. In *Proceedings of EMNLP*.

Regina Barzilay and Lillian Lee. 2003. Learning to paraphrase: An unsupervised approach using multiple-sequence alignment. In *Proceedings of HLT-NAACL*.

Regina Barzilay and Kathleen McKeown. 2001. Extracting paraphrases from a parallel corpus. In *Proceedings of ACL*.

Regina Barzilay, Kathleen McKeown, and Michael Elhadad. 1999. Information fusion in the context of multi-document summarization. In *Proceedings of ACL*, College Park, MD.

Anja Belz and Eric Kow. 2010. Extracting parallel fragments from comparable corpora for data-to-text generation. In *Proceedings of the 6th International Natural Language Generation Conference*, Stroudsburg, PA, USA.

Chris Callison-Burch. 2008. Syntactic constraints on paraphrases extracted from parallel corpora. In *Proceedings of EMNLP*.

I. Dagan, O. Glickman, and B. Magnini. 2005. The pascal recognising textual entailment challenge. In *Proceedings of the RTE Workshop*.

Georgiana Dinu and Rui Wang. 2009. Inference rules and their application to recognizing textual entailment.

In *Proceedings of EACL*, Athens, Greece. Association of Computational Linguistics.

William B. Dolan and Chris Brockett. 2005. Automatically constructing a corpus of sentential paraphrases. In *Proceedings of the IWP2005*.

Bill Dolan, Chris Quirk, and Chris Brockett. 2004. Unsupervised construction of large paraphrase corpora: Exploiting massively parallel news sources. In *Proceedings of COLING*.

Pascale Fung and Percy Cheung. 2004a. Mining very non-parallel corpora: Parallel sentence and lexicon extraction via bootstrapping and EM. In *Proceedings of EMNLP*.

Pascale Fung and Percy Cheung. 2004b. Multi-level bootstrapping for extracting parallel sentences from a quasi-comparable corpus. In *Proceedings of COLING*.

P. Fung and Y. Y. Lo. 1998. An IR approach for translating new words from nonparallel, comparable texts. In *Proceedings of ACL*.

Ali Ibrahim, Boris Katz, and Jimmy Lin. 2003. Extracting structural paraphrases from aligned monolingual corpora. In *Proceedings of ACL*.

Philipp Koehn and Kevin Knight. 2000. Estimating word translation probabilities from unrelated monolingual corpora using the EM algorithm. In *Proceedings of the National Conference on Artificial Intelligence*.

Percy Liang, Ben Taskar, and Dan Klein. 2006. Alignment by agreement. In *Proceedings of NAACL*.

Dekang Lin and Patrick Pantel. 2001. Dirt - discovery of inference rules from text. In *Proceedings of the ACM SIGKDD*.

Yuval Marton, Chris Callison-Burch, and Philip Resnik. 2009. Improved statistical machine translation using monolingually-derived paraphrases. In *Proceedings of EMNLP*, Singapore.

Dragos Munteanu and Daniel Marcu. 2005. Improving machine translation performance by exploiting comparable corpora. *Computational Linguistics*, 31(4), December.

Dragos Stefan Munteanu and Daniel Marcu. 2006. Extracting parallel sub-sentential fragments from non-parallel corpora. In *Proceedings of ACL*.

Chris Quirk, Chris Brockett, and William B. Dolan. 2004. Monolingual machine translation for paraphrase generation. In *Proceedings of the 2004 Conference on Proceedings of the Conference on Empirical Methods in Natural Language Processing*, Barcelona, Spain.

Chris Quirk, Raghavendra Udupa, and Arul Menezes. 2007. Generative models of noisy translations with applications to parallel fragment extraction. In *Proceedings of MT Summit XI*, Copenhagen, Denmark.

G. Salton and M. J. McGill. 1983. *Introduction to modern information retrieval*. ISBN 0-07-054484-0. McGraw-Hill.

Y. Shinyama and S. Sekine. 2003. Paraphrase acquisition for information extraction. In *Proceedings of International Workshop on Paraphrasing*.

Yusuke Shinyama, Satoshi Sekine, and Kiyoshi Sudo. 2002. Automatic paraphrase acquisition from news articles yusuke shinyama satoshi sekine automatic paraphrase acquisition from news articles. In *Proceedings of Human Language Technology Conference*, San Diego, USA.

Jason R. Smith, Chris Quirk, and Kristina Toutanova. 2010. Extracting parallel sentences from comparable corpora using document level alignment. In *Human Language Technologies: The 2010 Annual Conference of the North American Chapter of the Association for Computational Linguistics*, Stroudsburg, PA, USA. Association of Computational Linguistics.

Rion Snow, Brendan O'Connor, Daniel Jurafsky, and Andrew Y. Ng. 2008. Cheap and fast - but is it good? Evaluating non- expert annotations for natural language tasks. In *Proceedings of EMNLP*.

Stephan Vogel. 2003. Using noisy bilingual data for statistical machine translation. In *Proceedings of EACL*.

Dekai Wu and Pascale Fung. 2005. Inversion transduction grammar constraints for mining parallel sentences from quasi-comparable corpora. In *Proceedings of IJCNLP*, Jeju Island, Korea.

Shiqi Zhao, Haifeng Wang, Ting Liu, and Sheng Li. 2008. Pivot approach for extracting paraphrase patterns from bilingual corpora. In *Proceedings of ACL*.

Extracting Parallel Phrases from Comparable Data

Sanjika Hewavitharana and **Stephan Vogel**
Language Technologies Institute
Carnegie Mellon University
Pittsburgh, PA 15213, USA
{sanjika,vogel+}@cs.cmu.edu

Abstract

Mining parallel data from comparable corpora is a promising approach for overcoming the data sparseness in statistical machine translation and other NLP applications. Even if two comparable documents have few or no parallel sentence pairs, there is still potential for parallelism in the sub-sentential level. The ability to detect these phrases creates a valuable resource, especially for low-resource languages. In this paper we explore three phrase alignment approaches to detect parallel phrase pairs embedded in comparable sentences: the standard phrase extraction algorithm, which relies on the Viterbi path; a phrase extraction approach that does not rely on the Viterbi path, but uses only lexical features; and a binary classifier that detects parallel phrase pairs when presented with a large collection of phrase pair candidates. We evaluate the effectiveness of these approaches in detecting alignments for phrase pairs that have a known alignment in comparable sentence pairs. The results show that the Non-Viterbi alignment approach outperforms the other two approaches on F1 measure.

1 Introduction

Statistical Machine Translation (SMT), like many natural language processing tasks, relies primarily on parallel corpora. The translation performance of SMT systems directly depends on the quantity and the quality of the available parallel data. However, such corpora are only available in large quantities for a handful of languages, including English, Arabic, Chinese and some European languages. Much of this data is derived from parliamentary proceedings, though a limited amount of newswire text is also available. For most other languages, especially for less commonly used languages, parallel data is virtually non-existent.

Comparable corpora provide a possible solution to this data sparseness problem. Comparable documents are not strictly parallel, but contain rough translations of each other, with overlapping information. A good example for comparable documents is the newswire text produced by multilingual news organizations such as AFP or Reuters. The degree of parallelism can vary greatly, ranging from *noisy parallel* documents that contain many parallel sentences, to *quasi parallel* documents that may cover different topics (Fung and Cheung, 2004). The Web is by far the largest source of comparable data. Resnik and Smith (2003) exploit the similarities in URL structure, document structure and other clues for mining the Web for parallel documents. Wikipedia has become an attractive source of comparable documents in more recent work (Smith et al., 2010).

Comparable corpora may contain parallel data in different levels of granularity. This includes: parallel documents, parallel sentence pairs, or parallel sub-sentential fragments. To simplify the process and reduce the computational overhead, the parallel sentence extraction is typically divided into two tasks. First, a document level alignment is identified between comparable documents, and second, the parallel sentences are detected within the identified document pairs. Cross-lingual information retrieval methods (Munteanu and Marcu, 2005) and

Proceedings of the 4th Workshop on Building and Using Comparable Corpora, pages 61–68,
49th Annual Meeting of the Association for Computational Linguistics,
Portland, Oregon, 24 June 2011. ©*2011 Association for Computational Linguistics*

1.

واضف انها تهدف لصرف انتباه الراي العام عن الاعمال الوحشية المتزايدة التي يرتكبها النظام الاسرائيلي ضد الفلسطينيين في الاراضي المحتلة

[He] added that it aims to divert public attention from the growing atrocities committed by the Israeli regime against the Palestinians in the occupied territories.

" Iran considers these remarks as interference in its internal affairs , " Kharazi said , **adding that they are aimed at detracting public opinion from heightened atrocities committed by the Israeli regime against the Palestinians in occupied lands .**

2.

واضاف " لكن حتي الان لم نواجه مشكلات "

But "Until now we did not have problems"

" **but up to now , we didn't meet any problems** ; the afghan people are very kind to us , " he said.

3.

تعد هذه هي اول زيارة لموسي على العراق **منذ توليه الامانة العامة للجامعة العربيةفي مايو الماضي**

This is the first visit by Moussa *to Iraq,* ***since he became the General Secretary of the Arab League in last May.***

This was also the first such visit by Moussa himself , the former Egyptian foreign minister , **since he assumed the post as AL chief in may last year .**

Figure 1: Sample comparable sentences that contain parallel phrases

other similarity measures (Fung and Cheung, 2004) have been used for the document alignment task. Zhao and Vogel (2002) have extended parallel sentence alignment algorithms to identify parallel sentence pairs within comparable news corpora. Tillmann and Xu (2009) introduced a system that performs both tasks in a single run without any document level pre-filtering. Such a system is useful when document level boundaries are not available in the comparable corpus.

Even if two comparable documents have few or no parallel sentence pairs, there could still be parallel sub-sentential fragments, including word translation pairs, named entities, and long phrase pairs. The ability to identify these pairs would create a valuable resource for SMT, especially for low-resource languages. The first attempt to detect sub-sentential fragments from comparable sentences is (Munteanu and Marcu, 2006). Quirk et al. (2007) later extended this work by proposing two generative models for comparable sentences and showed improvements when applied to cross-domain test data. In both these approaches the extracted fragment data was used as additional training data to train alignment models. Kumano et al. (2007) have proposed a phrasal alignment approach for comparable corpora using the joint probability SMT model. While this approach is appealing for low-resource scenarios as it does not require any seed parallel corpus, the high computational cost is a deterrent in its applicability to large corpora.

In this paper we explore several phrase alignment approaches to detect parallel phrase pairs embedded in comparable sentence pairs. We assume that comparable sentence pairs have already been detected. Our intention is to use the extracted phrases directly in the translation process, along with other phrase pairs extracted from parallel corpora. In particular, we study three alignment approaches:

- the standard phrase extraction algorithm, which relies on the Viterbi path of the word alignment;
- a phrase extraction approach that does not rely on the Viterbi path, but only uses lexical features;
- and a binary classifier to detect parallel phrase pairs when presented with a large collection of phrase pair candidates.

We evaluate the effectiveness of these approaches in detecting alignments for phrase pairs that have a known translation a comparable sentence pair. Section 2 introduces the phrase alignment problem in comparable sentences and discusses some of the challenges involved. It also explains the different alignment approaches we explore. Section 3 presents the experimental setup and the results of the evaluation. We conclude, in section 4, with an analysis of the results and some directions for future work.

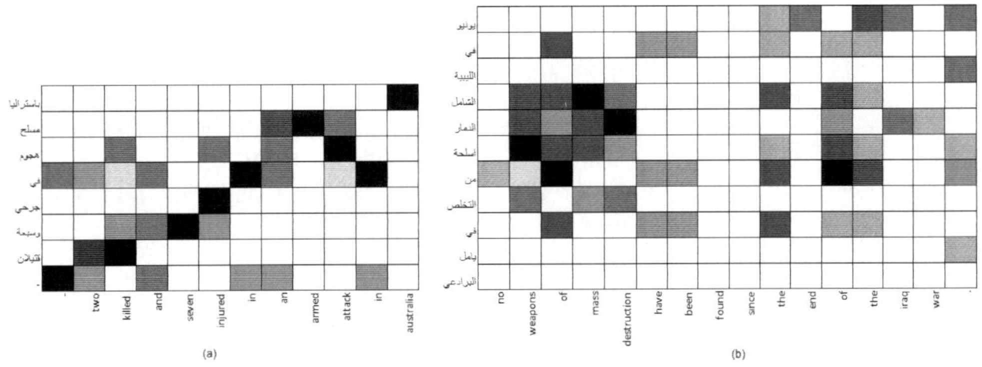

Figure 2: Word-to-word alignment pattern for (a) a parallel sentence pair (b) a non-parallel sentence pair

2 Parallel Phrase Extraction

Figure 1 shows three sample sentences that were extracted from Gigaword Arabic and Gigaword English collections. For each comparable sentence pair, the Arabic sentence is shown first, followed by its literal English translation (in Italics). The English sentence is shown next. The parallel sections in each sentence are marked in boldface. In the first two sentences pairs, the English sentence contains the full translation of the Arabic sentence, but there are additional phrases on the English side that are not present on the Arabic sentence. These phrases appear at the beginning of sentence 1 and at the end of sentence 2. In sentence 3, there are parallel phrases as well as phrases that appear only on one side. The phrase "to Iraq" appears only on the Arabic sentence while the phrase "the former Egyptian foreign minister" appears only on the English side.

Standard word alignment and phrase alignment algorithms are formulated to work on parallel sentence pairs. Therefore, these standard algorithms are not well suited to operate on partially parallel sentence pairs. Presence of non-parallel phrases may result in undesirable alignments.

Figure 2 illustrates this phenomenon. It compares a typical word alignment pattern in a parallel sentence pair (a) to one in a non-parallel sentence pair (b). The darkness of a square indicates the strength of the word alignment probability between the corresponding word pair. In 2(a), we observe high probability word-to-word alignments (dark squares) over the entire length of the sentences. In 2(b), we see one dark area above "weapons of mass destruction", corresponding to the parallel phrase pair, and some scattered dark spots, where high frequency English words pair with high frequency Arabic words. This spurious alignments pose problems to the phrase alignment, and indicate that word alignment probabilities alone might not be sufficient.

Our aim is to identify such parallel phrase pairs from comparable sentence pairs. In the following subsections we briefly explain the different phrase alignment approaches we use.

2.1 Viterbi Alignment

Here we use the typical phrase extraction approach used by Statistical Machine Translation systems: obtain word alignment models for both directions (source to target and target to source), combine the Viterbi paths using one of many heuristics, and extract phrase pairs from the combined alignment. We used Moses toolkit (Koehn et al., 2007) for this task. To obtain the word alignments for comparable sentence pairs, we performed a forced alignment using the trained models.

2.2 Binary Classifier

We used a Maximum Entropy classifier as our second approach to extract parallel phrase pairs from comparable sentences. Such classifiers have been used in the past to detect parallel sentence pairs in large collections of comparable documents (Munteanu and Marcu, 2005). Our classifier is similar, but we apply it at phrase level rather than at sentence level. The classifier probability is defined as:

$$p(c|S,T) = \frac{exp\left(\sum_{i=1}^{n} \lambda_i f_i(c,S,T)\right)}{Z(S,T)}, \quad (1)$$

where $S = s_1^L$ is a source phrase of length L and $T = t_1^K$ is a target phrase of length K. $c \in \{0,1\}$ is a binary variable representing the two classes of phrases: *parallel* and *not parallel*. $p(c|S,T) \in [0,1]$ is the probability where a value $p(c=1|S,T)$ close to 1.0 indicates that S and T are translations of each other. $f_i(c,S,T)$ are feature functions that are co-indexed with respect to the class variable c. The parameters λ_i are the weights for the feature functions obtained during training. $Z(S,T)$ is the normalization factor. In the feature vector for phrase pair (S,T), each feature appears twice, once for each class $c \in \{0,1\}$.

The feature set we use is inspired by Munteanu and Marcu (2005) who define the features based on IBM Model-1 (Brown et al., 1993) alignments for source and target pairs. However, in our experiments, the features are computed primarily on IBM Model-1 probabilities (i.e. lexicon). We do not explicitly compute IBM Model-1 alignments. To compute coverage features, we identify alignment points for which IBM Model-1 probability is above a threshold. We produce two sets of features based on IBM Model-1 probabilities obtained by training in both directions. All the features have been normalized with respect to the source phrase length L or the target phrase length K. We use the following 11 features:

1. Lexical probability (2): IBM Model-1 log probabilities $p(S|T)$ and $p(T|S)$
2. Phrase length ratio (2): source length ratio K/L and target length ratio L/K
3. Phrase length difference (1): source length minus target length, $L-K$
4. Number of words covered (2): A source word s is said to be covered if there is a target word $t \in T$ such that $p(s|t) > \epsilon$, where $\epsilon = 0.5$. Target word coverage is defined accordingly.
5. Number of words not covered (2): This is computed similarly to 4. above, but this time counting the number of positions that are not covered.
6. Length of the longest covered sequence of words (2)

To train the classifier, we used parallel phrases pairs extracted from a manually word-aligned corpus. In selecting negative examples, we followed the same approach as in (Munteanu and Marcu, 2005): pairing all source phrases with all target phrases, but filter out the parallel pairs and those that have high length difference or a low lexical overlap, and then randomly select a subset of phrase pairs as the negative training set. The model parameters are estimated using the GIS algorithm.

2.3 Non-Viterbi (PESA) Alignment

A phrase alignment algorithm called "PESA" that does not rely on the Viterbi path is described in (Vogel, 2005). PESA identifies the boundaries of the target phrase by aligning words inside the source phrase with words inside the target phrase, and similarly for the words outside the boundaries of the phrase pair. It does not attempt to generate phrase alignments for the full sentence. Rather, it identifies the best target phrase that matches a given source phrase. PESA requires a statistical word-to-word lexicon. A seed parallel corpus is required to automatically build this lexicon.

This algorithm seems particularly well suited in extracting phrase pairs from comparable sentence pairs, as it is designed to not generate a complete word alignment for the entire sentences, but to find only the target side for a phrase embedded in the sentence. We briefly explain the PESA alignment approach below.

Instead of searching for all possible phrase alignments in a parallel sentence pair, this approach finds the alignment for a single source phrase $S = s_1 \dots s_l$. Assume that we have a parallel sentence pair (s_1^J, t_1^I) which contains the source phrase S in the source sentence s_1^J. Now we want to find the target phrase $T = t_1 \dots t_k$ in the target sentence t_1^I which is the translation of the source phrase.
A constrained IBM Model-1 alignment is now applied as follows:

- Source words inside phrase boundary are aligned only with the target words inside the phrase boundary. Source words outside the phrase boundary are only aligned with target words outside the phrase boundary.

- Position alignment probability for the sentence, which is $1/I$ in IBM Model-1, is modified to be $1/k$ inside the source phrase and to $1/(I-k)$ outside the phrase.

Figure 3 shows the different regions. Given the source sentence and the source phrase from position j_1 to j_2, we want to find the boundaries of the target phrase, i_1 and i_2. The dark area in the middle is the phrase we want to align. The size of the blobs in each box indicates the lexical strength of the word pair.

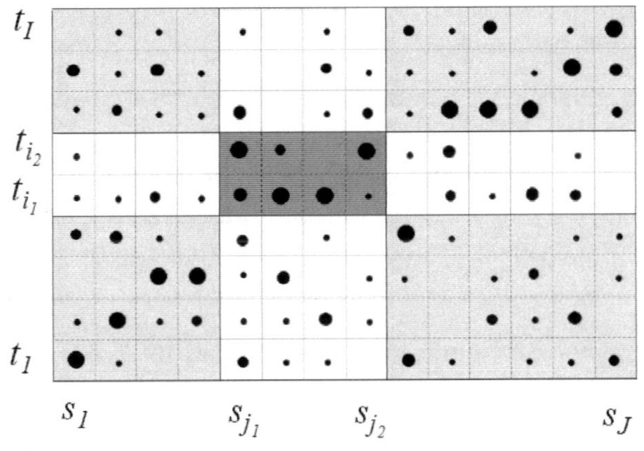

Figure 3: PESA Phrase alignment

The constrained alignment probability is calculated as follows:

$$p(s|t) = \left(\prod_{j=1}^{j_1-1} \sum_{i \notin (i_1 \dots i_2)} \frac{1}{I-k} p(s_j|t_i)\right) \times \left(\prod_{j=j_1}^{j_2} \sum_{i=i_1}^{i_2} \frac{1}{k} p(s_j|t_i)\right) \times \left(\prod_{j=j_2+1}^{J} \sum_{i \notin (i_1 \dots i_2)} \frac{1}{I-k} p(s_j|t_i)\right) \quad (2)$$

$p(t|s)$ is similarly calculated by switching source and target sides in equation 2:

$$p(t|s) = \left(\prod_{i=1}^{i_1-1} \sum_{i \notin (j_1 \dots j_2)} \frac{1}{J-l} p(t_i|s_j)\right) \times \left(\prod_{i=i_1}^{i_2} \sum_{j=j_1}^{j_2} \frac{1}{l} p(t_i|s_j)\right) \times \left(\prod_{i=i_2+1}^{I} \sum_{j \notin (j_1 \dots j_2)} \frac{1}{J-l} p(t_i|s_j)\right) \quad (3)$$

To find the optimal target phrase boundaries, we interpolate the two probabilities in equations 2 and 3 and select the boundary (i_1, i_2) that gives the highest probability.

$$(i_1, i_2) = \underset{i_1, i_2}{\operatorname{argmax}} \; \{(1-\lambda)\, log(p(s|t)) + \lambda\, log(p(t|s))\} \quad (4)$$

The value of λ is estimated using held-out data.

PESA can be used to identify all possible phrase pairs in a given parallel sentence pair by iterating over every source phrase. An important difference is that each phrase is found independently of any other phrase pair, whereas in the standard phrase extraction they are tied through the word alignment of the sentence pair.

There are several ways we can adapt the non-Viterbi phrase extraction to comparable sentence.

- Apply the same approach assuming the sentence pair as parallel. The inside of the source phrase is aligned to the inside of the target phrase, and the outside, which can be non-parallel, is aligned the same way.

- Disregard the words that are outside the phrase we are interested in. Find the best target phrase by aligning only the inside of the phrase. This will considerably speed-up the alignment process.

3 Experimental Results

3.1 Evaluation Setup

We want to compare the performance of the different phrase alignment methods in identifying parallel phrases embedded in comparable sentence pairs.

	1	2	3	4	5	6	7	8	9	10	All
test set	2,826	3,665	3,447	3,048	2,718	2,414	2,076	1,759	1,527	1,378	24,858
test set (found)	2,746	2,655	1,168	373	87	29	7	2	1	0	7,068

Table 1: N-gram type distribution of manually aligned phrases set

Using a manually aligned parallel corpus, and two monolingual corpora, we obtained a test corpus as follows: From the manually aligned corpus, we obtain parallel phrase pairs (S, T). Given a source language corpus $\mathcal{S}$ and a target language corpus $\mathcal{T}$, for each parallel phrase pair (S, T) we select a sentence s from $\mathcal{S}$ which contains S and a target sentence t from $\mathcal{T}$ which contains T. These sentence pairs are then non-parallel, but contain parallel phrases, and for each sentence pair the correct phrase pair is known. This makes it easy to evaluate different phrase alignment algorithms.

Ideally, we would like to see the correct target phrase T extracted for a source phrase S. However, even if the boundaries of the target phrase do not match exactly, and only a partially correct translation is generated, this could still be useful to improve translation quality. We therefore will evaluate the phrase pair extraction from non-parallel sentence pairs also in terms of partial matches.

To give credit to partial matches, we define precision and recall as follows: Let W and G denote the extracted target phrase and the correct reference phrase, respectively. Let M denote the tokens in W that are also found in the reference G. Then

$$Precision = \frac{|M|}{|W|} * 100 \quad (5)$$

$$Recall = \frac{|M|}{|G|} * 100 \quad (6)$$

These scores are computed for each extracted phrase pair, and are averaged to produce precision and recall for the complete test set. Finally, precision and recall are combined to generated the F-1 score in the standard way:

$$F1 = \frac{2 \cdot Precision \cdot Recall}{Precision + Recall} \quad (7)$$

3.2 Evaluation

We conducted our experiments on Arabic-English language pair. We obtained manual alignments for 663 Arabic-English sentence pairs. From this, we selected 300 sentences, and extracted phrase pairs up to 10 words long that are consistent with the underlying word alignment. From the resulting list of phrase pairs, we removed the 50 most frequently occurring pairs as well as those only consisting of punctuations. Almost all high frequency phrases are function words, which are typically covered by the translation lexicon. Line 1 in Table 1 gives the n-gram type distribution for the source phrases.

Using the phrase pairs extracted from the manually aligned sentences, we constructed a comparable corpus as follows:

1. For each Arabic phrase, we search the Arabic Gigaword[1] corpus for sentences that contain the phrase and select up to 5 sentences. Similarly, for each corresponding English phrase we select up to 5 sentences from English Gigaword[2].

2. For each phrase pair, we generate the Cartesian product of the sentences and produce a sentence pair collection. I.e. up to 25 comparable sentence pairs were constructed for each phrase pair.

3. We only select sentences up to 100 words long, resulting in a final comparable corpus consisting of 170K sentence pairs.

Line 2 in Table 1 gives the n-gram type distribution for the phrase pairs for which we found both a source sentence and a target sentence in the monolingual corpora. As expected, the longer the phrases, the less likely it is to find them in even larger corpora.

We consider the resulting set as our comparable corpus which we will use to evaluate all alignment approaches. In most sentence pairs, except for the phrase pair that we are interested in, the rest of the sentence does not typically match the other side.

[1]Arabic Gigaword Fourth Edition (LDC2009T30)

[2]English Gigaword Fourth Edition (LDC2009T13)

Lexicon	Viterbi				Classifier				PESA			
	Exact	P	R	F1	Exact	P	R	F1	Exact	P	R	F1
Lex-Full	43.56	65.71	57.99	61.61	54.46	81.79	85.29	85.29	67.94	93.34	86.80	90.22
Lex-1/3	42.95	65.68	56.69	60.85	53.57	81.32	88.34	84.69	67.28	93.23	86.17	89.56
Lex-1/9	41.10	63.60	51.15	56.70	52.38	80.30	86.64	83.35	65.81	91.95	84.73	88.19
Lex-1/27	41.02	62.10	49.38	55.01	52.51	80.51	83.84	82.14	63.23	89.41	82.06	85.57
Lex-BTEC	19.10	26.94	23.63	25.18	18.76	45.90	36.17	40.46	17.45	46.70	36.28	40.83

Table 2: Results for Alignment Evaluation of test phrases

We obtained the Viterbi alignment using standard word alignment techniques: IBM4 word alignment for both directions, Viterbi path combination using heuristics ('grow-diag-final') and phrase extraction from two-sided training, as implemented in the Moses package (Koehn et al., 2007). Because the non-parallel segments will lead the word alignment astray, this may have a negative effect on the alignment in the parallel sections. Alignment models trained on parallel data are used to generate the Viterbi alignment for the comparable sentences. We then extract the target phrases that are aligned to the embedded source phrases. A phrase pair is extracted only when the alignment does not conflict with other word alignments in the sentence pair. The alignments are not constrained to produce contiguous phrases. We allow unaligned words to be present in the phrase pair. For each source phrase we selected the target phrase that has the least number of unaligned words.

The classifier is applied at the phrase level. We generate the phrase pair candidates as follows: For a given target sentence we generate all n-grams up to length 10. We pair each n-gram with the source phrase embedded in the corresponding source sentence to generate a phrase pair. From the 170 thousand sentence pairs, we obtained 15.6 million phrase pair candidates. The maximum entropy classifier is then applied to the phrase pairs. For each source phrase, we pick the target candidate for which $p(c = 1, S, T)$ has the highest value.

For the PESA alignment we used both inside and outside alignments, using only lexical probabilities. For each source phrase pair, we select the best scoring target phrase.

As our goal is to use these methods to extract parallel data for low resource situations, we tested each method with several lexica, trained on different amounts of initial parallel data. Starting from the full corpus with 127 million English tokens, we generated three additional parallel corpora with 1/3, 1/9 and 1/27 of the original size. The 1/9 and 1/27 corpora (with 13 million and 4 million English words) can be considered *medium* and *small* sized corpora, respectively. These two corpora are a better match to the resource levels for many languages. We also used data from the BTEC (Kikui et al., 2003) corpus. This corpus contains conversational data from the travel domain, which is from a different genre than the document collections. Compared to other corpora, it is much smaller (about 190 thousand English tokens).

Table 2 gives the results for all three alignment approaches. Results are presented as percentages of: exact matches found (Exact), precision (P), recall (R) and F1. The Viterbi alignment gives the lowest performance. This shows that the standard phrase extraction procedure, which works well for parallel sentence, is ill-suited for partially parallel sentences. Despite the fact that the classifier incorporates several features including the lexical features, the performance of the PESA alignment, which uses only the lexical features, has consistently higher precision and recall than the classifier. This demonstrates that computing both inside and outside probabilities for the sentence pair helps the phrase extraction. The classifier lacks this ability because the phrase pair is evaluated in isolation, without the context of the sentence.

Except for the BTEC corpus, the performance degradation is minimal as the lexicon size is reduced. This shows that the approaches are robust for smaller parallel amounts of parallel data.

Instead of using token precision, an alternative

method of evaluating partial matches, is to give credit based on the length of the overlap between the extracted phrase and the reference. Precision and recall can then be defined based on the longest common contiguous subsequence, similar to (Bourdaillet et al., 2010). Results obtained using this methods were similar to the results in Table 2.

4 Conclusion and Future Work

In this paper we explored several phrase alignment approaches for extracting phrase pairs that are embedded inside comparable sentence pairs. We used the standard Viterbi phrase alignment, a maximum entropy classifier that works on phrase pairs, and a non-Viterbi PESA alignment in the evaluation process. The results show that PESA outperforms both the Viterbi approach and the classifier, in both precision and recall.

We plan to extend the PESA framework to use not only lexical features, but other features similar to the ones used in the classifier. We believe this will further improve the alignment accuracy.

While this paper focuses on comparisons of different phrase alignment approaches in a realistic, yet controlled manner by selecting appropriate comparable sentence pairs for given phrase pairs, future experiments will focus on finding new phrase pairs from comparable corpora and evaluating the potential utility of the extracted data in the context of an end-to-end machine translation system.

References

Julien Bourdaillet, Stéphane Huet, Philippe Langlais, and Guy Lapalme. 2010. TransSearch: from a bilingual concordancer to a translation finder. *Machine Translation*, 24(3-4):241–271, dec.

Peter F. Brown, Stephen A. Della Pietra, Vincent J. Della Pietra, and Robert L. Mercer. 1993. The mathematics of statistical machine translation: Parameter estimation. *Computational Linguistics*, 19(2):263–311.

Pascale Fung and Percy Cheung. 2004. Mining very non-parallel corpora: Parallel sentence and lexicon extraction via bootstrapping and EM. In *In Proceedings of the Conference on Empirical Methods in Natural Language Processing*, pages 57–63, Barcelona, Spain.

Genichiro Kikui, Eiichiro Sumita, Toshiyuki Takezawa, and Seiichi Yamamoto. 2003. Creating corpora for speech-to-speech translation. In *In Proc. of EUROSPEECH 2003*, pages 381–384, Geneva.

Philipp Koehn, Hieu Hoang, Alexandra Birch, Chris Callison-Burch, Marcello Federico, Nicola Bertoldi, Brooke Cowan, Wade Shen, Christine Moran, Richard Zens, Chris Dyer, Ondrej Bojar, Alexandra Constantin, and Evan Herbst. 2007. Moses: Open source toolkit for statistical machine translation. In *Proceedings of the 45th Annual Meeting of the Association for Computational Linguistics*, Prague, Czech Republic, June.

Tadashi Kumano, Hideki Tanaka, and Takenobu Tokunaga. 2007. Extracting phrasal alignments from comparable corpora by using joint probability smt model. In *In Proceedings of the International Conference on Theoretical and Methodological Issues in Machine Translation*, Skvde, Sweden, September.

Dragos Stefan Munteanu and Daniel Marcu. 2005. Improving machine translation performance by exploiting non-parallel corpora. *Computational Linguistics*, 31(4):477–504.

Dragos Stefan Munteanu and Daniel Marcu. 2006. Extracting parallel sub-sentential fragments from non-parallel corpora. In *Proceedings of the 21st International Conference on Computational Linguistics and the 44th Annual Meeting of the Association for Computational Linguistics*, pages 81–88, Sydney, Australia.

Chris Quirk, Raghavendra U. Udupa, and Arul Menezes. 2007. Generative models of noisy translations with applications to parallel fragment extraction. In *Proceedings of the Machine Translation Summit XI*, pages 377–384, Copenhagen, Denmark.

Philip Resnik and Noah Smith. 2003. The web as a parallel corpus. *Computational Linguistics*, 29(3):349–380.

Jason R. Smith, Chris Quirk, and Kristina Toutanova. 2010. Extracting parallel sentences from comparable corpora using document level alignment. In *Proceedings of the Human Language Technologies/North American Association for Computational Linguistics*, pages 403–411.

Christoph Tillmann and Jian-Ming Xu. 2009. A simple sentence-level extraction algorithm for comparable data. In *Companion Vol. of NAACL HLT 09*, Boulder, CA, June.

Stephan Vogel. 2005. PESA: Phrase pair extraction as sentence splitting. In *Proceedings of the Machine Translation Summit X*, Phuket, Thailand, September.

Bing Zhao and Stephan Vogel. 2002. Full-text story alignment models for chinese-english bilingual news corpora. In *Proceedings of the ICSLP '02*, September.

Active Learning with Multiple Annotations for Comparable Data Classification Task

Vamshi Ambati, Sanjika Hewavitharana, Stephan Vogel and Jaime Carbonell
{vamshi,sanjika,vogel,jgc}@cs.cmu.edu
Language Technologies Institute, Carnegie Mellon University
5000 Forbes Avenue, Pittsburgh, PA 15213, USA

Abstract

Supervised learning algorithms for identifying comparable sentence pairs from a dominantly non-parallel corpora require resources for computing feature functions as well as training the classifier. In this paper we propose active learning techniques for addressing the problem of building comparable data for low-resource languages. In particular we propose strategies to elicit two kinds of annotations from comparable sentence pairs: class label assignment and parallel segment extraction. We also propose an active learning strategy for these two annotations that performs significantly better than when sampling for either of the annotations independently.

1 Introduction

The state-of-the-art Machine Translation (MT) systems are statistical, requiring large amounts of parallel corpora. Such corpora needs to be carefully created by language experts or speakers, which makes building MT systems feasible only for those language pairs with sufficient public interest or financial support. With the increasing rate of social media creation and the quick growth of web media in languages other than English makes it relevant for language research community to explore the feasibility of Internet as a source for parallel data. (Resnik and Smith, 2003) show that parallel corpora for a variety of languages can be harvested on the Internet. It is to be observed that a major portion of the multilingual web documents are created independent of one another and so are only mildly parallel at the document level.

There are multiple challenges in building comparable corpora for consumption by the MT systems. The first challenge is to identify the parallelism between documents of different languages which has been reliably done using cross lingual information retrieval techniques. Once we have identified a subset of documents that are potentially parallel, the second challenge is to identify comparable sentence pairs. This is an interesting challenge as the availability of completely parallel sentences on the internet is quite low in most language-pairs, but one can observe very few comparable sentences among comparable documents for a given language-pair. Our work tries to address this problem by posing the identification of comparable sentences from comparable data as a supervised classification problem. Unlike earlier research (Munteanu and Marcu, 2005) where the authors try to identify parallel sentences among a pool of comparable documents, we try to first identify comparable sentences in a pool with dominantly non-parallel sentences. We then build a supervised classifier that learns from user annotations for comparable corpora identification. Training such a classifier requires reliably annotated data that may be unavailable for low-resource language pairs. Involving a human expert to perform such annotations is expensive for low-resource languages and so we propose active learning as a suitable technique to reduce the labeling effort.

There is yet one other issue that needs to be solved in order for our classification based approach to work for truly low-resource language pairs. As we will describe later in the paper, our comparable sentence classifier relies on the availability of an ini-

Proceedings of the 4th Workshop on Building and Using Comparable Corpora, pages 69–77,
49th Annual Meeting of the Association for Computational Linguistics,
Portland, Oregon, 24 June 2011.

tial seed lexicon that can either be provided by a human or can be statistically trained from parallel corpora (Och and Ney, 2003). Experiments show that a broad coverage lexicon provides us with better coverage for effective identification of comparable corpora. However, availability of such a resource can not be expected in very low-resource language pairs, or even if present may not be of good quality. This opens an interesting research question - Can we also elicit such information effectively at low costs? We propose active learning strategies for identifying the most informative comparable sentence pairs which a human can then extract parallel segments from.

While the first form of supervision provides us with class labels that can be used for tuning the feature weights of our classifier, the second form of supervision enables us to better estimate the feature functions. For the comparable sentence classifier to perform well, we show that both forms of supervision are needed and we introduce an active learning protocol to combine the two forms of supervision under a single joint active learning strategy.

The rest of the paper is organized as follows. In Section 2 we survey earlier research as relevant to the scope of the paper. In Section 3 we discuss the supervised training setup for our classifier. In Section 4 we discuss the application of active learning to the classification task. Section 5 discusses the case of active learning with two different annotations and proposes an approach for combining them. Section 6 presents experimental results and the effectiveness of the active learning strategies. We conclude with further discussion and future work.

2 Related Work

There has been a lot of interest in using comparable corpora for MT, primarily on extracting parallel sentence pairs from comparable sources (Zhao and Vogel, 2002; Fung and Yee, 1998). Some work has gone beyond this focussing on extracting subsentential fragments from noisier comparable data (Munteanu and Marcu, 2006; Quirk et al., 2007). The research conducted in this paper has two primary contributions and so we will discuss the related work as relevant to each of them.

Our first contribution in this paper is the application of active learning for acquiring comparable data in the low-resource scenario, especially relevant when working with low-resource languages. There is some earlier work highlighting the need for techniques to deal with low-resource scenarios.(Munteanu and Marcu, 2005) propose bootstrapping using an existing classifier for collecting new data. However, this approach works when there is a classifier of reasonable performance. In the absence of parallel corpora to train lexicons human constructed dictionaries were used as an alternative which may, however, not be available for a large number of languages. Our proposal of active learning in this paper is suitable for highly impoverished scenarios that require support from a human.

The second contribution of the paper is to extend the traditional active learning setup that is suitable for eliciting a single annotation. We highlight the needs of the comparable corpora scenario where we have two kinds of annotations - class label assignment and parallel segment extraction and propose strategies in active learning that involve multiple annotations. A relevant setup is *multitask learning* (Caruana, 1997) which is increasingly becoming popular in natural language processing for learning from multiple learning tasks. There has been very less work in the area of multitask active learning. (Reichart et al., 2008) proposes an extension of the single-sided active elicitation task to a multi-task scenario, where data elicitation is performed for two or more independent tasks at the same time. (Settles et al., 2008) propose elicitation of annotations for image segmentation under a multi-instance learning framework.

Active learning with multiple annotations also has similarities to the recent body of work in learning from instance feedback and feature feedback (Melville et al., 2005). (Druck et al., 2009) propose active learning extensions to the gradient approach of learning from feature and instance feedback. However, in the comparable corpora problem although the second annotation is geared towards learning better features by enhancing the coverage of the lexicon, the annotation itself is not on the features but for extracting training data that is then used to train the lexicon.

3 Supervised Comparable Sentence Classification

In this section we discuss our supervised training setup and the classification algorithm. Our classifier tries to identify comparable sentences from among a large pool of noisy comparable sentences. In this paper we define comparable sentences as being translations that have around fifty percent or more translation equivalence. In future we will evaluate the robustness of the classifier by varying levels of noise at the sentence level.

3.1 Training the Classifier

Following (Munteanu and Marcu, 2005), we use a Maximum Entropy classifier to identify comparable sentences. The classifier probability can be defined as:

$$Pr(c_i|S,T) = \frac{1}{Z(S,T)} exp\left(\sum_{j=1}^{n} \lambda_j f_{ij}(c_i, S, T)\right)$$

where (S, T) is a sentence pair, c_i is the class, f_{ij} are feature functions and $Z(S)$ is a normalizing factor. The parameters λ_i are the weights for the feature functions and are estimated by optimizing on a training data set. For the task of classifying a sentence pair, there are two classes, $c_0 = comparable$ and $c_1 = non\ parallel$. A value closer to one for $Pr(c_1|S,T)$ indicates that (S, T) are comparable.

To train the classifier we need comparable sentence pairs and non-parallel sentence pairs. While it is easy to find negative examples online, acquiring comparable sentences is non-trivial and requires human intervention. (Munteanu and Marcu, 2005) construct negative examples automatically from positive examples by pairing all source sentences with all target sentences. We, however, assume the availability of both positive and negative examples to train the classifier. We use the GIS learning algorithm for tuning the model parameters.

3.2 Feature Computation

The features are defined primarily based on translation lexicon probabilities. Rather than computing word alignment between the two sentences, we use lexical probabilities to determine alignment points as follows: a source word s is aligned to a target word t if $p(s|t) > 0.5$. Target word alignment is computed similarly. Long contiguous sections of aligned words indicate parallelism. We use the following features:

- Source and target sentence length ratio
- Source and target sentence length difference
- Lexical probability score, similar to IBM model 1
- Number of aligned words
- Longest aligned word sequence
- Number of un-aligned words

Lexical probability score, and alignment features generate two sets of features based on translation lexica obtained by training in both directions. Features are normalized with respect to the sentence length.

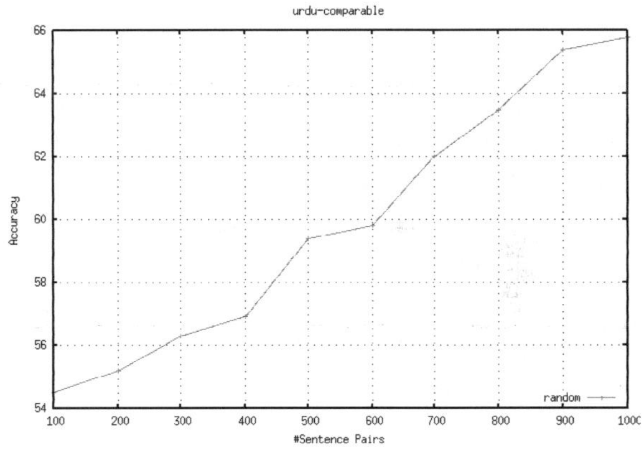

Figure 1: Seed parallel corpora size vs. Classifier performance in Urdu-English language pair

In our experiments we observe that the most informative features are the ones involving the probabilistic lexicon. However, the comparable corpora obtained for training the classifier cannot be used for automatically training a lexicon. We, therefore, require the availability of an initial seed parallel corpus that can be used for computing the lexicon and the associated feature functions. We notice that the size of the seed corpus has a large influence on the accuracy of the classifier. Figure 1 shows a plot with the initial size of the corpus used to construct the probabilistic lexicon on x-axis and its effect on the accuracy of the classifier on y-axis. The sentences were drawn randomly from a large pool of Urdu-English parallel corpus and it is clear that a larger pool of parallel sentences leads to a better lexicon and an improved classifier.

4 Active Learning with Multiple Annotations

4.1 Cost Motivation

Lack of existing annotated data requires reliable human annotation that is expensive and effort-intensive. We propose active learning for the problem of effectively acquiring multiple annotations starting with unlabeled data. In active learning, the learner has access to a large pool of unlabeled data and sometimes a small portion of seed labeled data. The objective of the active learner is then to select the most informative instances from the unlabeled data and seek annotations from a human expert, which it then uses to retrain the underlying supervised model for improving performance.

A meaningful setup to study multi annotation active learning is to take into account the cost involved for each of the annotations. In the case of comparable corpora we have two annotation tasks, each with cost models $Cost_1$ and $Cost_2$ respectively. The goal of multi annotation active learning is to select the optimal set of instances for each annotation so as to maximize the benefit to the classifier. Unlike the traditional active learning, where we optimize the number of instances we label, here we optimize the selection under a provided budget B_k per iteration of the active learning algorithm.

4.2 Active Learning Setup

We now discuss our active learning framework for building comparable corpora as shown in Algorithm 1. We start with an unlabeled dataset $U_0 = \{x_j =< s_j, t_j >\}$ and a seed labeled dataset $L_0 = \{(< s_j, t_j >, c_i)\}$, where $c \in 0, 1$ are class labels with 0 being the non-parallel class and 1 being the comparable data class. We also have $T_0 = \{< s_k, t_k >\}$ which corresponds to parallel segments or sentences identified from L_0 that will be used in training the probabilistic lexicon. Both T_0 and L_0 can be very small in size at the start of the active learning loop. In our experiments, we tried with as few as 50 to 100 sentences for each of the datasets.

We perform an iterative budget motivated active learning loop for acquiring labeled data over k iterations. We start the active learning loop by first training a lexicon with the available T_k and then using that we train the classifier over L_k. We, then score all the sentences in the U_k using the model θ and apply our selection strategy to retrieve the best scoring instance or a small batch of instances. In the simplest case we annotate this instance and add it back to the tuning set C_k for re-training the classifier. If the instance was a comparable sentence pair, then we could also perform the second annotation conditioned upon the availability of the budget. The identified sub-segments (ss_i , tt_i) are added back to the training data T_k used for training the lexicon in the subsequent iterations.

Algorithm 1 ACTIVE LEARNING SETUP

Given Unlabeled Comparable Corpus: U_0
Given Seed Parallel Corpus: T_0
Given Tuning Corpus: L_0
for $k = 0$ to K **do**
  Train Lexicon using T_k
  θ = Tune Classifier using C_k
  while $Cost < B_k$ **do**
    i = Query(U_k,L_k,T_k,θ)
    c_i = Human Annotation-1 (s_i, t_i)
    (ss_i ,tt_i) = Human Annotation-2 x_i
    $L_k = C_k \cup (s_i, t_i, c_i)$
    $T_k = T_k \cup (ss_i, tt_i)$
    $U_k = U_k$ - x_i
    $Cost = Cost_1 + Cost_2$
  end while
end for

5 Sampling Strategies for Active Learning

5.1 Acquiring Training Data for Classifier

Our selection strategies for obtaining class labels for training the classifier uses the model in its current state to decide on the informative instances for the next round of iterative training. We propose the following two sampling strategies for this task.

5.1.1 Certainty Sampling

This strategy selects instances where the current model is highly confident. While this may seem redundant at the outset, we argue that this criteria can be a good sampling strategy when the classifier is weak or trained in an impoverished data scenario. Certainty sampling strategy is a lot similar to the idea of unsupervised approaches like boosting or self-training. However, we make it a semi-supervised approach by having a human in the loop to provide affirmation for the selected instance. Consider the following scenario. If we select an instance that our current model prefers and obtain a contradicting label from the human, then this instance has a maximal impact on the decision boundary of the classifier. On the other hand, if the label is reaffirmed by a human, the overall variance reduces and in the process, it also helps in assigning higher preference for the configuration of the decision boundary. (Melville et al., 2005) introduce a certainty sampling strategy for the task of feature labeling in a text categorization task. Inspired by the same we borrow the name and also apply this as an instance sampling approach. Given an instance x and the classifier posterior distribution for the classes as $P(.)$, we select the most informative instance as follows:

$$x* = arg\,max_x P(c = 1|x)$$

5.1.2 Margin-based Sampling

The certainty sampling strategy only considers the instance that has the best score for the comparable sentence class. However we could benefit from information about the second best class assigned to the same instance. In the typical multi-class classification problems, earlier work shows success using such a 'margin based' approach (Scheffer et al., 2001), where the difference between the probabilities assigned by the underlying model to the first best and second best classes is used as the sampling criteria.

Given a classifier with posterior distribution over classes for an instance $P(c = 1|x)$, the margin based strategy is framed as $x* = arg\,min_x P(c_1|x) - P(c_2|x)$, where c_1 is the best prediction for the class and c_2 is the second best prediction under the model. It should be noted that for binary classification tasks with two classes, the margin sampling approach reduces to an uncertainty sampling approach (Lewis and Catlett, 1994).

5.2 Acquiring Parallel Segments for Lexicon Training

We now propose two sampling strategies for the second annotation. Our goal is to select instances that could potentially provide parallel segments for improved lexical coverage and feature computation.

5.2.1 Diversity Sampling

We are interested in acquiring clean parallel segments for training a lexicon that can be used in feature computation. It is not clear how one could use a comparable sentence pair to decide the potential for extracting a parallel segment. However, it is highly likely that if such a sentence pair has new coverage on the source side, then it increases the chances of obtaining new coverage. We, therefore, propose a diversity based sampling for extracting instances that provide new vocabulary coverage . The scoring function $tc\_score(s)$ is defined below, where $Voc(s)$ is defined as the vocabulary of source sentence s for an instance $x_i =< s_i, t_i >$, T is the set of parallel sentences or segments extracted so far.

$$tc\_score(s) = \sum_{s=1}^{|T|} sim(s, s') * \frac{1}{|T|} \quad (1)$$

$$sim(s, s') = |(Voc(s) \cap Voc(s')| \quad (2)$$

5.2.2 Alignment Ratio

We also propose a strategy that provides direct insight into the coverage of the underlying lexicon and prefers a sentence pair that is more likely to be comparable. We call this *alignment ratio* and it can be easily computed from the available set of features discussed in Section 3 as below:

$$a\_score(s) = \frac{\#unalignedwords}{\#alignedwords} \quad (3)$$

$$s* = arg\,max_s a\_score(s) \quad (4)$$

This strategy is quite similar to the diversity based approach as both prefer selecting sentences that have a potential to offer new vocabulary from the comparable sentence pair. However while the diversity approach looks only at the source side coverage and does not depend upon the underlying lexicon, the alignment ratio utilizes the model for computing coverage. It should also be noted that while we have coverage for a word in the sentence pair, it may not make it to the probabilistically trained and extracted lexicon.

5.3 Combining Multiple Annotations

Finally, given two annotations and corresponding sampling strategies, we try to jointly select the sentence that is best suitable for obtaining both the annotations and is maximally beneficial to the classifier. We select a single instance by combining the scores from the different selection strategies as a geometric mean. For instance, we consider a margin based sampling ($margin$) for the first annotation and a diversity sampling (tc_score) for the second annotation, we can jointly select a sentence that maximizes the combined score as shown below:

$$total\_score(s) = margin(s) * tc\_score(s) \quad (5)$$

$$s* = arg\,max_s total\_score(s) \quad (6)$$

6 Experiments and Results

6.1 Data

This research primarily focuses on identifying comparable sentences from a pool of dominantly non-parallel sentences. To our knowledge, there is a dearth of publicly available comparable corpora of this nature. We, therefore, simulate a low-resource scenario by using realistic assumptions of noise and parallelism at both the corpus-level and the sentence-level. In this section we discuss the process and assumptions involved in the creation of our datasets and try to mimic the properties of real-world comparable corpora harvested from the web.

We first start with a sentence-aligned parallel corpus available for the language pair. We then divide the corpus into three parts. The first part is called the 'sampling pool' and is set aside to use for drawing sentences at random. The second part is used to act as a non-parallel corpus. We achieve non-parallelism by randomizing the mapping of the target sentences with the source sentences. This is a slight variation of the strategy used in (Munteanu and Marcu, 2005) for generating negative examples for their classifier. The third part is used to synthesize a comparable corpus at the sentence-level. We perform this by first selecting a parallel sentence-pair and then padding either sides by a source and target segment drawn independently from the sampling pool. We control the length of the non-parallel portion that is appended to be lesser than or equal to the original length of the sentence. Therefore, the resulting synthesized comparable sentence pairs are guaranteed to contain at least 50% parallelism.

We use this dataset as the unlabeled pool from which the active learner selects instances for labeling. Since the gold-standard labels for this corpus are already available, which gives us better control over automating the active learning process, which typically requires a human in the loop. However, our active learning strategies are in no way limited by the simulated data setup and can generalize to the real world scenario with an expert providing the labels for each instance.

We perform our experiments with data from two language pairs: Urdu-English and Spanish-English. For Urdu-English, we use the parallel corpus NIST 2008 dataset released for the translation shared task. We start with 50,000 parallel sentence corpus from the released training data to create a corpus of 25,000 sentence pairs with 12,500 each of comparable and non-parallel sentence pairs. Similarly, we use 50,000 parallel sentences from the training data released by the WMT 2008 datasets for Spanish-English to create a corpus of 25,000 sentence pairs. We also use two held-out data sets for training and tuning the classifier, consisting of 1000 sentence pairs (500 non-parallel and 500 comparable).

6.2 Results

We perform two kinds of evaluations: the first, to show that our active learning strategies perform well across language pairs and the second, to show that multi annotation active learning leads to a good improvement in performance of the classifier.

6.2.1 How does the Active Learning perform?

In section 5, we proposed multiple active learning strategies for both eliciting both kinds of annotations. A good active learning strategy should select instances that contribute to the maximal improvement of the classifier. The effectiveness of active learning is typically tested by the number of queries the learner asks and the resultant improvement in the performance of the classifier. The classifier performance in the comparable sentence classification task can be computed as the F-score on the held out dataset. For this work, we assume that both the annotations require the same effort level and so assign uniform cost for eliciting each of them. Therefore the number of queries is equivalent to the total cost of supervision.

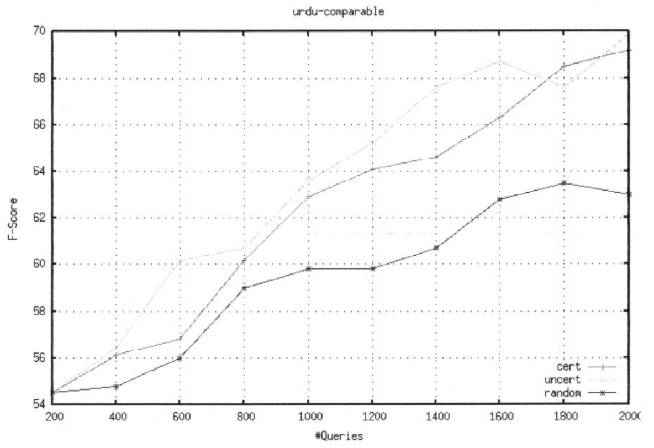

Figure 2: Active learning performance for the comparable corpora classification in Urdu-English language-pair

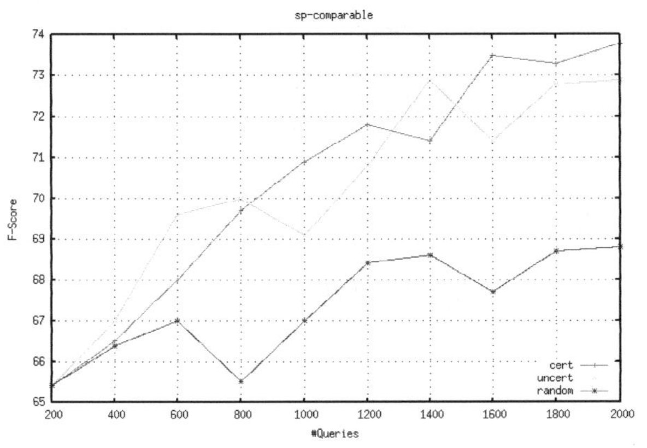

Figure 3: Active learning performance for the comparable corpora classification in Spanish-English language-pair

Figure 2 shows our results for the Urdu-English language pair, and Figure 3 plots the Spanish-English results with the x-axis showing the total number of queries posed to obtain annotations and the y-axis shows the resultant improvement in accuracy of the classifier. In these experiments we do not actively select for the second annotation but acquire the parallel segment from the same sentence. We compare this over a random baseline where the sentence pair is selected at random and used for eliciting both annotations at the same time.

Firstly, we notice that both our active learning strategies: certainty sampling and margin-based sampling perform better than the random baseline. For the Urdu-English language pair we can see that for the same effort expended (i.e 2000 queries) the classifier has an increase in accuracy of 8 absolute points. For Spanish-English language pair the accuracy improvement is 6 points over random baseline. Another observation from Figure 3 is that for the classifier to reach an fixed accuracy of 68 points, the random sampling method requires 2000 queries while the from the active selection strategies require significantly less effort of about 500 queries.

6.2.2 Performance of Joint Selection with Multiple Annotations

We now evaluate our joint selection strategy that tries to select the best possible instance for both the annotations. Figure 4 shows our results for the Urdu-English language pair, and Figure 5 plots the Spanish-English results for active learning with multiple annotations. As before, the x-axis shows the total number of queries posed, equivalent to the cumulative effort for obtaining the annotations and the y-axis shows the resultant improvement in accuracy of the classifier.

We evaluate the multi annotation active learning against two single-sided baselines where the sampling focus is on selecting instances according to strategies suitable for one annotation at a time. The best performing active learning strategy for the class label annotations is the certainty sampling (annot1) and so for one single-sided baseline, we use this baseline. We also obtain the second annotation for the same instance. By doing so, we might be selecting an instance that is sub-optimal for the second annotation and therefore the resultant lexicon may not maximally benefit from the instance. We also observe, from our experiments, that the diversity based sampling works well for the second annotation and alignment ratio does not perform as well. So, for the second single-sided baseline we use the diversity based sampling strategy (annot2) and get the first annotation for the same instance. Finally we compare this with the joint selection approach proposed earlier that combines both the annotation strategies (annot1+annot2). In both the language pairs we notice that joint selection for both annotations performs better than the baselines.

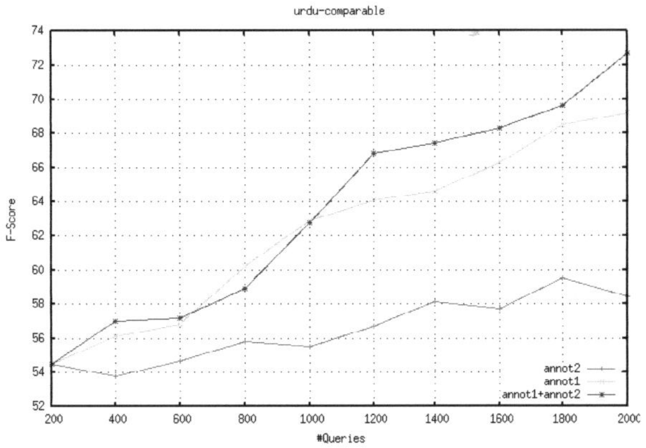

Figure 4: Active learning with multiple annotations and classification performance in Urdu-English

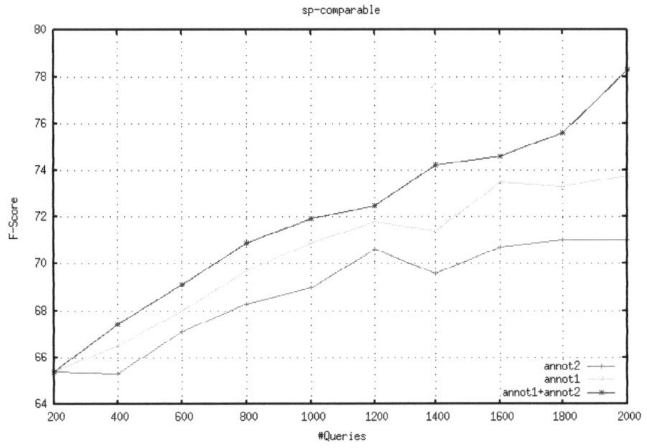

Figure 5: Active learning with multiple annotations and classification performance in Spanish-English

7 Conclusion and Future Work

In this paper, we proposed active learning with multiple annotations for the challenge of building comparable corpora in low-resource scenarios. In particular, we identified two kinds of annotations: class labels (for identifying comparable vs. non-parallel data) and clean parallel segments within the comparable sentences. We implemented multiple independent strategies for obtaining each of the abve in a cost-effective manner. Our active learning experiments in a simulated low-resource comparable corpora scenario across two language pairs show significant results over strong baselines. Finally we also proposed a joint selection strategy that selects a single instance which is beneficial to both the annotations. The results indicate an improvement over single strategy baselines.

There are several interesting questions for future work. Throughout the paper we assumed uniform costs for both the annotations, which will need to be verified with human subjects. We also hypothesize that obtaining both annotations for the same sentence may be cheaper than getting them from two different sentences due to the overhead of context switching. Another assumption is that of the existence of a single contiguous parallel segment in a comparable sentence pair, which needs to be verified for corpora on the web.

Finally, active learning assumes availability of an expert to answer the queries. Availability of an expert for low-resource languages and feasibility of running large scale experiments is difficult. We, therefore, have started working on crowdsourcing these annotation tasks on Amazon Mechanical Turk (MTurk) where it is easy to find people and quickly run experiments with real people.

Acknowledgement

This material is based upon work supported in part by the U. S. Army Research Laboratory and the U. S. Army Research Office under grant W911NF-10-1-0533, and in part by NSF under grant IIS 0916866.

References

Peter F. Brown, Stephen A. Della Pietra, Vincent J. Della Pietra, and Robert L. Mercer. 1993. The mathematics of statistical machine translation: Parameter estimation. *Computational Linguistics*, 19(2):263–311.

Rich Caruana. 1997. Multitask learning. In *Machine Learning*, pages 41–75.

Gregory Druck, Burr Settles, and Andrew McCallum. 2009. Active learning by labeling features. In *Proceedings of Conference on Empirical Methods in Nat-*

ural Language Processing (EMNLP 2009), pages 81–90.

Jenny Rose Finkel and Christopher D. Manning. 2010. Hierarchical joint learning: Improving joint parsing and named entity recognition with non-jointly labeled data. In *Proceedings of ACL 2010*.

Pascale Fung and Lo Yen Yee. 1998. An IR approach for translating new words from nonparallel, comparable texts. In *Proceedings of the 36th Annual Meeting of the Association for Computational Linguistics*, pages 414–420, Montreal, Canada.

David D. Lewis and Jason Catlett. 1994. Heterogeneous uncertainty sampling for supervised learning. In *In Proceedings of the Eleventh International Conference on Machine Learning*, pages 148–156. Morgan Kaufmann.

Prem Melville, Foster Provost, Maytal Saar-Tsechansky, and Raymond Mooney. 2005. Economical active feature-value acquisition through expected utility estimation. In *UBDM '05: Proceedings of the 1st international workshop on Utility-based data mining*, pages 10–16, New York, NY, USA. ACM.

Dragos Stefan Munteanu and Daniel Marcu. 2005. Improving machine translation performance by exploiting non-parallel corpora. *Computational Linguistics*, 31(4):477–504.

Dragos Stefan Munteanu and Daniel Marcu. 2006. Extracting parallel sub-sentential fragments from non-parallel corpora. In *Proceedings of the 21st International Conference on Computational Linguistics and the 44th Annual Meeting of the Association for Computational Linguistics*, pages 81–88, Sydney, Australia.

Franz Josef Och and Hermann Ney. 2003. A systematic comparison of various statistical alignment models. *Computational Linguistics*, 29(1):19–51.

Sinno Jialin Pan and Qiang Yang. 2010. A survey on transfer learning. *IEEE Transactions on Knowledge and Data Engineering*, 22(10):1345–1359, October.

Chris Quirk, Raghavendra U. Udupa, and Arul Menezes. 2007. Generative models of noisy translations with applications to parallel fragment extraction. In *Proceedings of the Machine Translation Summit XI*, pages 377–384, Copenhagen, Denmark.

Roi Reichart, Katrin Tomanek, Udo Hahn, and Ari Rappoport. 2008. Multi-task active learning for linguistic annotations. In *Proceedings of ACL-08: HLT*, pages 861–869, Columbus, Ohio, June. Association for Computational Linguistics.

Philip Resnik and Noah A. Smith. 2003. The web as a parallel corpus. *Comput. Linguist.*, 29(3):349–380.

Tobias Scheffer, Christian Decomain, and Stefan Wrobel. 2001. Active hidden markov models for information extraction. In *IDA '01: Proceedings of the 4th International Conference on Advances in Intelligent Data Analysis*, pages 309–318, London, UK. Springer-Verlag.

Burr Settles, Mark Craven, and Soumya Ray. 2008. Multiple-instance active learning. In *In Advances in Neural Information Processing Systems (NIPS*, pages 1289–1296. MIT Press.

Bing Zhao and Stephan Vogel. 2002. Full-text story alignment models for chinese-english bilingual news corpora. In *Proceedings of the ICSLP '02*, September.

How Comparable are Parallel Corpora? Measuring the Distribution of General Vocabulary and Connectives

Bruno Cartoni
Linguistics Department
University of Geneva
2, rue de Candolle
CH – 1211 Geneva 4

Sandrine Zufferey
Linguistics Department
University of Geneva
2, rue de Candolle
CH – 1211 Geneva 4

{bruno.cartoni|sandrine.zufferey}@unige.ch

Thomas Meyer
Idiap Research Institute
Rue Marconi 19
CH – 1920 Martigny

Andrei Popescu-Belis
Idiap Research Institute
Rue Marconi 19
CH – 1920 Martigny

{thomas.meyer|andrei.popescu-belis}@idiap.ch

Abstract

In this paper, we question the homogeneity of a large parallel corpus by measuring the similarity between various sub-parts. We compare results obtained using a general measure of lexical similarity based on χ^2 and by counting the number of discourse connectives. We argue that discourse connectives provide a more sensitive measure, revealing differences that are not visible with the general measure. We also provide evidence for the existence of specific characteristics defining translated texts as opposed to non-translated ones, due to a universal tendency for explicitation.

1 Introduction

Comparable corpora are often considered as a solution to compensate for the lack of parallel corpora. Indeed, parallel corpora are still perceived as the gold standard resource for many multilingual natural language processing applications, such as statistical machine translation.

The aim of this paper is to assess the homogeneity of the widely used Europarl parallel corpus (Koehn 2005) by comparing a distributional measure of lexical similarity with results focused on a more specific measure, the frequency of use of discourse connectives. Various perspectives can be taken to assess the homogeneity of this corpus. First, we evaluate the (dis)similarities between translated and original language (Experiment 1) and then the (dis)similarities between texts translated from different source languages (Experiment 2).

Analyzing the use of discourse connectives such as *because* and *since* in English highlights important differences between translated and original texts. The analysis also reveals important differences when comparing, for a given language, texts that have been translated from various source languages. The different distribution of connectives in original vs. translated French, as well as across varieties of French translated from various source languages (English, German, Italian and Spanish), are all the more intriguing that they are not matched by a distributional difference of the general vocabulary in these corpora. We will indeed show that a well-known method (Kilgarriff 2001) designed to compare corpora finds that the original French and the various translated portions of Europarl are rather similar, regardless of their source language.

The paper is structured as follows: we first present related work on the characterization of translated text (Section 2). In Section 3, we argue that analyzing discourse connectives sheds new light on text (dis)similarity. Section 4 presents the Europarl parallel corpus and its sub-parts that have been used in our studies, as well as the methodology and measures that have been applied to assess text similarities. Section 5 presents our main findings and Section 6 discusses our results, drawing methodological conclusions about the use of parallel corpora.

Proceedings of the 4th Workshop on Building and Using Comparable Corpora, pages 78–86,
49th Annual Meeting of the Association for Computational Linguistics,
Portland, Oregon, 24 June 2011. ©*2011 Association for Computational Linguistics*

2 Previous Work

Existing studies on translated corpora are mainly designed to automatically identify the presence of so-called "translationese" or "third code", in other words, a text style deemed to be specific to translated texts, as in (Baroni and Bernardini 2005) or in (Ilisei et al. 2010). In the literature, many possible characteristics of translationese have been identified, such as those listed in (Baker 1996): translations are simpler than original texts (Laviosa-Braithwaite 1996); translations are more explicit than original texts due to an increase of cohesion markers (Blum-Kulka 1986); and the items that are unique in the target system (i.e. that do not have exact equivalents in the source language) are under-represented in translations (Tirkkonen-Condit 2000).

In the field of natural language processing, several studies on parallel corpora have shown that when building a statistical machine translation system, knowing which texts have been originally written in a given language and which ones are translations has an impact on the quality of the system (Ozdowska 2009). A recent study using machine learning has confirmed the universal of simplification as a feature of translated texts (Ilisei et al. 2010).Corpora can be compared using similarity measures. Most of these measures are based on lexical frequency. Kilgariff (2001) provides a comprehensive review of the different methods for computing similarity.

In this study, we chose to use the CBDF measure (Chi-by-degrees-of-freedom), as proposed in (Kilgariff 1997), to assess the similarity of our sub-corpora, as explained in Section 4.3. We compare this measure with another marker of text diversity (connectives), as explained in the following section.

3 Discourse Connectives as Markers of Text Diversity

Discourse connectives like *but*, *because* or *while* form a functional category of lexical items that are very frequently used to mark coherence relations such as *explanation* or *contrast* between units of text or discourse (e.g. Halliday & Hassan 1976; Mann & Thomson 1992; Knott & Dale 1994; Sanders 1997). One of the unique properties of discourse connectives is that the relation they convey can in many cases be inferred even when they are removed, as illustrated in (1) and (2):

1 Max fell because Jack pushed him.

2 Max fell. Jack pushed him.

The causal relation conveyed by *because* in (1) is also inferable when the connective is absent by using world knowledge about the possible relation between the fact of pushing someone and this person's fall in (2). In other words, contrary to most other lexical items, connectives can be used or left out without producing ungrammatical results or losing important aspects of meaning. At a macro-textual level, it is however clear that a text containing no connective at all would become rather difficult to understand. Several psycho-linguistic studies have indeed stressed the role of connectives for processing (Millis & Just 1994; Noordman & Blijzer 2000). But the point we want to make here is that in most texts or discourses, some coherence relations are conveyed by the use of connectives while others are not, depending on what the author/speaker feels necessary to mark explicitly.

Another consequence of the fact that connectives are optional is that their use in translation can vary tremendously between the source and the target texts. Studies that have examined at the use of connectives in translation have indeed found that connectives were often removed or added in the target texts, and that the type of coherence relation conveyed was sometimes even modified due to the actual choice of connectives in the target system (Altenberg 1986; Baker 1993; Lamiroy 1994; Halverson 2004). For all these reasons, discourse connectives appear to be particularly interesting to investigate in relation to corpus homogeneity.

In this study, we focus more particularly on the category of causal connectives, that is to say connectives such as *because* and *since* in English. This particular category seemed especially appropriate for our purposes for a number of reasons. First, causal connectives form a well-defined cluster in many languages and can be studied comprehensively. Second, causal relations are amongst the most basic ones for human cognition and in consequence causal connectives are widely used in almost all text types (Sanders & Sweetser 2009). Lastly, causal connectives have been found to be more volatile in translation than other categories, such as for example concessive connectives like *but*, *however*, etc. (Halverson 2004; Altenberg 1986).

From a quantitative perspective, function words are usually very frequent whereas most content words tend to be in the tail of the distribution. This provides another reason to treat connectives as a key feature for assessing text similarities.

4 Corpora and Methodology

4.1 Corpora

Our analysis is based on the Europarl corpus (Koehn 2005), a resource initially designed to train statistical machine translation systems. Europarl is a multilingual corpus that contains the minutes of the European Parliament. At the parliament, every deputy usually speaks in his/her own language, and all statements are transcribed, and then translated into the other official languages of the European Union (a total of 11 languages for this version of the corpus – version 5). Based on this data, several parallel bilingual corpora can be extracted, but caution is necessary because the exact status of every text, original or translated, is not always clearly stated. However, for a number of statements, a specific tag provides this information.

From this multilingual corpus, we extracted for our first experiment two parallel and "directional" corpora (En-Fr and Fr-En). By "directional" we mean that the original and translated texts are clearly identified in these corpora. Namely, in the English-French subset, the original speeches were made in English (presumably mostly by native speakers), and then translated into French, while the reverse is true for French-English. Still, for many applications, these would appear as two undifferentiated subsets of an English-French parallel corpus.

Since language tags are scarcely present, we automatically gathered all the tag information in all the language-specific files, correcting all the tags and discarding texts with contradictory information. Therefore, these extracted directional corpora are made of discontinuous sentences, because of the very nature of this multilingual corpus. In one single debate, each speaker speaks in his/her own language, and when extracting statements of one particular language, discourse cohesion across speakers is lost. However, this has no incidence at the global level on the quantitative distribution of connectives.

We have focused our investigation on the years 1996 to 1999 of the Europarl corpus. Indeed, statistical investigations and information gathered at the European Parliament revealed that the translation policy had changed over the years. The 1996-1999 period appeared to contain the most reliable translated data of the whole corpus.

For Experiment 1, we extracted two parallel directional corpora made of two languages – French and English – in order to compare translated and original texts in both languages, as shown in Figure 1.

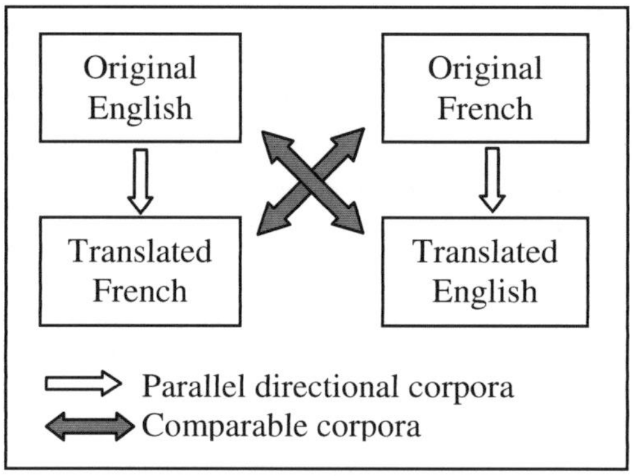

Figure 1: Parallel and comparable corpora extracted from Europarl

Table 1 gives the number of tokens in the English-French and in the French-English parallel directional corpora.

Parallel corpus	Token in ST	Token in TT
English-French (EF)	1,412,316	1,583,775
French-English (FE)	1,257,879	1,188,923

Table 1: Number of tokens in Source Texts (ST) and Translated Texts (TT) of the parallel directional corpora.

Following the same methodology, we extracted for Experiment 2 other parallel directional corpora, again with French as a target language (also from the 1996-1999 period), as shown in Figure 2. Table 2 presents the sizes of these four additional comparable corpora.

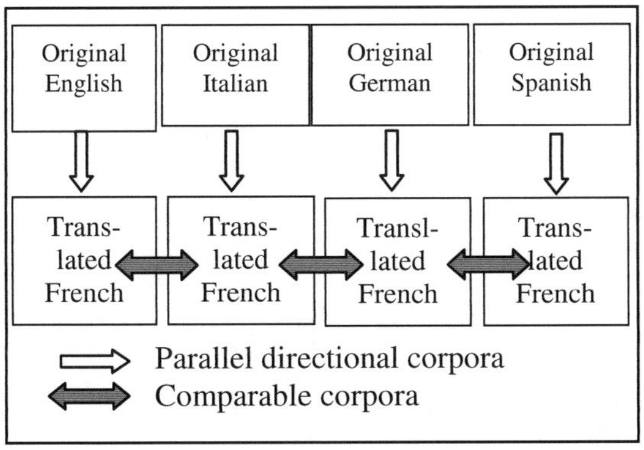

Figure 2: Parallel and comparable corpora for Translated French

Parallel corpus	Token in ST	Token in TT
German-French (DF)	1,254,531	1,516,634
Italian-French (IF)	552,242	624,534
Spanish-French (SF)	597,607	633,918

Table 2: Number of tokens in Source Texts (ST) and Translated Texts (TT) of the three additional parallel directional corpora of translated French.

These parallel directional corpora have been used as comparable corpora in our study because they are written in the same language and are of the same genre, but do not have the same "status", since some are original texts while others are translations, as shown in . Moreover, for comparison purposes, we have also used a sub-part of Europarl which was originally produced in French (noted OF), corresponding to the French part of the French-English corpus described in Table 1

All the experiments described below are based on these comparable corpora, i.e. on the translated vs. original corpus (for French and English) and on the different corpora of translated French (with Italian, English, Spanish and German as source languages).

4.2 First Measure: CBDF Measure

Following a proposal by Kilgarriff (2001), who criticizes a number of simpler techniques, we have measured corpus similarity by computing the χ^2 statistic over the 500 most frequent words from the two corpora to be compared, which were limited to 200,000 words each, so that comparison with the values given by Kilgarriff was possible. The value was normalized by the number of degrees of freedom, which is $(500-1) \times (2-1) = 499$, hence its name. As shown by Kilgarriff with artificially designed corpora, for which the similarity level was known in advance, the χ^2 statistic is a reliable indicator of similarity. Moreover, Kilgarriff (2001: Table 10, page 260) provides a table with the χ^2 values for all 66 pairs of 200,000-word corpora selected from 12 English corpora, which we will use for comparison below. The table also lists internal homogeneity values for each corpus, obtained by averaging the χ^2 statistic over each 200,000-word corpus split several times in half. In fact, as the same method is used for computing both similarity and homogeneity, only 100,000-word fragments are used for similarity, as stated by Kilgarriff.

The CBDF similarity values between 100,000-word subsets of Original French (OF), French translated from English (EF), from Italian (IF), from German (DF), and from Spanish (SF) are shown in Table 4 below. Taking OF vs. EF as an example, these values are computed by summing up, for all of the most frequent 500 words in OF+EF, the difference between the observed and the expected number of occurrences in each of OF and EF, more precisely $(o - e)^2 / e$, and then dividing the sum by 499. The expected number is simply the average of OF and EF occurrences, which is the best guess given the observations. The lower the result, the closer the two corpora are considered to be, in terms of lexical distribution, as shown by Kilgarriff (2001).

For measuring homogeneity, we sliced each corpus in 10 equal parts, and computed the score by randomly building 10 different corpus configurations and calculating the average of the values.

4.3 Second Measure: Counting Connectives

As explained above, we focused our experiments on comparing frequencies of causal connectives. For French, our list of items included *parce que*, *puisque*, *car*, and *étant donné que*. For English, we included *because*, *since*, and *given that*[1]. In the case of *since*, we manually annotated its two meanings in order to distinguish its causal uses from its temporal ones, and retained only its causal uses in our counts.

To count the number of occurrences for each causal connective in each sub-part of the corpus, we first pre-processed the corpora to transform each connective as one word-form (e.g. *étant donné que* became *étantdonnéque*, and *puisqu'* became *puisque.*). Then, we counted each connective, and normalized the figures to obtain a ratio of connectives per 100,000 tokens.

Moreover, when comparing French sub-corpora translated from different source languages, we also computed the rank of each connective in the frequency list extracted from each corpus. Comparing these ranks provided important information about their respective frequencies.

We have found that the frequency of each connective does not vary significantly throughout the corpus (years 1996-1999), which tends to prove that the use of connectives does not depend crucially on the style of a particular speaker or translator.

5 Results

This section presents the results of the CBDF measure for each corpus (Section 5.1), and shows how the frequencies of connectives reveal differences between translated and original texts (Section 5.2) and between texts translated from various source languages (Section 5.3).

5.1 Text Similarity according to CBDF

For Experiment 1, we have compared the differences between original and translated texts, for English and French. The values of CBDF similarity resulting from this comparison are shown in Table 3. Compared to the different scores computed by Kilgarriff, these scores indicate that the two pairs of corpora are both quite similar.

[1] The English causal connective *for* is more difficult to address because of its ambiguity with the homographic preposition. However, on a sample of 500 tokens of *for* randomly extracted from Europarl, we found only two occurrences of the connective *for*, leading us to exclude this connective from our investigation.

	CBDF
Original English – Translated English	13.28
Original French – Translated French	12.28

Table 3: CBDF between original and translated texts

The similarities between sub-corpora of French translated from different source languages (Experiment 2) are shown in Table 4. The values comparing the same portion (e.g. OF/OF) indicate the homogeneity score of the respective sub-corpus.

	OF	EF	DF	IF	SF
OF	*2.64*				
EF	6.00	*3.34*			
DF	5.11	4.83	*2.74*		
IF	4.88	6.30	4.99	*2.86*	
SF	5.34	5.43	5.36	4.43	*2.22*

Table 4: Values of CBDF (χ^2 statistic normalized by degrees of freedom) for all pairs of source-specific 200,000-word subsets from Europarl. The lower the value, the more similar the subsets.

Looking at the values in Table 4, we can see that the similarity score between OF and EF is 6.00, which, compared to Kilgarriff's values for British corpora, is lower than all but two of the 66 pairs of corpora he compared. Most of the values observed by Kilgarriff are in fact between 20 and 40, and the similarity we found for OF vs. EF is, for instance, in the same range as the one for the journal *The Face* vs. *The Daily Mirror*, a tabloid, and higher than the similarity of two broadsheet newspapers (i.e., they get a lower CBDF value). Therefore, we can conclude that OF and EF are very similar from a word distribution point of view.

As for the other pairs, they are all in the same range of similarity, again much more similar than the corpora cited in Kilgarriff's Table 10. Regarding internal comparisons, OF/EF appears as the second most dissimilar pair, preceded only by IF/EF (French translated from Italian vs. from English). The most similar pair is Original French vs. French translated from Italian, which is not surprising given that the two languages are closely related. Also similar to OF/IF are the IF/SF and EF/DF pairs, reflecting the similarity of translations from related languages.

Homogeneity values are higher than similarity values (the χ^2 scores are lower). These values are again comparable, albeit clearly lower, than those found by Kilgarriff, and presumably account for the lower variety of parliamentary discourse. Still, these values are similar to those of the most homogeneous subset used by Kilgarriff, the *Dictionary of National Biography* (1.86) or the *Computergram* (2.20).

Figures on the distribution of connectives, presented in the next section, tend to show that these sub-corpora are however not as similar as they may seem at a first view.

5.2 Text Similarities Measured with the Use of Causal Connectives: Experiment 1

In Experiment 1, we highlight the differences in the use of causal connectives between original English and translated English. Figure 3 shows the discrepancy between the use of the same connectives in original and translated texts. Among these connectives, *since* is the only truly ambiguous word. We have therefore also evaluated the proportion of causal uses of *since* among all the uses of the word *since*. In original English, this proportion is 31.8% and doubles in translated English to reach 67.7%.

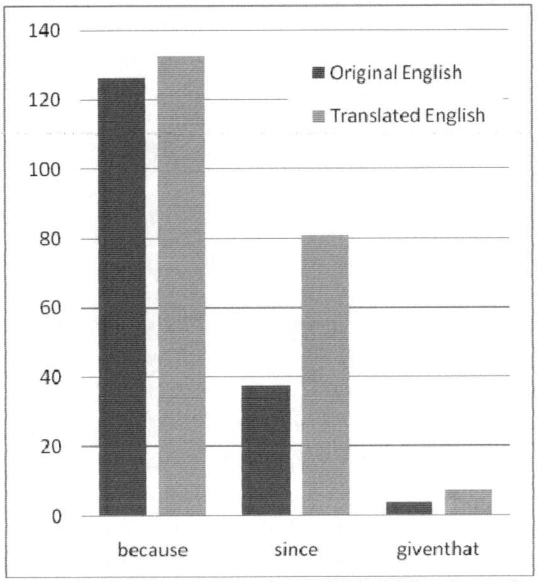

Figure 3: Ratio connectives/100,000 tokens in original and translated English.

These figures show that original and translated texts differ, at least in terms of the number of causal connectives they contain. While *because* seems equally used in original and translated English, *since* and *given that* are used three times more frequently in translated than in original texts. This variability is also noticeable when comparing original and translated uses of French connectives, as shown in Figure 4.

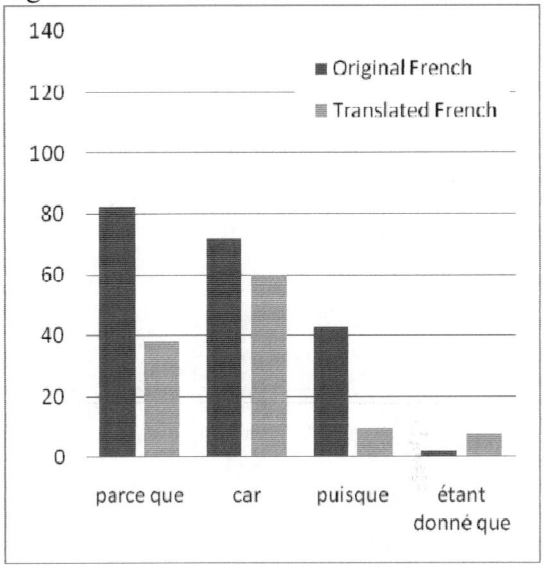

Figure 4: Ratio connectives/100’000 tokens in original and translated French.

For French, while *car* seems to be equally used in both sub-parts of the corpus, *parce que* is used twice less frequently in translated than in original texts. This discrepancy is even bigger in the case of *puisque*, which is used five times less frequently in translated than in original texts. The reverse phenomenon is observed for *étant donné que,* which is used four times more frequently in translated than in original texts.

By looking at the translation of every connective, we were able to count the number of connectives inserted in the target language, that is to say when there was a connective in the target system but no connective in the original text. Conversely, we have also counted the number of connectives removed in the target text, when a connective in the source language was not translated at all. Overall, we found that connectives were inserted much more often than removed during the process of translation. In the case of English as a target language, 65 connectives were inserted while 35 were removed. In the case of French, 46 connectives were inserted while 11 were removed.

5.3 Text similarities measured by the use of causal connectives: Experiment 2

When comparing the number of occurrences of French causal connectives across texts translated from different languages, the differences are striking. Indeed, every source language seems to increase the use of one specific connective in the French translations.

Figure 5 presents the ratio of connectives per 100'000 token. The data compares the use of connectives in French translated from English, Italian, Spanish and German.

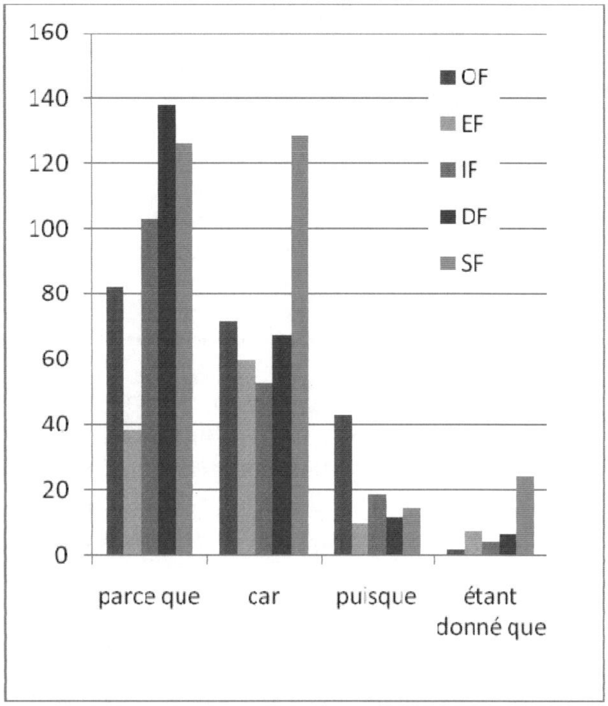

Figure 5: Connectives per 100,000 tokens in French texts translated from various source languages (for each connective, from left to right OF, EF, IF, DF, SF)

Table 5 provides the *rank* of every connective in the word frequency list (sorted by decreasing frequency) computed for each sub-corpus. Grey cells indicate the most frequent connective in each sub-corpus.

	OF	EF	IF	DF	SF
parce que	**115**	292	**99**	159	87
car	136	**172**	201	**82**	**85**
puisque	235	1070	601	886	790
étant donné que	3882	1368	2104	1450	459

Table 5: Rank of the connectives in word frequency list for each corpus. Note that the order varies with the source language.

These figures show that the distribution of every connective differs radically according to the source language. Every source language seems to increase the use of one specific connective. When German is the source language, *car* is used twice more often than when English or Italian are the source languages. When Italian is the source language, *parce que* is used twice as often and when English is the source language, *étant donné que* is again used twice as often. Overall, *puisque* is the only connective that does not seem to be enhanced by any of the source languages, which confirms some prior linguistic analyses of this item, showing that *puisque* does not have exact equivalents in other close languages (Degand 2004; Zufferey to appear).

6 Discussion

We have compared the use of discourse connectives in different sub-parts of the Europarl parallel corpus with the use of general vocabulary, as computed by a measure of lexical homogeneity. Our main finding is that even though the lexical measure showed the similarity of these sub-parts, the use of discourse connectives varied tremendously between the various sub-parts of our corpus.

One of the reasons why connectives show more variability than many other lexical items is that they are almost always optional. In other words, as argued in Section 3, for every individual use of a connective, the translator has the option to use another connective in the target language or to leave the coherence relation it conveys implicit. Coherence marking is therefore a global rather than a local textual strategy.

Given that connectives can be used or left out without producing ungrammatical results, studying their variability between comparable corpora provides interesting indications about their global homogeneity. The significant variability that we report between comparable (monolingual) sub-parts of the Europarl corpus indicates that they are not as homogeneous as global lexical measures like the CBDF tend to indicate. In other words, the various sub-parts of the corpus are not equivalents of one another for all purposes, and should not be used as such without caution. These differences were noticeable both by the different number of every connective used in every sub-part of the corpus, but also by the rather different frequency rank that was measured for every one of them in these same sub-parts.

From a translation perspective, our study also provides some further confirmation for the existence of specific characteristics that define translated texts (i.e. "translationese" or "third code"). More specifically, our study corroborates the explicitation hypothesis (Blum-Kulka 1986), positing that translated texts are more explicit than original ones due to an increase of cohesion markers. Connectives are part of the lexical markers that contribute to textual coherence, and we found that they are indeed more numerous in translated than in original texts. For English as a target language, translators have inserted twice as many connectives as they have removed. For French, this proportion raises to four times more insertions than omissions.

However, our data also indicates that the source language has an important influence on the nature of its translation. Indeed, for the use of connectives, we report important variations between texts translated into French from various source languages. More interestingly still, every source language triggered the use of one specific connective over the others. This connective was always specific to one particular source language.

It is also noteworthy that the similarity between texts translated into French, as measured with the CBDF, is greater when the source languages are typologically related. In our corpora of translated French, we found that texts were more similar when comparing the portion translated from Spanish and Italian (Romance languages) and when comparing texts translated from English and German (Germanic languages). This result makes intuitive sense and provides further confirmation of the reliability of this measure to assess global similarity between portions of texts.

7 Conclusion

The Europarl corpus is mostly used in NLP research without taking into account the direction of translation, in other words, without knowing which texts were originally produced in one language and which ones are translations. The experiments reported in this paper show that this status has a crucial influence of the nature of texts and should therefore be considered. Moreover, we have shown that translated texts from different source languages are not homogeneous either, therefore there is no unique translationese, and we identified some characteristics that vary according to the source language.

Our study also indicates that global measures of corpus similarity are not always sensitive enough to detect all forms of lexical variation, notably in the use of discourse connectives. However, the variability observed in the use of these items should not be discarded, both because of their rather frequent use and because they form an important aspect of textual strategies involving cohesion.

Acknowledgments

This study was partially funded by the Swiss National Science Foundation through the COMTIS Sinergia project (www.idiap.ch/comtis). The authors would particularly like to thank Adam Kilgarriff for his explanations regarding the CBDF measure.

References

Altenberg Bengt. 1986. Contrastive linking in spoken and written English. In Tottie G. & Bäcklund U. (Eds.), English in Speech and writing: a symposium. Uppsala, 13-40.

Baker Mona. 1993. In Other Words. A coursebook on translation. Routledge, London/New York.

Baker Mona. 1996. Corpus-based translation studies: The challenges that lie ahead. In Somers H. (Ed.) Terminology, LSP and Translation. Studies in language engineering in honour of Juan C. Sager. John Benjamins, Amsterdam, 175-186.

Baroni Marco and Bernardini Silvia. 2006. A new approach to the study of translationese: Machine-learning the difference between original and translated text. *Literary and Linguistic Computing* 21(3). 259-274

Degand Liesbeth. 2004. Contrastive analyses, translation and speaker involvement: the case of *puisque* and *aangezien*. In Achard, M. & Kemmer, S. (Eds.), Language, Culture and Mind. The University of Chicago Press, Chicago, 251-270.

Halliday Michael and Hasan Ruqaiya. 1976. *Cohesion in English*. Longman, London

Halverson Sandra. 2004. Connectives as a translation problem. In Kittel, H. et al. (Eds.) An International Encyclopedia of Translation Studies. Walter de Gruyter, Berlin/New York, 562-572.

Ilisei Iustina, Inkpen Diana, Corpas Pastor Gloria and Mitkov Russlan. 2010 Identification of Translationese: A Machine Learning Approach. In Gelbukh, A. (Ed), Computational Linguistics and Intelligent Text Processing Lecture Notes in Computer Science. Springer, Berlin / Heidelberg, 503-511

Kilgarriff Adam. 2001. Comparing Corpora. *Intl. Journal of Corpus Linguistics* 6(1): 1-37.

Kilgariff Adam. 1997. Using word frequency lists to measure corpus homogeneity and similarity between corpora. In *Fifth ACL Workshop on Very Large Corpora*, Beijing.

Knott Alistair and Dale Robert. 1994. Using linguistic phenomena to motivate a set of coherence relations. *Discourse processes* 18(1), 35-62.

Koehn Philipp. 2005. Europarl: A Parallel Corpus for Statistical Machine Translation, *MT Summit 2005*.

Lamiroy Beatrice. 1994. Pragmatic connectives and L2 acquisition. The case of French and Dutch. *Pragmatics* 4(2), 183-201.

Laviosa-Braithwaite Sara. 1996. The English Comparable Corpus (ECC): A Resource and a Methodology for the Empirical Study of Translation. PhD Thesis, Manchester, UMIST.

Mann William and Thomson Sandra. 1992. Relational Discourse Structure: A Comparison of Approaches to Structuring Text by 'Contrast'. In Hwang S. & Merrifield W. (Eds.), Language in Context: Essays for Robert E. Longacre. SIL, Dallas, 19-45.

Millis Keith & Just Marcel. 1994. The influence of connectives on sentence comprehension. *Journal of Memory and Language* 33 (1): 128-147.

New Boris, Pallier Christophe, Brysbaert Marc, Ferr Ludovic and Holloway Royal. 2004. Lexique~2: A New French Lexical Database. *Behavior Research Methods, Instruments, & Computers*, 36 (3): 516-524.

Noordman Leo and de Blijzer Femke. 2000. On the processing of causal relations. In E. Couper-Kuhlen & B. Kortmann (Eds.) Cause, Condition, Concession, Contrast. Mouton de Gruyter, Berlin. 35-56.

Ozdowska Sylvia. 2009. Données bilingues pour la TAS français-anglais : impact de la langue source et direction de traduction originales sur la qualité de la traduction. Proceedings of Traitement Automatique des Langues Naturelles, TALN'09, Senlis, France.

Sanders Ted. 1997. Semantic and pragmatic sources of coherence: On the categorization of coherence relations in context. *Discourse Processes* 24: 119–147.

Sanders Ted and Sweetser Eve (Eds) 2009. Causal Categories in Discourse and Cognition. Mouton de Gruyter, Berlin.

Tirkkonen-Condit Sonja. 2000. In search of translation universals: non-equivalence or « unique » items in a corpus test. Paper presented at the UMIST/UCL Research Models in Translation Studies Conference, Manchester, UK, April 2000.

Zufferey Sandrine to appear. "Car, parce que, puisque" Revisited. Three empirical studies on French causal connectives. *Journal of Pragmatics*.

Identifying Parallel Documents from a Large Bilingual Collection of Texts: Application to Parallel Article Extraction in Wikipedia.

Alexandre Patry
KeaText
845, Boulevard Dcarie, bureau 202
Saint-Laurent, Canada H4L 3L7
alexandre.patry@keatext.com

Philippe Langlais
DIRO/RALI
Université de Montréal
Montréal, Canada H3C3J7
felipe@iro.umontreal.ca

Abstract

While several recent works on dealing with large bilingual collections of texts, *e.g.* (Smith et al., 2010), seek for extracting **parallel sentences** from comparable corpora, we present PARADOCS, a system designed to recognize pairs of **parallel documents** in a (large) bilingual collection of texts. We show that this system outperforms a fair baseline (Enright and Kondrak, 2007) in a number of controlled tasks. We applied it on the French-English cross-language linked article pairs of `Wikipedia` in order see whether parallel articles in this resource are available, and if our system is able to locate them. According to some manual evaluation we conducted, a fourth of the article pairs in `Wikipedia` are indeed in translation relation, and PARADOCS identifies parallel or noisy parallel article pairs with a precision of 80%.

1 Introduction

There is a growing interest within the Machine Translation (MT) community to investigate *comparable corpora*. The idea that they are available in a much larger quantity certainly contributes to foster this interest. Still, *parallel corpora* are playing a crucial role in MT. This is therefore not surprising that the number of *bitexts* available to the community is increasing.

Callison-Burch et al. (2009) mined from institutional websites the 10^9 word parallel corpus[1] which gathers 22 million pairs of (likely parallel) French-English sentences. Tiedemann (2009) created the Opus corpus,[2] an open source parallel corpus gathering texts of various sources, in several languages pairs. This is an ongoing effort currently gathering more than 13 Gigabytes of compressed files. The Europarl corpus[3] (Koehn, 2005) gathers no less than 2 Gigabytes of compressed documents in 20 language pairs. Some other bitexts are more marginal in nature. For instance, the novel *1984* of George Orwel has been organized into an English-Norvegian bitext (Erjavec, 2004) and *Beyaz Kale* of Orhan Pamuk as well as *Sofies Verden* of Jostein Gaardner are available for the Swedish-Turk language pair (Megyesi et al., 2006).

A growing number of studies investigate the extraction of near parallel material (mostly sentences) from comparable data. Among them, Munteanu et al. (2004) demonstrate that a classifier can be trained to recognize parallel sentences in comparable corpora mined from news collections. A number of related studies (see section 5) have also been proposed; some of them seeking to extract parallel sentences from cross-language linked article pairs in `Wikipedia`[4] (Adafre and de Rijke, 2006; Smith et al., 2010). None of these studies addresses specifically the issue of discovering parallel pairs of articles in `Wikipedia`.

In this paper, we describe PARADOCS, a system capable of mining parallel documents in a collection, based on lightweight content-based features extracted from the documents. On the contrary to other systems designed to target parallel corpora (Chen

[1] http://www.statmt.org/wmt10

[2] http://opus.lingfil.uu.se/

[3] http://www.statmt.org/europarl/

[4] http://fr.wikipedia.org/

Proceedings of the 4th Workshop on Building and Using Comparable Corpora, pages 87–95,
49th Annual Meeting of the Association for Computational Linguistics,
Portland, Oregon, 24 June 2011. ©*2011 Association for Computational Linguistics*

and Nie, 2000; Resnik and Smith, 2003), we do not assume any specific naming conventions on filenames or URLs.

The reminder of this article is organized as follows. In the next section, we describe our approach to mining parallel documents in a bilingual collection of texts. We test our approach on the Europarl corpus in section 3. We present in section 4 the application of our system to a subpart of the French-English articles of Wikipedia. We describe related work in section 5, summarize our work in section 6 and present future works in section 7.

2 PARADOCS

In order to identify pairs of parallel documents in a bilingual collection of texts, we designed a system, named PARADOCS, which is making as few assumptions as possible on the language pair being considered, while still making use of the content of the documents in the collection. Our system is built on three lightweight components. The first one searches for target documents that are more likely parallel to a given source document (section 2.1). The second component classifies (candidate) pairs of documents as parallel or not (section 2.2). The third component is designed to filter out some (wrongly) recognized parallel pairs, making use of collection-level information (section 2.3).

2.1 Searching Candidate Pairs

In a collection containing n documents in a given language, and m in another one, scoring each of the $n \times m$ potential pairs of source-target documents becomes rapidly intractable. In our approach, we resort to an information retrieval system in order to select the target documents that are most likely parallel to a given source one. In order to do so, we index target documents t in the collection thanks to an *indexing strategy* ϕ that will be described shortly. Then, for a source document s, we first index it, that is, we compute $\phi(s)$, and query the retrieval engine with $\phi(s)$, which in turn returns the N most similar target documents found in the collection. In our experiments, we used the Lucene[5] retrieval library.

[5]http://lucene.apache.org

We tested two indexing strategies: one reduces a document to the sequence of hapax words it contains ($\phi \equiv$hap), the other one reduces it to its sequence of numerical entities ($\phi \equiv$num). Hapax words have been found very useful in identifying parallel pairs of documents (Enright and Kondrak, 2007) as well as for word-aligning bitexts (Lardilleux and Lepage, 2007). Following Enright and Kondrak (2007), we define hapax words as blank separated strings of more than 4 characters that appear only once in the document being indexed. Also, we define a numerical entity as a blank separated form containing at least one digit. It is clear from this description that our indexing strategies can easily be applied to many different languages.

2.2 Identifying candidate pairs

Each candidate pair delivered by Lucene, is classified as parallel or not by a classifier trained in a supervised way to recognize parallel documents. Here again, we want our classifier to be as agnostic as possible to the pair of languages considered. This is why we adopted very light feature extractors ψ which are built on three types of entities in documents: numerical entities ($\psi \equiv$num), hapax words ($\psi \equiv$hap) and punctuation marks[6] ($\psi \equiv$punc). For each sequence of entities $\psi(s)$ and $\psi(t)$ of a source document s and a target document t respectively, we compute the three following features:

- the normalized edit-distance between the two representations:

  $$\sigma = ed(\psi(s), \psi(t))/max(|\psi(s)|, |\psi(t)|)$$

  where $|\psi(d)|$ stands for the size of the sequence of entities contained in d. Intuitively, σ gives the proportion of entities shared across documents,

- the total number of entities in the representation of both documents:

  $$|\psi(s)| + |\psi(t)|$$

  We thought this information might complement the one of σ which is relative to the document's sequence length.

[6]We only considered the 6 following punctuation marks that are often preserved in translation: . ! ? ( ) :

- A binary feature which fires whenever the pair of documents considered receives the smaller edit-distance among all the pairs of documents involving this source document:

$$\delta(s,t) = \begin{cases} 1 & \text{if } \mathrm{ed}\,(\psi(s), \psi(t)) \leq \mathrm{ed}\,(\psi(s), \psi(t')) \;\forall\, t' \\ 0 & \text{otherwise} \end{cases}$$

  Intuitively, the target document considered is more likely the good one if it has with the source document the smallest edit distance. Since we do compute edit-distance for all the candidate documents pairs, this feature comes at no extra computational cost.

We compute these three features for each sequence of entities considered. For instance, if we represent a document according to its sequence of numerical entities and its hapax words, we do compute a total of 6 features.[7]

It is fair to say that our feature extraction strategy is very light. In particular, it does not capitalize on an existing bilingual lexicon. Preliminary experiments with features making use of such a lexicon turned out to be less successful, due to issues in the coverage of the lexicon (Patry and Langlais, 2005).

To create and put to the test our classifier, we used the free software package `Weka` (Hall et al., 2009), written in Java.[8] This package allows the easy experimentation of numerous families of classifiers. We investigated logistic regression (`logit`), naive bayes models (`bayes`), adaboost (`ada`), as well as decision tree learning (`j48`).

2.3 Post-treatments

The classifiers we trained label each pair of documents independently of other candidate pairs. This independence assumption is obviously odd and leads to situations where several target documents are paired to a given source document and vice-versa. Several solutions can be applied; we considered two simple ones in this work. The first one, hereafter named `nop`, consists in doing nothing; therefore leaving potential duplicates source or target documents. The second solution, called `dup`, filters out pairs sharing documents. Another solution we did not implement would require to keep from the set of pairs concerning a given source document the one with the best score as computed by our classifier. We leave this as future work.

3 Controlled Experiments

We checked the good behavior of PARADOCS in a controlled experimental setting, using the `Europarl` corpus. This corpus is organized into bitexts, which means that we have a ground truth against which we can evaluate our system.

3.1 Corpus

We downloaded version 5 of the `Europarl` corpus.[9] Approximatively 6 000 documents are available in 11 languages (including English), that is, we have 6 000 bitexts in 10 language pairs where English is one of the languages. The average number of sentences per document is 273. Some documents contain problems (encoding problems, files ending unexpectedly, etc.). We did not try to cope with this. In order to measure how sensible our approach is to the size of the documents, we considered several slices of them (from 10 to 1000 sentences). [10]

3.2 Protocol

We tested several experimental conditions, varying the language pairs considered (en-da, -de, -el, -es, -fi, -fr, -it, -nl, -pt and -sv) as well as the document length (10, 20, 30, 50, 70, 100 and 1 000 sentences). We also tested several system configurations, varying the indexing strategy (`num`, `hap`), the entities used for representing documents (`hap`, `num`, `num+hap`, `num+punc`), the classifier used (`logit`, `ada`, `bayes`, and `j48`), as well as the post-filtering strategy (`nop`, `dup`). This means that we conducted no less than 4 480 experiments.

Because we know which documents are parallel, we can compute precision (percentage of identified parallel pairs that are truly parallel) and recall (percentage of true parallel pairs identified) for each configuration.

---

[7] We tried with less success to compute a single set of features from a representation considering all entities.

[8] `www.cs.waikato.ac.nz/ml/weka/`

[9] `http://www.statmt.org/europarl`

[10] We removed the first sentences of each document, since they may contain titles or other information that may artificially ease pairing.

Since our approach requires to train a classifier, we resorted in this experiment to a 5-fold cross-validation procedure where we trained our classifiers on 4/5 of the corpus and tested on the remaining part. The figures reported in the reminder of this section are averaged over the 5 folds. Also, all configurations tested in this section considered the $N = 20$ most similar target documents returned by the retrieval engine for each source document.

3.3 Results

3.3.1 Search errors

We first measured search errors observed during step 1 of our system. There are actually two types of errors: one when no document is returned by `Lucene` (`nodoc`) and one when none of the target documents returned by the retrieval engine are sanctioned ones (`nogood`). Figure 1 shows both error types for the Dutch-English language pair, as a function of the document length.[11] Clearly, search errors are more important when documents are short. Approximatively a tenth of the source documents of (at most) 100 sentences do not receive by `Lucene` any target document. For smaller documents, this happens for as much as a third of the documents. Also, it is interesting to note that in approximatively 6% of the cases where `Lucene` returns target documents, the good one is not present. Obviously we pay the prize of our lightweight indexation scheme. In order to increase the recall of our system, `nodoc` errors could be treated by employing an indexing strategy which would use more complex features, such as sufficiently rare words (possibly involving a keyword test, *e.g.* tf.idf). This is left as future work.

3.3.2 Best System configuration

In order to determine the factors which influence the most our system, we varied the language pairs (10 values) and the length of the documents (7 values) and counted the number of times a given system configuration obtained the best f-measure over the 70 tests we conducted. We observed that most of the time, the configurations recording the best f-measure are those that exploit numerical entities (both at indexing time and feature extraction time). Actually, we observed that computing features on hapax words or punctuation marks on top of numerical entities do not help much. One possible explanation is that often, and especially within the `Europarl` corpus, hapax words correspond to numerical entities. Also, we noted that frequently, the wining configuration is the one embedding a logistic regression classifier, tightly followed by the decision tree learner.

[11]Similar figures have been observed for other language pairs.

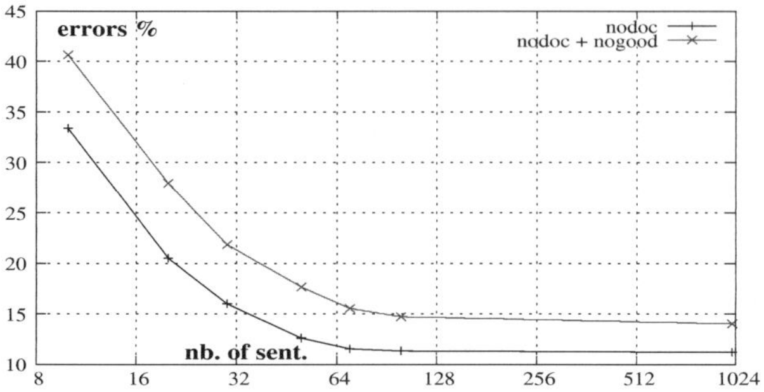

Figure 1: Percentage of Dutch documents for which `Lucene` returns no English document (`nodoc`), or no correct document (`nodoc+nogood`) as a function of the document size counted in sentences.

3.3.3 Sensitivity to the language pair

We also tested the sensibility of our approach to the language pair being considered. Apart from the fact that the French-English pair was the easiest to deal with, we did not notice strong differences in performance among language pairs. For documents of at most 100 sentences, the worst f-measure (0.93) is observed for the Dutch/English language pair, while the best one (0.95) is observed for the French-English pair. Slightly larger differences were measured for short documents.

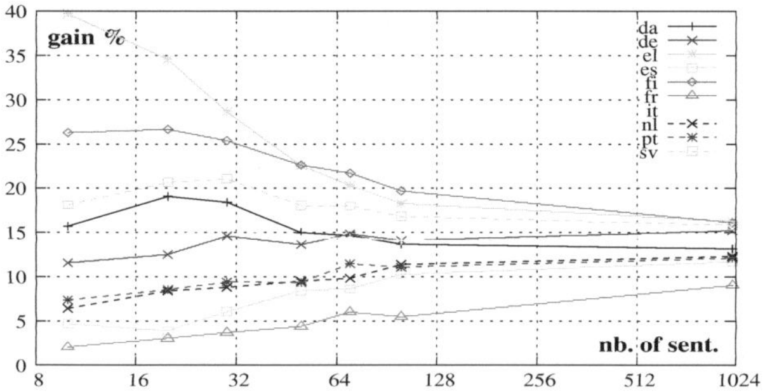

Figure 2: Absolute gains of the best variant of our system over the approach described by Enright and Kondrak (2007).

3.3.4 Sanity check

We conducted a last sanity check by comparing our approach to the one of (Enright and Kondrak, 2007). This approach simply ranks the candidate pairs in decreasing order of the number of hapax words they share. The absolute gains of our approach over theirs are reported in Figure 2, as a function of the document length and the language pair considered. Our system systematically outperforms the hapax approach of (Enright and Kondrak, 2007) regardless of the length of the documents and the language pairs considered. An average absolute gain of 13.6% in f-measure is observed for long documents, while much larger gains are observed for shorter ones. It has to be noted, that our approach requires to train a classifier, which makes it potentially less useful in some situations. Also, we used the best of our system in this comparison.

4 Experiments with Wikipedia

Many articles in `Wikipedia` are available in several languages. Often, they are explicitly marked as linked across languages. For instance, the English article *[Text_corpus]* is linked to the French one *[Corpus]*, but they are not translation of each other, while the English article *[Decline_of_the_Roman_Empire]* and the French one *[Déclin_de_l'empire_romain_d'Occident]* are parallel.[12]

4.1 Resource

During summer 2009, we collected all French-English cross-language linked articles from `Wikipedia`. A very straightforward preprocessing stage involving simple regular expressions removed part of the markup specific to this resource. We ended up with 537 067 articles in each language. The average length of the English pages is 711 words, while the average for French is 445 words. The difference in length among linked articles has been studied by Filatova (2009) on a small excerpt of bibliographical articles describing 48 persons listed in the biography generation task (Task 5) of DUC 2004.[13]

[12] At least they were at the time of redaction.

[13] `http://duc.nist.gov/duc2004/tasks.html/`

4.2 Parallelness of cross-language linked article pairs in FR-EN `Wikipedia`.

In this experiment, we wanted to measure the proportion of cross-language linked article pairs in `Wikipedia` that are in translation relation. In order to do so, we manually evaluated 200 pairs of articles in our French-English `Wikipedia` repository.

A web interface was developed in order to annotate each pair, following the distinction introduced by Fung and Cheung (2004): `parallel` indicates sentence-aligned texts that are in translation relation; `noisy` characterizes two documents that are nevertheless mostly bilingual translations of each other; `topic` corresponds to documents which share similar topics, but that are not translation of each others and `very-non` that stands for rather unrelated texts.

The results of the manual evaluation are reported in the left column of table 1. We observe that a fourth of the pairs of articles are indeed parallel or noisy parallel. This figure quantifies the observation made by Adafre and de Rijke (2006) that while some articles in `Wikipedia` tend to be translations of each other, the majority of the articles tend to be written independently of each other. To the best of our knowledge, this is the first time someone is measuring the degree of parallelness of `Wikipedia` at the article level.

If our sample is representative (something which deserves further investigations), it means that more than 134 000 pairs of documents in the French-English `Wikipedia` are parallel or noisy parallel.

We would like to stress that, while conducting the manual annotation, we frequently found difficult to label pairs of articles with the classes proposed by Fung and Cheung (2004). Often, we could spot a few sentences translated in pairs that we rated `very-non` or `topic`. Also, it was hard to be consistent over the annotation session with the distinction made between those two classes. Many articles are divided into sub-topics, some of which being covered in the other article, some being not.

4.3 Parallelness of the article pairs identified by PARADOCS

We applied PARADOCS to our `Wikipedia` collection. We indexed the French pages with the `Lucene`

Type	Wikipedia		PARADOCS	
	Count	Ratio	Count	Ratio
very-non	92	46%	5	2.5%
topic	58	29%	34	17%
noisy	22	11%	39	19.5%
parallel	28	14%	122	61%
Total	200		200	

Table 1: Manual analysis of 200 pairs cross-language linked in Wikipedia (left) and 200 pairs of articles judged parallel by our system (right).

toolkit using the num indexing scheme. Each English article was consequently transformed with the same strategy before querying Lucene, which was asked to return the $N = 5$ most similar French articles. We limited the retrieval to 5 documents in this experiment in order to reduce computation time. As a matter of fact, running our system on Wikipedia took 1.5 days of computation on 8 nodes of a pentium cluster. Most of this time was devoted to compute edit-distance features.

Each candidate pair of articles was then labeled as parallel or not by a classifier we trained to recognize parallel documents in an in-house collection of French-English documents we gathered in 2009 from a website dedicated to Olympic games.[14] Using a classifier trained on a different task gives us the opportunity to see how our system would do if used out-of-the-box. A set of 1844 pairs of documents have been automatically aligned (at the document level) thanks to heuristics on URL names; then manually checked for parallelness. The best classifier we developed on this collection (thanks to a 5-fold cross-validation procedure) was a decision tree classifier (j48) which achieves an average f-measure of 90% (92.7% precision, and 87.4% recall). This is the classifier we used in this experiment.

From the 537 067 English documents of our collection, 106 896 (20%) did not receive any answer from Lucene (nodoc). A total of 117 032 pairs of documents were judged by the classifier as parallel. The post-filtering stage (dup) eliminated slightly less than half of them, leaving us with a total of 61 897 pairs. We finally eliminated those pairs that were not cross-language linked in Wikipedia. We ended up with a set of 44 447 pairs of articles identified as parallel by our system.

Since there is no reference telling us which cross-language linked articles in Wikipedia are indeed parallel, we resorted to a manual inspection of a random excerpt of 200 pairs of articles identified as parallel by our system. The sampling was done in a way that reflects the distribution of the scores of the classifier over the pairs of articles identified as parallel by our system.

The results of this evaluation are reported in the right column of table 1. First, we observe that 20% (2.5+17) of the pairs identified as parallel by our system are at best topic aligned. One explanation for this is that topic aligned articles often share numbers (such as dates), sometimes in the same order, especially in bibliographies that are frequent in Wikipedia. Clearly, we are paying the prize of a lightweight content-oriented system. Second, we observe that 61% of the annotated pairs were indeed parallel, and that roughly 80% of them were parallel or noisy parallel. Although PARADOCS is not as accurate as it was on the Europarl corpus, it is still performing much better than random.

4.4 Further analysis

We scored the manually annotated cross-language linked pairs described in section 4.2 with our classifier. The cumulative distribution of the scores is reported in table 2. We observe that 64% (100-35.7%) of the parallel pairs are indeed rated as parallel ($p \geq 0.5$) by our classifier. This percentage is much lower for the other types of article pairs. On the contrary, for very non-parallel pairs, the classi-

	$p \leq 0.1$	$p \leq 0.2$	$p < 0.5$	avr.
very-non	1.1%	91.4%	92.5%	0.25
topic	1.7%	74.6%	78.0%	0.37
noisy	13.6%	77.3%	90.9%	0.26
parallel	7.1%	25.0%	35.7%	0.71

Table 2: Cumulative distribution and average score given by our classifier to the 200 manually annotated pairs of articles cross-language linked in Wikipedia.

[14] http://www.olympic.org

fier assigns a score lower than 0.2 in more than 91% of the cases. This shows that the score given by the classifier correlates to some extent with the degree of parallelness of the article pairs.

Among the 28 pairs of cross-language linked article pairs manually labelled as parallel (see table 1), only 2 pairs were found parallel by PARADOCS, even if 18 of them received a score of 1 by the classifier. This discrepancy is explained in part by the filter (`dup`) which is too drastic since it removes all the pairs sharing one document. We already discussed alternative strategies. The retrieval stage of our system is as well responsible of some failures, especially since we considered the 5 first French documents returned by `Lucene`. We further inspected the 10 (28-18) pairs judged parallel but scored by our classifier as non parallel. We observed several problems; the most frequent one being a failure of our pre-processing step which leaves undesired blocs of text in one of the article, but not in the other (recall we kept the preprocessing very agnostic to the specificities of `Wikipedia`). These blocs might be infoboxes or lists recapitulating important dates, or even sometimes HTML markup. The presence of numerical entities in those blocs is confounding the classifier.

5 Related Work

Pairing parallel documents in a bilingual collection of texts has been investigated by several authors. Most of the previous approaches for tackling this problem capitalize on naming conventions (on file URL names) for pairing documents. This is for instance the case of PTMINER (Chen and Nie, 2000) and STRAND (Resnik and Smith, 2003), two systems that are intended to mine parallel documents over the Web. Since heuristics on URL names does not ensure parallelness, other cues, such as the ratio of the length of the documents paired or their HTML structure, are further being used. Others have proposed to use features computed after sentence aligning a candidate pair of documents (Shi et al., 2006), a very time consuming strategy (that we tried without success). Others have tried to use bilingual lexicons in order to compare document pairs; this is for instance the case of the BITS system (Ma and Liberman, 1999). Also, Enright and Kondrak (2007) propose a very lightweight content-based approach to pairing documents, capitalizing on the number of hapax words they share. We show in this study, that this approach can easily be outperformed.

Zhao and Vogel (2002) were among the first to report experiments on harvesting comparable news collections in order to extract parallel sentences. With a similar goal, Munteanu et al. (2004) proposed to train in a supervised way (using some parallel data) a classifier designed to recognize parallel sentences. They applied their classifier on two monolingual news corpora in Arabic and English, covering similar periods, and showed that the parallel material extracted, when added to an in-domain parallel training corpus of United Nation texts, improved significantly an Arabic-to-English SMT system tested on news data. Still, they noted that the extracted material does not come close to the quality obtained by adding a small out-domain parallel corpus to the in-domain training material. Different variants of this approach have been tried afterwards, *e.g.* (Abdul-Rauf and Schwenk, 2009).

To the best of our knowledge, Adafre and de Rijke (2006) where the first to look at the problem of extracting parallel sentences from `Wikipedia`. They compared two approaches for doing so that both search for parallel sentence pairs in cross-language linked articles. The first one uses an MT engine in order to translate sentences of one document into the language of the other article; then parallel sentences are selected based on a monolingual similarity measure. The second approach represents each sentence of a pair of documents in a space of hyperlink anchored texts. An initial lexicon is collected from the title of the articles that are linked across languages (they also used the `Wikipedia`'s redirect feature to extend the lexicon with synonyms). This lexicon is used for representing sentences in both languages. Whenever the anchor text of two hyperlinks, one in a source sentence, and one in a target sentence is sanctioned by the lexicon, the ID of the lexicon entry is used to represent each hyperlink, thus making sentences across languages sharing some representation. They concluded that the latter approach returns fewer incorrect pairs than the MT based approach.

Smith et al. (2010) extended these previous lines of work in several directions. First, by training a global classifier which is able to capture the tendency of parallel sentences to appear in chunks. Second, by applying it at large on Wikipedia. In their work, they extracted a large number of sentences identified as parallel from linked pairs of articles. They show that this extra materiel, when added to the training set, improves a state-of-the-art SMT system on out-domain test sets, especially when the in-domain training set is not very large.

The four aforementioned studies implement some heuristics in order to limit the extraction of parallel sentences to some fruitful document pairs. For news collections, the publication time can for instance be used for narrowing down the search; while for Wikipedia articles, the authors concentrate on document pairs that are linked across languages. PARADOCS could be used for narrowing the search space down to a set of parallel or closely parallel document pairs. We see several ways this could help the process of extracting parallel fragments. For one thing, we know that extracting parallel sentences from a parallel corpus is something we do well, while extracting parallel sentences from a comparable corpus is a much riskier enterprise (not even mentioning time issues). As a matter of fact, Munteanu et al. (2004) mentioned the inherent noise present in pairs of sentences extracted from comparable corpora as a reason why a large set of extracted sentence pairs does not contribute to improve an SMT system more that a small but highly specific parallel dataset. Therefore, a system like ours could be used to decide which sort of alignment technique should be used, given a pair of documents. For another thing, one could use our system to delimit a set of fruitful documents to harvest in the first place. The material acquired this way could then be used to train models that could be employed for extracting noisiest document pairs, hopefully for the sake of the quality of the material extracted.

6 Conclusion

We have described a system for identifying parallel documents in a bilingual collection. This system does not presume specific information, such as file (or URL) naming conventions, which can sometime be useful for mining parallel documents. Also, our system relies on a very lightweight set of content-based features (basically numerical entities and possibly hapax words), therefore our claim of a language neutral system.

We conducted a number of experiments on the Europarl corpus in order to control the impact of some of its hyper-parameters. We show that our approach outperforms the fair baseline described in (Enright and Kondrak, 2007). We also conducted experiments in extracting parallel documents in Wikipedia. We were satisfied by the fact that we used a classifier trained on another task in this experiment, but still got good results (a precision of 80% if we consider noisy parallel document pairs as acceptable). We conducted a manual evaluation of some cross-language linked article pairs and found that 25% of those pairs were indeed parallel or noisy parallel. This manually annotated data that can be downloaded at http://www.iro.umontreal.ca/~felipe/bucc11/.

7 Future Work

In their study on infobox arbitrage, Adar et al. (2009) noted that currently, cross-language links in Wikipedia are essentially made by volunteers, which explains why many such links are missing. Our approach lends itself to locate missing links in Wikipedia. Another extension of this line of work, admittedly more prospective, would be to detect recent vandalizations (modifications or extensions) operated on one language only of a parallel pair of documents.

Also, we think that there are other kinds of data on which our system could be invaluable. This is the reason why we refrained in this work to engineer features tailored for a specific data collection, such as Wikipedia. One application of our system we can think of, is the organization of (proprietary) translation memories. As a matter if fact, many companies do not organize the flow of the documents they handle in a systematic way and there is a need for tools able to spot texts that are in translation relation.

Acknowledgments

We are grateful to Fabienne Venant who participated in the manual annotation we conducted in this study.

References

Sadaf Abdul-Rauf and Holger Schwenk. 2009. On the use of comparable corpora to improve smt performance. In *Proceedings of the 12th Conference of the European Chapter of the Association for Computational Linguistics*, EACL '09, pages 16–23.

Sisay Fissaha Adafre and Maarten de Rijke. 2006. Finding Similar Sentences across Multiple Languages in Wikipedia. In *11th EACL*, pages 62–69, Trento, Italy.

Eytan Adar, Michael Skinner, and Daniel S. Weld. 2009. Information arbitrage across multi-lingual wikipedia. In *Proceedings of the Second ACM International Conference on Web Search and Data Mining*, WSDM '09, pages 94–103.

Chris Callison-Burch, Philipp Koehn, Christof Monz, and Josh Schroeder. 2009. Findings of the 2009 Workshop on Statistical Machine Translation. In *Proceedings of the Fourth Workshop on Statistical Machine Translation*, pages 1–28, Athens, Greece, March. Association for Computational Linguistics.

Jiang Chen and Jian-Yun Nie. 2000. Parallel Web text mining for cross-language IR. In *RIAO*, pages 62–67, Paris, France.

Jessica Enright and Gregorz Kondrak. 2007. A Fast Method for Parallel Document Identification. In *NAACL HLT 2007, Companion Volume*, pages 29–32, Rochester, NY.

Tomaz Erjavec. 2004. MULTEXT-East Version 3: Multilingual Morphosyntactic Specifications, Lexicons and Corpora. In *LREC*, Lisbon, Portugal.

Elena Filatova. 2009. Directions for exploiting asymmetries in multilingual wikipedia. In *Third International Cross Lingual Information Access Workshop*, pages 30–37, Boulder, Colorado.

Pascale Fung and Percy Cheung. 2004. Mining very-non-parallel corpora: Parallel sentence and lexicon extraction via bootstrapping and EM. In Dekang Lin and Dekai Wu, editors, *Proceedings of EMNLP 2004*, pages 57–63, Barcelona, Spain, July. Association for Computational Linguistics.

Mark Hall, Eibe Frank, Geoffrey Holmes, Bernhard Pfahringer, Peter Reutemann, and Ian H. Witten. 2009. The WEKA Data Mining Software: An Update. *SIGKDD Explorations*, 11, Issue 1(10–18).

Philipp Koehn. 2005. Europarl: A multilingual corpus for evaluation of machine translation. In *10th Machine Translation Summit*, Phuket, Thailand, sep.

Adrien Lardilleux and Yves Lepage. 2007. The contribution of the notion of hapax legomena to word alignment. In *3rd Language & Technology Conference (LTC'07)*, pages 458–462, Poznań Poland.

Xiaoyi Ma and Mark Liberman. 1999. Bits: A method for bilingual text search over the web. In *Machine Translation Summit VII*, Singapore, sep.

Beata Bandmann Megyesi, Eva Csato Johansson, and Anna Sgvall Hein. 2006. Building a Swedish-Turkish Parallel Corpus. In *LREC*, Genoa, Italy.

Dragos Stefan Munteanu, Alexander Fraser, and Daniel Marcu. 2004. Improved machine translation performance via parallel sentence extraction from comparable corpora. In Daniel Marcu Susan Dumais and Salim Roukos, editors, *HLT-NAACL 2004: Main Proceedings*, pages 265–272, Boston, Massachusetts, USA, May. Association for Computational Linguistics.

Alexandre Patry and Philippe Langlais. 2005. Automatic identification of parallel documents with light or without linguistic resources. In *18th Annual Conference on Artificial Intelligence (Canadian AI)*, pages 354–365, Victoria, British-Columbia, Canada.

Philip Resnik and Noah A. Smith. 2003. The web as a parallel corpus. *Computational Linguistics*, 29:349–380. Special Issue on the Web as a Corpus.

Lei Shi, Cheng Niu, Ming Zhou, and Jianfeng Gao. 2006. A dom tree alignment model for mining parallel data from the web. In *Proceedings of the 21st International Conference on Computational Linguistics (COLING) and the 44th annual meeting of the Association for Computational Linguistics (ACL)*, pages 489–496, Sydney, Australia.

Jason R. Smith, Chris Quirk, and Kristina Toutanova. 2010. Extracting parallel sentences from comparable corpora using document level alignment. In *Human Language Technologies: The 2010 Annual Conference of the NAACL*, HLT '10, pages 403–411.

Jörg Tiedemann. 2009. News from OPUS – A Collection of Multilingual Parallel Corpora with Tools and Interfaces. In N. Nicolov, K. Bontcheva, G. Angelova, and R. Mitkov, editors, *Recent Advances in Natural Language Processing*, pages 237–248. John Benjamins, Amsterdam/Philadelphia.

Bing Zhao and Stephan Vogel. 2002. Adaptive parallel sentences mining from web bilingual news collection. In *Proceedings of the 2002 IEEE International Conference on Data Mining*, ICDM '02, pages 745–748, Maebashi City, Japan.

Comparable Fora

Johanka Spoustová   Miroslav Spousta
Institute of Formal and Applied Linguistics
Faculty of Mathematics and Physics,
Charles University Prague, Czech Republic
{johanka,spousta}@ufal.mff.cuni.cz

Abstract

As the title suggests, our paper deals with web discussion fora, whose content can be considered to be a special type of comparable corpora. We discuss the potential of this vast amount of data available now on the World Wide Web nearly for every language, regarding both general and common topics as well as the most obscure and specific ones. To illustrate our ideas, we propose a case study of seven wedding discussion fora in five languages.

1 Introduction to comparable corpora

Nearly every description of comparable corpora begins with the EAGLES (Expert Advisory Group on Language Engineering Standards) definition:[1]

"A comparable corpus is one which selects similar texts in more than one language or variety. The possibilities of a comparable corpus are to compare different languages or varieties in similar circumstances of communication, but avoiding the inevitable distortion introduced by the translations of a parallel corpus."

(Maia, 2003), which also became nearly standard during the recent years, emphasizes the fact that comparable monolingual corpora usually provide us with much better linguistic quality and representativeness than translated parallel corpora. The other advantages over the parallel corpora, i.e. amount and availability, are obvious.

Nowadays, the most popular usage of comparable corpora is improving machine translation, more precisely, compensating the lack of parallel training data. The articles (Munteanu et al., 2004), (Munteanu and Marcu, 2005) and (Munteanu and Marcu, 2006) are introducing algorithms for extracting parallel sentences and sub-sentential fragments from comparable corpora and using the automatically extracted parallel data for improving statistical machine translation algorithms performance.

Present day most popular comparable corpora come either from the newswire resources (AFP, Reuters, Xinhua), leading to data sets like LDC English, Chinese and Arabic Gigaword, or from Wikipedia. Mining Wikipedia became very popular in the recent years. For example, (Tomás et al., 2008) is exploring both parallel and comparable potential of Wikipedia, (Filatova, 2009) examines multilingual aspects of a selected subset of Wikipedia and (Gamallo and López, 2010) describes converting Wikipedia into "CorpusPedia".

2 Introduction to fora

Just to avoid confusion: In this article, we focus only on fora or boards, i.e. standalone discussion sites on a stated topic. We are not talking about comments accompanying news articles or blog posts.

The internet discussion fora cover, in surprisingly big amounts of data and for many languages, the most unbelievable topics (real examples from the authors' country). People, who eat only uncooked ("raw") food. People, who eat only cooked food. Mothers with young children, women trying to conceive, communities of people absolutely avoiding sex. Fans of Volvo, BMW, Maserati, Trabant cars. Probably also in your country mothers like to talk

[1] http://www.ilc.cnr.it/EAGLES96/corpustyp/node21.html

Proceedings of the 4th Workshop on Building and Using Comparable Corpora, pages 96–101,
49th Annual Meeting of the Association for Computational Linguistics,
Portland, Oregon, 24 June 2011.

about their children and men like to compare their engine's horse power.

Everyone who has any specific interest or hobby and is friendly with the web, probably knows at least one discussion forum focused on his/her favourite topic, inhabited by intelligent, friendly debaters producing interesting, on-topic content. These types of fora often have very active administrators, who clean the discussions from off-topics, vulgarities, move the discussion threads into correct thematic categories etc. The administrators' "tidying up" effort can be even regarded as a kind of annotation.

The rapidly growing amount of web discussion fora was until now linguistically exploited only in a strictly monolingual manner. To the best of our (and Google Scholar) knowledge, nobody has published any work regarding the possibility of using internet discussion fora as a multilingual source of data for linguistic or machine translation purposes.

2.1 Forum structure

A typical forum is divided into thematic categories (larger fora split into boards and boards into categories). Every category usually contains from tens to thousands of separate discussions. A discussion consists of messages (posts) and sometimes its content is further arranged using threads.

A discussion should be placed in appropriate category and messages in the discussion should hold onto the discussion topic, otherwise the administrator removes the inappropriate messages or even the whole discussion.

Fora usually have an entire off-topic category where their members can talk about anything "out-of-domain".

To avoid spam, usually only registered members can contribute. Some fora keep their memberlist visible to the public, some do not.

3 Why comparable fora?

Besides their amount and availability, comparable fora have a few other advantages over other types of comparable corpora.

They contain "spontaneous writing" – an original, previously unpublished content, which is almost certainly not a translation of other language original. This is obviously not the case of parallel corpora, and we cannot be sure even for other popular comparable corpora. A journalist may be inspired by a news agency report or by another media source, and a Wikipedia author must also reconcile his claims with existing resources, which more or less affects his writing style.

The other advantage is easier domain classification, or more effective pre-selection before running an automatic parallel sentences alignment. A generic newspaper article is provided only with a title, language and release date. A Wikipedia entry has a title, history and is classified into a thematic category. Fora messages have both dates, titles and category classifications and they are available in much larger amounts than Wikipedia entries and are covering more thematic domains than news articles.

4 A case study: wedding sites

As a topic of our case study, we have chosen an event which occurs to most of the people at least once in their life – a wedding.

4.1 General overview

We looked over five language mutations of the same forum operated by Asmira Company – Finalstitch.co.uk (EN), Braupunkt.de (DE), Fairelanoce.fr (FR), Mojasvadba.sk (SK), Beremese.cz (CZ); and two other fora, Brides.com/forums (EN2) and Organisation-mariage.net (FR2), which seem to be larger and more popular in the target countries.

We have manually examined fora sizes and possibilities of their alignment on the category level.

Tables 1 and 2 summarize the total number of discussions and messages contained in selected categories, shared by most of the fora. For the Asmira fora, we omitted the discussions accessible both from CZ and SK sites.

If we assume average length of a message to be about 60 words (see below), the proposed sites give us a few millions of words of multilingual comparable corpora in each category (focussed on very restricted topic, such as wedding clothes, or hairdressing & make-up) even for "non-mainstream" languages, such as Czech or Slovak.

4.2 Quantitative characteristics

In order to learn more about the amount and textual quality of the data, we have downloaded all the con-

<table>
<tr><th></th><th>EN</th><th>DE</th><th>FR</th><th>CZ</th><th>SK</th><th>EN2</th><th>FR2</th></tr>
<tr><td>Ceremony and reception</td><td>389</td><td>280</td><td>232</td><td>1 532</td><td>2 345</td><td>N/A</td><td>1 536</td></tr>
<tr><td>Wedding-preparations</td><td>474</td><td>417</td><td>654</td><td>916</td><td>1270</td><td>13632</td><td>1 873</td></tr>
<tr><td>Date & location</td><td>63</td><td>119</td><td>154</td><td>839</td><td>529</td><td>371</td><td>N/A</td></tr>
<tr><td>Beauty</td><td>68</td><td>47</td><td>74</td><td>472</td><td>794</td><td>2 858</td><td rowspan="2">2 452</td></tr>
<tr><td>Wedding clothing</td><td>291</td><td>166</td><td>200</td><td>715</td><td>1 108</td><td>10 832</td></tr>
<tr><td>After the wedding</td><td>37</td><td>47</td><td>47</td><td>236</td><td>245</td><td>1 530</td><td>390</td></tr>
</table>

Table 1: Total number of discussions in the selected wedding fora.

<table>
<tr><th></th><th>EN</th><th>DE</th><th>FR</th><th>CZ</th><th>SK</th><th>EN2</th><th>FR2</th></tr>
<tr><td>Ceremony and reception</td><td>3 863</td><td>3 947</td><td>4 174</td><td>43 436</td><td>64 273</td><td>N/A</td><td>19 002</td></tr>
<tr><td>Wedding-preparations</td><td>4 908</td><td>4 987</td><td>8 867</td><td>51 880</td><td>27 837</td><td>130 408</td><td>24 585</td></tr>
<tr><td>Date & location</td><td>1 004</td><td>1 988</td><td>3 178</td><td>550 969</td><td>279 091</td><td>24 513</td><td>N/A</td></tr>
<tr><td>Beauty</td><td>692</td><td>852</td><td>1 462</td><td>32 118</td><td>32 620</td><td>15 946</td><td rowspan="2">38 582</td></tr>
<tr><td>Wedding clothing</td><td>2 634</td><td>2 336</td><td>3 588</td><td>27 624</td><td>28 048</td><td>75 331</td></tr>
<tr><td>After the wedding</td><td>527</td><td>1 012</td><td>1 065</td><td>30 588</td><td>18 090</td><td>23 612</td><td>6 286</td></tr>
</table>

Table 2: Total number of messages in the selected wedding fora.

tent of the five Asmira fora, extracted their messages into five monolingual corpora and measured some basic characteristics of the texts. The downloading and extracting task needed about 20 minutes of coding and a few days of waiting for the result (we did not want to overload the fora webservers).

Table 3 shows us average messages lengths (in words) for particular categories of these fora.

In graphs 1, 2 and 3, we present normalized sentence length distributions for particular fora. For English and Czech, we added for comparison sentence length distributions of reference corpora of comparable sizes, i.e. The Penn Treebank, training set (Marcus et al., 1994), for English and The Czech National Corpus, SYN2005 (CNC, 2005), for Czech.

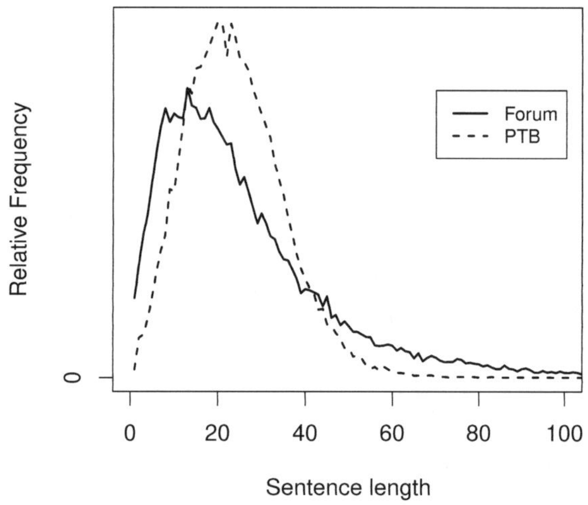

Figure 1: The EN forum and The Penn Treebank - sentence length distributions.

4.3 Examples of similar discussion topics

The category distinction may be still too coarse for potential alignment. The site FR2 has a joint category for Beauty and Wedding clothing, and on the contrary, it has separate categories for Wedding and Reception. Therefore, we tried to examine the fora on a deeper level. In table 4, we present some examples of discussions on the same topic.

As you can guess, fully automatic alignment of the discussion titles will not be an easy task. On the other side, every machine translation specialist must shiver with pleasure when seeing some of the discussion titles to be almost translations of each other, and it would be a sin to leave these data unexploited.

	EN	DE	FR	CZ	SK
Ceremony and reception	70.0	68.7	51.9	59.7	56.9
Wedding-preparations	73.8	62.5	55.1	63.7	62.3
Date & location	59.2	56.4	61.7	52.0	48.8
Beauty	67.7	61.3	53.4	65.8	56.6
Wedding clothing	61.1	60.4	42.1	57.0	50.0
After the wedding	71.8	69.5	52.0	66.8	68.6

Table 3: Average messages lengths (in words) for the selected wedding fora categories.

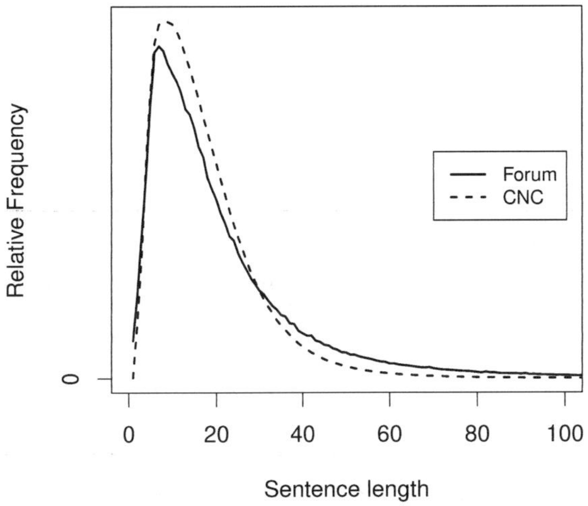

Figure 2: The CZ forum and The Czech National Corpus - sentence length distributions.

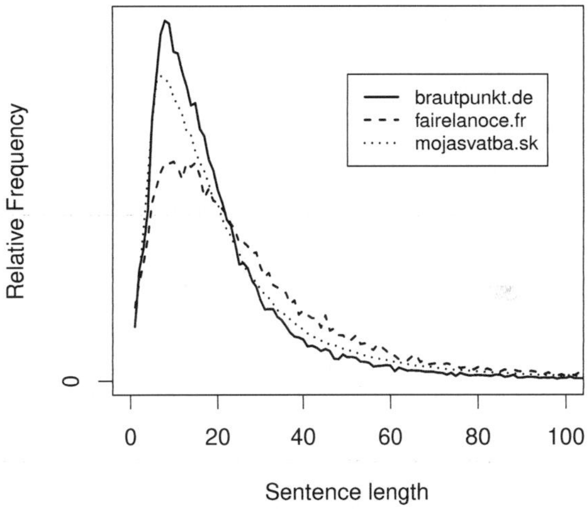

Figure 3: The DE, FR and SK fora - sentence length distributions.

5 Technical issues

Of course, language mutations of the same forum (sharing the same category structure and running on the same forum engine) are a "researcher's dream" and not the case of the majority of potential comparable fora.

You will probably ask two questions: 1) How to effectively extract messages from a site with undocumented structure? 2) How to put together comparable fora in multiple languages and how to align their category hierarchy?

5.1 Messages mining

According to an internet source [2], about 96 % of internet discussion fora are powered by two most popular forum systems, phpBB and vBulletin, and another 3 % are powered by Simple Machines Forum, MyBB and Invision Power Board.

Our observation is, that small hobby fora run mostly on unadapted ("as is") phpBB or another free system, while large commercial fora often have their own systems.

If you intend to automatically process only a few selected fora, you will probably use XPath queries on the HTML Document Object Model. According to our experience, it is very easy and straightforward task to write a single wrapper for a particular forum. But it would be nice, of course, to have a general solution which does not rely on a fixed forum structure. Unfortunately, general web page cleaning algorithms, e.g. Victor (Spousta et al., 2008), are not

[2] http://www.qualityposts.com/ForumMarketShare.php

EN2	How to set up a budget
DE	Budget?
FR2	Financement mariage
CZ	Jaký máte rozpočet na svatbu???
SK	Svadobny rozpocet
EN	Mobile hair and makeup
DE	Friseur und Kosmetik daheim?
FR2	Estheticienne a domicile?
CZ	Nalíčení plus účes doma - Praha
SK	Licenie a uces - v den svadby a doma
EN	Hair extensions?
DE	Echthaar-Clip-Extensions
FR2	Extensions pour cheveux
CZ	Prodlužování vlasů
SK	Predlzovanie vlasov
EN	Where should we go for our honeymoon?
DE	Habt ihr Tipps für eine schöne Hochzeitsreise???
FR2	Quelle destination pour le voyage de noce?
CZ	Svatební cesta
SK	Kam idete na svadobnú cestu?

Table 4: Examples of similar discussions.

very succesfull with this type of input (i.e. ten to fifty rather small textual portions on one page).

However, there are some invariants shared among all types of fora [3]. The content is automatically generated and therefore all the messages on one page (can be generalized to one site) usually "look similar", in terms of HTML structure. (Limanto et al., 2005) exploits this fact and introduces a subtree-matching algorithm for detecting messages on a discussion page. (Li et al., 2009) proposes more complex algorithm which extracts not only the messages content but also the user profile information.

5.2 Fora coupling

The task of optimal fora, categories, discussions, sentences and phrases alignment remains open. Our article is meant to be an inspiration, thus for now, we will not provide our reader with any surprising practical solutions, only with ideas.

The sentence and sub-sentence level can be maintained by existing automatic aligners. For the rest, we believe that combined use of hierarchical structure of the fora together with terms, named entities or simple word translations can help. For example, nearly every EU top level domain hosts a "Volvo Forum" or "Volvo Club", and each Volvo Forum contains some portion of discussions mentioning model names, such as V70 or S60, in their titles.

Besides, according to our case study, the amount of acquired data compared to the amount of human effort should be reasonable even when coupling the fora sites and their top categories manually. Present day approaches to acquiring comparable corpora also require some human knowledge and effort, e.g. you need to pick out manually the most reliable and appropriate news resources.

6 Conclusion

We have proposed an idea of using co-existent web discussion fora in multiple languages addressing the same topic as comparable corpora. Our case study shows that using this approach, one can acquire large portions of comparable multilingual data with minimal effort. We also discussed related technical issues.

You may ask, whether the forum language is the right (addition to a) training set for a machine translation system. The answer may depend on, what type of system it is and what type of input do you want to translate. If you need to translate parliamentary proceedings, you will surely be more satisfied with parliament-only training data. But do you want an anything-to-speech machine translation system to talk to you like a parliamentary speaker, or like a Wikipedia author, or like a friend of yours from your favourite community of interest?

We hope that our article drew the attention of the linguistic audience to this promising source of comparable texts and we are looking forward to seeing some interesting resources and applications.

Acknowledgments

The research described here was supported by the project *GA405/09/0278* of the Grant Agency of the Czech Republic.

[3]and some other types of web sites, eg. e-shops or blogs

References

CNC, 2005. *Czech National Corpus – SYN2005*. Institute of Czech National Corpus, Faculty of Arts, Charles University, Prague, Czech Republic.

Elena Filatova. 2009. Directions for exploiting asymmetries in multilingual wikipedia. In *Proceedings of the Third International Workshop on Cross Lingual Information Access: Addressing the Information Need of Multilingual Societies*, CLIAWS3 '09, pages 30–37, Stroudsburg, PA, USA. Association for Computational Linguistics.

Pablo Gamallo and Isaac González López. 2010. Wikipedia as multilingual source of comparable corpora. In *Proceedings of the LREC Workshop on Building and Using Comparable Corpora*, pages 30–37.

Suke Li, Liyong Tang, Jianbin Hu, and Zhong Chen. 2009. Automatic data extraction from web discussion forums. *Frontier of Computer Science and Technology, Japan-China Joint Workshop on*, 0:219–225.

Hanny Yulius Limanto, Nguyen Ngoc Giang, Vo Tan Trung, Jun Zhang, Qi He, and Nguyen Quang Huy. 2005. An information extraction engine for web discussion forums. In *Special interest tracks and posters of the 14th international conference on World Wide Web*, WWW '05, pages 978–979, New York, NY, USA. ACM.

Belinda Maia. 2003. What are comparable corpora? In *Proceedings of the Workshop on Multilingual Corpora: Linguistic requirements and technical perspectives, at the Corpus Linguistics 2003*, pages 27–34, Lancaster, UK, March.

Mitchell P. Marcus, Mary Ann Marcinkiewicz, and Beatrice Santorini. 1994. Building a large annotated corpus of English: The Penn Treebank. *Computational Linguistics*, 19(2):313–330.

Dragos Stefan Munteanu and Daniel Marcu. 2005. Improving machine translation performance by exploiting non-parallel corpora. *Computational Linguistics*, 31(4).

Dragos Stefan Munteanu and Daniel Marcu. 2006. Extracting parallel sub-sentential fragments from non-parallel corpora. In *Proceedings of the 21st International Conference on Computational Linguistics and 44th Annual Meeting of the Association for Computational Linguistics*, pages 81–88, Sydney, Australia, July. Association for Computational Linguistics.

Dragos Stefan Munteanu, Alexander Fraser, and Daniel Marcu. 2004. Improved machine translation performance via parallel sentence extraction from comparable corpora. In *HLT-NAACL 2004: Main Proceedings*, pages 265–272, Boston, Massachusetts, USA, May. Association for Computational Linguistics.

Miroslav Spousta, Michal Marek, and Pavel Pecina. 2008. Victor: the web-page cleaning tool. In *Proceedings of the Web as Corpus Workshop (WAC-4)*, Marrakech, Morocco.

Jesús Tomás, Jordi Bataller, Francisco Casacuberta, and Jaime Lloret. 2008. Mining wikipedia as a parallel and comparable corpus. *Language Forum*, 34.

Unsupervised Alignment of Comparable Data and Text Resources

Anja Belz **Eric Kow**
School of Computing, Engineering and Mathematics
University of Brighton
Brighton BN2 4GJ, UK
{A.S.Belz,E.Y.Kow}@brighton.ac.uk

Abstract

In this paper we investigate automatic data-text alignment, i.e. the task of automatically aligning data records with textual descriptions, such that data tokens are aligned with the word strings that describe them. Our methods make use of log likelihood ratios to estimate the strength of association between data tokens and text tokens. We investigate data-text alignment at the document level and at the sentence level, reporting results for several methodological variants as well as baselines. We find that log likelihood ratios provide a strong basis for predicting data-text alignment.

1 Introduction

Much of NLP system building currently uses aligned parallel resources that provide examples of the inputs to a system and the outputs it is intended to produce. In Machine Translation (MT), such resources take the form of sentence-aligned parallel corpora of source-language and target-language texts; in parsing and surface realisation, parse-annotated corpora of naturally occurring texts are used, where in parsing, the inputs are the sentences in the texts and the outputs are the parses represented by the annotations on the sentences, and in surface realisation, the roles of inputs and outputs are reversed.

In MT parallel resources exist, and in fact are produced in large quantities daily, and in some cases (e.g. multilingual parliamentary proceedings) are publicly available. Moreover, even if resources are created specifically for system building (e.g. NIST's OpenMT evaluations) the cost is offset by the fact that the resulting translation system can be expected to generalise to new domains to some extent.

While parse-annotated corpora are in the first instance created by hand, here too, parsers and surface realisers built on the basis of such corpora are expected to generalise beyond the immediate corpus domain.

In data-to-text generation, as in parsing, parallel resources do not occur naturally and have to be created manually. The associated cost is, however, incurred for every new task, as systems trained on a given parallel data-text resource cannot be expected to generalise beyond task and domain. Automatic data-text alignment methods, i.e. automatic methods for creating parallel data-text resources, would be extremely useful for system building in this situation, but no such methods currently exist.

In MT there have been recent efforts (reviewed in the following section) to automatically produce aligned parallel corpora from comparable resources where texts in two different languages are about similar topics, but are not translations of each other). Taking our inspiration from this work in MT, in this paper we investigate the feasibility of automatically creating aligned parallel data-text resources from comparable data and text resources available on the web. This task of automatic data-text alignment, previously unexplored as far as we are aware, is the task of automatically aligning data records with textual descriptions, such that data tokens are aligned with the word strings that describe them. For example, the data tokens `height_metres=250` might be aligned with the word string *with an altitude of 250*

Proceedings of the 4th Workshop on Building and Using Comparable Corpora, pages 102–109,
49th Annual Meeting of the Association for Computational Linguistics,
Portland, Oregon, 24 June 2011.

metres above sea level.

We start in Section 2 with an overview of data-to-text generation and of related work in MT. In Section 3 we describe our comparable data and text resources and the pre-processing methods we apply to them. In Section 4 we provide an overview of our unsupervised learning task and of the methodology we have developed for it. We then describe our methods and results for sentence selection (Section 5) and sentence-level data selection (Section 6) in more detail. We finish with a discussion of our results and some conclusions (Section 7).

2 Background and Related Research

Work in data-to-text generation has involved a variety of different domains, including generating weather forecasts from meteorological data (Sripada et al., 2003), nursing reports from intensive care data (Portet et al., 2009), and museum exhibit descriptions from database records (Isard et al., 2003; Stock et al., 2007); types of data have included dynamic time-series data (such as meteorological or medical data) and static database entries (as in museum exhibits).

The following is an example of an input/output pair from the M-PIRO project (Androutsopoulos et al., 2005), where the input is a database record for a museum artifact, and the output is a description of the artifact:

```
creation-period=archaic-period,
current-location=Un-museum-Pennsylvania,
painting-techinique-used=red-figure-technique,
painted-by=Eucharides, creation-time=between
(500 year BC)(480 year BC)
```

Classical kylix

This exhibit is a kylix; it was created during the archaic period and was painted with the red figure technique by Eucharides. It dates from between 500 and 480 B.C. and currently it is in the University Museum of Pennsylvania.

While data and texts in the three example domains cited above do occur naturally, two factors mean they cannot be used directly as target corpora or training data for building data-to-text generation systems: one, most are not freely available to researchers (e.g. by simply being available on the Web), and two, more problematically, the correspondence between inputs and outputs is not as direct as it is, say, between a source language text and its translation. In general, naturally occurring resources of data and related texts are not parallel, but are merely what has become known as *comparable* in the MT literature, with only a subset of data having corresponding text fragments, and other text fragments having no obvious corresponding data items. Moreover, data transformations may be necessary before corresponding text fragments can be identified.

In this paper we look at the possibility of automatically identifying parallel data-text fragments from comparable corpora in the case of data-to-text generation from static database records. Such a parallel data-text resource could then be used to train an existing data-to-text generation system, or even to build a new statistical generator from scratch, e.g. using techniques from statistical MT (Belz and Kow, 2009).

In statistical MT, the expense of manually creating new parallel MT corpora, and the need for very large amounts of parallel training data, has led to a sizeable research effort to develop methods for automatically constructing parallel resources. This work typically starts by identifying comparable corpora. Much of it has focused on identifying word translations in comparable corpora, e.g. Rapp's approach was based on the simple and elegant assumption that if words A_f and B_f have a higher than chance co-occurrence frequency in one language, then two appropriate translations A_e and B_e in another language will also have a higher than chance co-occurrence frequency (Rapp, 1995; Rapp, 1999). At the other end of the spectrum, Resnik and Smith (2003) search the Web to detect web pages that are translations of each other. Other approaches aim to identify pairs of sentences (Munteanu and Marcu, 2005) or sub-sentential fragments (Munteanu and Marcu, 2006) that are parallel within comparable corpora.

The latter approach is particularly relevant to our work. Munteanu and Marcu start by translating each document in the source language (SL) word for word into the target language (TL). The result is given to an information retrieval (IR) system as a query, and the top 20 results are retained and paired with the given SL document. They then obtain all sentence pairs from each pair of SL and TL documents, and discard those sentence pairs that have only a small number of words that are translations of each other. To the remaining sentences they then apply a fragment detection method which tries to distinguish between source fragments that have a translation on the target side, and fragments that do not.

The biggest difference between the MT situation and the data-to-text generation situation is that in the former, sentence-aligned parallel resources exist and can be used as a starting point. E.g. Munteanu and Marcu use an existing parallel Romanian-English corpus to (automatically) create a lexicon which is then used in various ways in their method. In data-to-text generation we have no analogous resources to help us get started. The approach to data-text alignment described in this paper therefore uses no prior knowledge, and all our learning methods are unsupervised.

3 Data and Texts about British Hills

As a source of data, we use the Database of British Hills (BHDB) created by Chris Crocker,[1] version 11.3, which contains measurements and other information about 5,614 British hills. We add some information to the BHDB records by performing reverse geocoding via the Google Map API[2] which allows us to convert latitude and longitude information from the hills database into country and region names. We add the latter to each database record.

On the text side, we use Wikipedia articles in the WikiProject British and Irish Hills (retrieved on 2009-11-09). At the time of retrieval there were 899 pages covered by this WikiProject, 242 of which were of quality category B or above.[3]

3.1 Aligning database entries with documents

Given that different hills can share the same name, and that the same hill can have several different names and spellings, matching up the data records in the BHDB with articles in Wikipedia is not entirely trivial. The method we use is to take a given hill's name from the BHDB record and to perform a search of Wikipedia with the hill's name as a search term, using the Mediawiki API. We then pair up the BHDB record with the Wikipedia article returned as the top search result.

[1]http://www.biber.fsnet.co.uk

[2]http://code.google.com/apis/maps/

[3]B = The article is mostly complete and without major issues, but requires some further work.

```
k-name v-name-Beacon_Fell
k-area v-area-Lakes:_S_Fells
k-height-metres v-height-metres-255
k-height-feet v-height-feet-837
k-feature v-feature-cairn
k-classification v-classification-WO
k-classification v-classification-Hu
k-locality v-locality-Skelwith
k-admin-area-level1 v-admin-area-level1-England
k-admin-area-level2 v-admin-area-level2-Cumbria
k-country v-country-United_Kingdom
```

Figure 1: Result of preprocessing BHDB record for Beacon Fell.

We manually evaluated the data-text pairs matched by this method, scoring each pair good/unsure/bad. We found that 759 pairs out of 899 (the number of Wikipedia articles in the WikiProject British and Irish Hills at the time of retrieval), or 84.4%, were categorised 'good' (i.e. they had been matched correctly), a further 89 pairs (9.8%) were categorised 'unsure', and the remainder was a wrong match. This gave us a corpus of 759 correctly matched data record/text pairs to work with.

We randomly selected 20 of the data record/text pairs for use as a development set to optimise modules on, and another 20 pairs for use as a test set, for which we did not compute scores until the methods were finalised. We manually annotated the 40 texts in the development and test sets to mark up which subsets of the data and which text substrings correspond to each other for each sentence (indicating parallel fragments as shown at the bottom of Figure 2).

3.2 Pre-processing of data records and texts

Database records: We perform three kinds of preprocessing on the data fields of the BHDB database records: (1) deletion; (2) structure flattening, and (3) data conversion including the reverse geocoding mentioned above (the result of these preprocessing steps for the English hill Beacon Fell can be seen in Figure 1).

Furthermore, for each data field `key = value` we separate out key and value, prefixing the key with `k-` and the value with `v-key` (e.g. `v-area` and `k-area-Berkshire`). Each data field is thus converted into two 'data tokens'.

Texts: For the texts, we first strip out Wikipedia mark-up to yield text-only versions. We then perform sentence splitting and tokenisation (with our own simple tools). Each text thus becomes a sequence of strings of 'text tokens'.

4 Task and Methodology Overview

Our aim is to automatically create aligned data-text resources where database records are paired with documents, and in each document, strings of word tokens are aligned with subsets of data tokens from the corresponding database record. The first two items shown in Figure 2 are the text of the Wikipedia article and the BHDB record about Black Chew Head (the latter cut down to the fields we actually use and supplemented by the administrative area information from reverse geocoding). The remainder of the figure shows fragments of text paired with subsets of data fields that could be extracted from the two comparable inputs.

How to get from a collection of texts and a separate but related collection of database records, to the parallel fragments shown at the bottom of Figure 2 is in essence the task we address. In order to do this automatically, we identify the following steps (the list includes, for the sake of completeness, the data record/document pairing and pre-processing methods from the previous section):

1. Identify comparable data and text resources and pair up individual data records and documents (Section 3).
2. Preprocess data and text, including e.g. tokenisation and sentence splitting (Section 3.2).
3. Select sentences that are likely to contain word strings that correspond to ('realise') any data fields (Section 5).
4. For each sentence selected in the previous step, select the subset of data tokens that are likely to be realised by the word strings in the sentence (Section 6).
5. Extract parallel fragments (future work).

5 Sentence Selection

The Wikipedia articles about British Hills in our corpus tend to have a lot of text in them for which the corresponding entry in BHDB contains no matching data. This is particularly true of longer articles about more well-known hills such as Ben Nevis. The article about the latter, for example, contains sections about the name's etymology, the geography, geology, climate and history, and even a section about the Ben Nevis Distillery and another about ships named after the hill, none of which the BHDB entry for Ben Nevis contains any data about. The task of sentence selection is to rule out such sections, and pick out those sentences that are likely to contain text that can be aligned with data. Using the example in Figure 2, the aim would be to select the first two sentences only.

Our sentence selection method consists of (i) estimating the strength of association between data and text tokens (Section 5.1); and (ii) selecting those sentences for further consideration that have sufficiently strong and/or numerous associations with data tokens (Section 5.2).

5.1 Computing positive and negative associations between data and text

We measure the strength of association between data tokens and text tokens using log-likelihood ratios which have been widely used for this sort of purpose (especially lexical association) since they were introduced to NLP (Dunning, 1993). They were e.g. used by Munteanu & Marcu (2006) to obtain a translation lexicon from word-aligned parallel texts.

We start by obtaining counts for the number of times each text token w co-occurs with each data token d, the number of times w occurs without d being present, the number of times d occurs without w, and finally, the number of times neither occurs. Co-occurrence here is at the document/data record level, i.e. a data token and a text token co-occur if they are present in the same document/data record pair (pairs as produced by the method described in Section 3). This allows us to compute log likelihood ratios for all data-token/text-token pairs, using one of the G^2 formulations from Moore (2004) which is shown in slightly different representation in Figure 3. The resulting G^2 scores tell us whether the frequency with which a data token d and a text token w co-occur deviates from that expected by chance.

If the G^2 score for a given (d, w) pair is greater than their joint probability $p(d)p(w)$, then the asso-

Wikipedia text:

Black Chew Head is the highest point (or county top) of Greater Manchester , and forms part of the Peak District , in northern England . Lying within the Saddleworth parish of the Metropolitan Borough of Oldham , close to Crowden , Derbyshire , it stands at a height of 542 metres above sea level . Black Chew Head is an outlying part of the Black Hill and overlooks the Chew Valley , which leads to the Dovestones Reservoir .

Entry from Database of British Hills:

name	area	height m	height ft	feature	classification	top	locality	adm_area1	adm_area2	country
Black Chew Head	Peak District	542	1778	fence	Dewey	Greater Manchester	Glossop	England	Derbyshire	UK

Parallel fragments:

name	area	top	adm_area1	adm_area2
Black Chew Head	Peak District	Greater Manchester	England	Derbyshire

Black Chew Head is the highest point (or county top) of Greater Manchester , and forms part of the Peak District , in northern England .

height (m)
542

it stands at a height of 542 metres above sea level .

Figure 2: Black Chew Head: Wikipedia article, entry in British Hills database (the part of it we use), and parallel fragments that could be extracted.

ciation is taken to be positive, i.e. w is likely to be part of a realisation of d, otherwise the association is taken to be negative, i.e. w is likely not to be part of a realisation of d.

Note that we use the notation G^2_+ below to denote a G^2 score which reflects a positive association.

5.2 Selecting sentences on the basis of association strength

In this step, we consider each sentence s in turn. We ignore those text tokens that have only negative associations with data tokens. For each of the remaining text tokens w^s in s we obtain $maxg2score(w^s)$, its highest G^2_+ score with any data token d in the set D of data tokens in the database record:

$$maxg2score(w^s) = \arg\max_{d \in D} G^2_+(d, w^s)$$

We then use these scores in two different ways to select sentences for further processing:

1. Thresholding: Select all sentences that have at least one text token w with $maxg2score(w) > t$, where t is a given threshold.

2. Greater-than-the-mean selection: Select all sentences whose mean $maxg2score$ (computed over all text tokens with positive association in the sentence) is greater than the mean of mean $maxg2scores$ (computed over all sentences in the corpus).

The reason why we are not interested in negative associations in sentence selection is that we want to identify those sentences that are likely to contain a text fragment of interest (characterised by high positive association scores), and such sentences may well also contain material unlikely to be of interest (characterised by negative association scores).

5.3 Results

Table 1 shows the results for sentence selection, in terms of Precision, Recall and F_1 Scores. In addition to the two methods described in the preceding section, we computed two baselines. Baseline 1 selects just the first sentence, which yields a Precision of 1 and a Recall of 0.141 for the test set (0.241 for the development set), indicating that in the manually aligned data, the first sentence is always selected and that less than a quarter of sentences selected are first sentences. Baseline 2 selects all sentences which yields a Recall of 1 and a Precision of 0.318 for the test set (0.377 for the development set), indicating that around one third of all sentences were selected in the manually aligned data.

Greater-than-the-mean selection roughly evens out Recall and Precision scores, with an F_1 Score above both baselines. As for thresholded selection, applying thresholds $t < 10$ results in all sentences being selected (hence the same R/P/F_1 scores as for Baseline 2).[4] Very high thresholds (500+) result in

[4]This ties in with Moore's result confirming previous anec-

$$G^2(d,w) = 2N\left(p(d,w)log\frac{p(d,w)}{p(d)p(w)} + p(d,\neg w)log\frac{p(d,\neg w)}{p(d)p(\neg w)} + p(\neg d,w)log\frac{p(\neg d,w)}{p(\neg d)p(w)} + p(\neg d,\neg w)log\frac{p(\neg d,\neg w)}{p(\neg d)p(\neg w)}\right)$$

Figure 3: Formula for computing G^2 from Moore (2004) (N is the sample size).

Selection Method	Development Set			Test Set		
	P	R	F_1	P	R	F_1
1st sentence only (Baseline 1)	1.000	0.241	0.388	1.000	0.141	0.247
All sentences (Baseline 2)	0.377	1.000	0.548	0.318	1.000	0.483
Greater-than-the-mean selection	0.516	0.590	0.551	0.474	0.634	0.542
Thresholded selection $t = 60$	0.487	0.928	0.639	0.423	0.965	0.588

Table 1: Sentence selection results in terms of Precision, Recall and F_1 Score.

very high Precision ($> .90$) with Recall dropping below 0.15. In the table, we show just the threshold that achieved the highest F_1 Score on the development set ($t = 60$).

Selecting a threshold on the basis of highest F_1 Score (rather than, say, $F_{0.5}$) in our case means we are favouring Recall over Precision, the intuition being that at this stage it is more important not to lose sentences that are likely to have useful realisations in them (than it is to get rid of sentences that are not).

6 Data Selection

For data selection, the aim is to select, for each sentence remaining after sentence selection, the subset of data tokens that are realised by (some part of) the sentence. In terms of Figure 2, the aim would be to select for each of sentence 1 and 2 the data tokens which are shown next to the fragment(s) extracted from it at the bottom of Figure 2. Looked at another way, we want to get rid of any data tokens that are not likely to be realised by any part of the sentence they are paired with.

We preform sentence selection separately for each sentence s, obtaining the subset D_s of data tokens likely to be realised by s, in one of the following two ways:

1. Individual selection: Retain all and only those data tokens that have a sufficiently strong positive association with at least one text token w^s:

$$D_s = \left\{d \middle| \exists w^s(G^2_+(d,w^s) > t)\right\}$$

dotal evidence that G^2 scores above 10 are a reliable indication of significant association (Moore, 2004, p. 239).

2. Pairwise selection: Consider each pair of key and value data tokens d_i^k, d_i^v that were originally derived from the same data field f_i. Retain all and only those pairs d_i^k, d_i^v where either d_i^k or d_i^v has a sufficiently strong association with at least one text token:

$$D_s = \Big\{d_i^k, d_i^v \Big| \exists w_j^s(G^2_+(d_i^k, w_j^s) > t) \vee \exists w_m^s(G^2_+(d_i^v, w_m^s) > t)\Big\}$$

Note that while previously each sentence in a text was associated with the same set of data tokens (the original complete set), after data selection each sentence is associated with its own set of data tokens which may be smaller than the original set.

If data selection produces an empty data token set D_s for a given sentence s, then s, along with its data token set D_s, are removed from the set of pairs of data token set and sentence.

We evaluate data selection for the baseline of selecting all sentences, and the above two methods in combination with different thresholds t. As the evaluation measure we use the Dice coefficient (a measure of set similarity), computed at the document level between (i) the union D of all sentence-level sets of data tokens selected by a given method and (ii) the corresponding reference data token set D^R, i.e. the set of data tokens in the manual annotations of the same text in the development/test data. Dice is defined as follows:

$$Dice(D, D^R) = \frac{2|D \cap D^R|}{|D| + |D^R|}$$

Table 6 shows results for the baseline and individual and pairwise data selection, on the development set

		Sentence selection method			
		Greater-than-the-mean	Thresholded, $t = 60$	All-sentences	1st-sentence
Dev Set	All data tokens	0.666	0.666	0.666	0.666
	Individual selection	$t = 0$: 0.666	$t = 0$: 0.666	$t = 0$: 0.666	$t = 0$: 0.666
	Pairwise selection	$t = 19$: 0.706	$t = 18$: 0.709	$t = 18$: 0.717	$t = 1$: 0.697
Test Set	All data tokens	0.716	0.748	0.748	0.748
	Individual selection	$t = 0$: 0.716	$t = 0$: 0.748	$t = 0$: 0.748	$t = 0$: 0.748
	Pairwise selection	$t = 19$: 0.751	$t = 18$: 0.777	$t = 18$: 0.775	$t = 1$: 0.767

Table 2: Data selection results in terms of Dice coefficient. Results shown for data selection methods preceded by different sentence selection methods.

(top half of the table), and on the test set (bottom half). In each case we show results for the given data selection method applied after each of the four different sentence selection methods described in Section 5: greater-than-the-mean, thresholded with $t = 60$, and the first-sentence-only and all-sentences baselines (these index the columns).

Again, we optimised the two non-baseline methods on the development set, finding the best threshold t separately for each combination of a given data selection method with a given sentence selection method. This yielded the t values shown in the cells in the table.

Looking at the results, selecting data tokens individually (second row in each half of Table 6) cannot improve Dice scores compared to leaving the original data token set in place (first row); this is the case across all four sentence selection methods. The pairwise data selection method (third row) achieves the best results, although it does not appear to make a real difference whether or not sentence selection is applied prior to data selection.

7 Conclusion

In this paper we have reported our work to date on data-text alignment, a previously unexplored problem as far as we are aware. We looked at alignment of two comparable resources (one a collection of data records about British Hills, the other a collection of texts about British Hills) at the data record/document level, where our simple search-based method achieved an accuracy rate of 84%. Next we looked at alignment at the data record/sentence level. Here we obtained a best F_1 score of 0.588 for sentence selection and a best mean Dice score of 0.777 for data selection.

The best performing methods described here provide a good basis for further development of our parallel fragment extraction methods, in particular considering that the methods start from nothing and obtain all knowledge about data-text relations in a completely unsupervised way. Our results show that log likelihood ratios, which have been widely used for measuring lexical association, but were so far unproven for the data-text situation, can provide a strong basis for identifying associations between data and text.

References

I. Androutsopoulos, S. Kallonis, and V. Karkaletsis. 2005. Exploiting owl ontologies in the multilingual generation of object descriptions. In *Proceedings of the 10th European Workshop on Natural Language Generationf (ENLG'05)*, pages 150–155.

Anja Belz and Eric Kow. 2009. System building cost vs. output quality in data-to-text generation. In *Proceedings of the 12th European Workshop on Natural Language Generation*, pages 16–24.

E. Briscoe, J. Carroll, and J. Graham. 2006. The second release of the rasp system. In *Proceedings of the COLING/ACL 2006 Interactive Presentation Sessions*.

Ted Dunning. 1993. Accurate methods for the statistics of surprise and coincidence. *Computational Linguistics*, 1:61–74.

A. Isard, J. Oberlander, I. Androutsopoulos, and C. Matheson. 2003. Speaking the users' languages. *IEEE Intelligent Systems Magazine: Special Issue "Advances in Natural Language Processing*, 18(1):40–45.

Robert C. Moore. 2004. On log-likelihood-ratios and the significance of rare events. In *Proceedings of the 9th Converence on Empirical Methods in Natural Language Processing (EMNLP'04)*, pages 333–340.

Dragos Munteanu and Daniel Marcu. 2005. Improving machine translation performance by exploiting non-parallel corpora. *Computational Linguistics*, 31:477–504.

Dragos Stefan Munteanu and Daniel Marcu. 2006. Extracting parallel sub-sentential fragments from non-parallel corpora. In *Proceedings of the 21st International Conference on Computational Linguistics and the 44th annual meeting of the Association for Computational Linguistics (COLING-ACL'06)*, pages 81–88, Morristown, NJ, USA. Association for Computational Linguistics.

F. Portet, E. Reiter, A. Gatt, J. Hunter, S. Sripada, Y. Freer, and C. Sykes. 2009. Automatic generation of textual summaries from neonatal intensive care data. *Artificial Intelligence*, 173:789–816.

Reinhard Rapp. 1995. Identifying word translations in non-parallel texts. In *Proceedings of the 33rd annual meeting on Association for Computational Linguistics*, pages 320–322, Morristown, NJ, USA. Association for Computational Linguistics.

Reinhard Rapp. 1999. Automatic identification of word translations from unrelated english and german corpora. In *Proceedings of the 37th annual meeting of the Association for Computational Linguistics on Computational Linguistics*, pages 519–526, Morristown, NJ, USA. Association for Computational Linguistics.

Philip Resnik and Noah Smith. 2003. The web as a parallel corpus. *Computational Linguistics*, 29:349–380.

S. Sripada, E. Reiter, J. Hunter, and J. Yu. 2003. Exploiting a parallel text-data corpus. In *Proceedings of Corpus Linguistics 2003*, pages 734–743.

Oliviero Stock, Massimo Zancanaro, Paolo Busetta adn Charles Callaway, Anbtonio Krüger, Michael Kruppa, Tsvi Kuflik, Elena Not, and Cesare Rocchi. 2007. Adaptive, intelligent presentation of information for the museum visitor in PEACH. *User Modeling and User-Adapted Interaction*, 17(3):257–304.

Cross-lingual Slot Filling from Comparable Corpora

Matthew Snover, Xiang Li, Wen-Pin Lin, Zheng Chen, Suzanne Tamang, Mingmin Ge, Adam Lee, Qi Li, Hao Li, Sam Anzaroot, Heng Ji
Computer Science Department
Queens College and Graduate Center
City University of New York
New York, NY 11367, USA
msnover@qc.cuny.edu, hengji@cs.qc.cuny.edu

Abstract

This paper introduces a new task of crosslingual slot filling which aims to discover attributes for entity queries from crosslingual comparable corpora and then present answers in a desired language. It is a very challenging task which suffers from both information extraction and machine translation errors. In this paper we analyze the types of errors produced by five different baseline approaches, and present a novel supervised rescoring based validation approach to incorporate global evidence from very large bilingual comparable corpora. Without using any additional labeled data this new approach obtained 38.5% relative improvement in Precision and 86.7% relative improvement in Recall over several state-of-the-art approaches. The ultimate system outperformed monolingual slot filling pipelines built on much larger monolingual corpora.

1 Introduction

The slot filling task at NIST TAC Knowledge Base Population (KBP) track (Ji et al., 2010) is a relatively new and popular task with the goal of automatically building profiles of entities from large amounts of unstructured data, and using these profiles to populate an existing knowledge base. These profiles consist of numerous slots such as "*title*", "*parents*" for persons and "*top-employees*" for organizations. A variety of approaches have been proposed to address both tasks with considerable success; nevertheless, all of the KBP tasks so far have been limited to monolingual processing. However, as the shrinking fraction of the world's Web pages are written in English, many slot fills can only be discovered from comparable documents in foreign languages. By comparable corpora we mean texts that are about similar topics, but are not in general translations of each other. These corpora are naturally available, for example, many news agencies release multi-lingual news articles on the same day. In this paper we propose a new and more challenging crosslingual slot filling task, to find information for any English query from crosslingual comparable corpora, and then present its profile in English.

We developed complementary baseline approaches which combine two difficult problems: information extraction (IE) and machine translation (MT). In this paper we conduct detailed error analysis to understand how we can exploit comparable corpora to construct more complete and accurate profiles.

Many correct answers extracted from our baselines will be reported multiple times in any external large collection of comparable documents. We can thus take advantage of such information redundancy to rescore candidate answers. To choose the best answers we consult large comparable corpora and corresponding IE results. We prefer those answers which frequently appear together with the query in certain IE contexts, including co-occurring names, coreference links, relations and events. For example, we prefer "*South Korea*" instead of "*New York Stock Exchange*" as the "*per:employee_of*" answer for "*Roh Moo-hyun*" using global evidence from employment relation extraction. Such global knowledge from comparable corpora

Proceedings of the 4th Workshop on Building and Using Comparable Corpora, pages 110–119,
49th Annual Meeting of the Association for Computational Linguistics,
Portland, Oregon, 24 June 2011. ©*2011 Association for Computational Linguistics*

provides substantial improvement over each individual baseline system and even state-of-the-art monolingual slot filling systems. Compared to previous methods of exploiting comparable corpora, our approach is novel in multiple aspects because it exploits knowledge from: (1) both local and global statistics; (2) both languages; and (3) both shallow and deep analysis.

2 Related Work

Sudo et al. (2004) found that for a crosslingual single-document IE task, source language extraction and fact translation performed notably better than machine translation and target language extraction. We observed the same results. In addition we also demonstrate that these two approaches are complementary and can be used to boost each other's results in a statistical rescoring model with global evidence from large comparable corpora.

Hakkani-Tur et al. (2007) described a filtering mechanism using two crosslingual IE systems for improving crosslingual document retrieval. Many previous validation methods for crosslingual QA, such as those organized by Cross Language Evaluation Forum (Vallin et al., 2005), focused on local information which involves only the query and answer (e.g. (Kwork and Deng, 2006)), keyword translation (e.g. (Mitamura et al., 2006)) and surface patterns (e.g. (Soubbotin and Soubbotin, 2001)). Some global validation approaches considered information redundancy based on shallow statistics including co-occurrence, density score and mutual information (Clarke et al., 2001; Magnini et al., 2001; Lee et al., 2008), deeper knowledge from dependency parsing (e.g. (Shen et al., 2006)) or logic reasoning (e.g. (Harabagiu et al., 2005)). However, all of these approaches made limited efforts at disambiguating entities in queries and limited use of fact extraction in answer search and validation.

Several recent IE studies have stressed the benefits of using information redundancy on estimating the correctness of the IE output (Downey et al., 2005; Yangarber, 2006; Patwardhan and Riloff, 2009; Ji and Grishman, 2008). Some recent research used comparable corpora to re-score name transliterations (Sproat et al., 2006; Klementiev and Roth, 2006) or mine new word translations (Fung and Yee, 1998; Rapp, 1999; Shao and Ng, 2004; Tao and Zhai, 2005; Hassan et al., 2007; Udupa et al., 2009; Ji, 2009). To the best of our knowledge, this is the first work on mining facts from comparable corpora for answer validation in a new crosslingual entity profiling task.

3 Experimental Setup

3.1 Task Definition

The goal of the KBP slot filling task is to extract facts from a large source corpus regarding certain attributes ("*slots*") of an entity, which may be a person or organization, and use these facts to augment an existing knowledge base (KB). Along with each slot answer, the system must provide the ID of a document which supports the correctness of this answer. KBP 2010 (Ji et al., 2010) defines 26 types of attributes for persons (such as the age, birthplace, spouse, children, job title, and employing organization) and 16 types of attributes for organizations (such as the top employees, the founder, the year founded, the headquarters location, and the subsidiaries).

The new problem we define in this paper is an extension of this task to a crosslingual paradigm. Given a query in a target language t and a collection of documents in a source language s, a system must extract slot answers about the query and present the answers in t. In this paper we examine a specific setting of s=Chinese and t=English.

To score crosslingual slot filling, we pool all the system responses and group equivalent answers into equivalence classes. Each system response is rated as correct, wrong, inexact or redundant. Given these judgments, we calculate the precision, recall and F-measure of each system, crediting only correct answers.

3.2 Data and Query Selection

We use the comparable corpora of English TDT5 (278,358 documents) and Chinese TDT5

(56,424 documents) as our source collection.

For query selection, we collected all the entities from the entire source collection and counted their frequencies. We then selected 50 informative entities (25 persons and 25 organizations) which were located in the middle range of frequency counts. Among the 25 person queries, half are Chinese-specific names, and half are non-Chinese names. The 25 organizations follow a representative distribution according to the entity subtypes defined in NIST Automatic Content Extraction (ACE) program[1].

3.3 Baseline Pipelines

3.3.1 Overview

We employ the following two types of baseline crosslingual slot filling pipelines to process Chinese documents. Figure 1 and Table 1 shows the five system pipelines we have used to conduct our experiments.

Type A Translate Chinese texts into English, and apply English slot filling systems to the translations.

Type B Translate English queries into Chinese, apply Chinese slot filling systems to Chinese texts, and translate answers back to English.

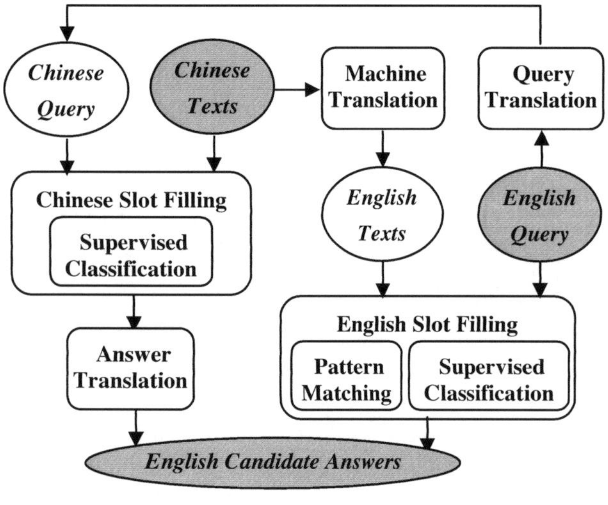

Figure 1: Overview of Baseline Crosslingual Slot Filling Pipelines

[1]http://www.itl.nist.gov/iad/mig/tests/ace/

Pipeline	Label		Components	Data
Mono-lingual	(1)		English Supervised Classification	English TDT5
	(2)		English Pattern Matching	
Cross-lingual	Type A	(3)	MT+English Supervised Classification	Chinese TDT5
		(4)	MT+English Pattern Matching	
	Type B	(5)	Query Translation +Chinese Supervised Classification +Answer Translation	

Table 1: Monolingual and Crosslingual Baseline Slot Filling Pipelines

3.3.2 Monolingual Slot Filling

We applied a state-of-the-art bilingual slot filling system (Chen et al., 2010) to process bilingual comparable corpora. This baseline system includes a supervised ACE IE pipeline and a bottom-up pattern matching pipeline. The IE pipeline includes relation extraction and event extraction based on maximum entropy models that incorporate diverse lexical, syntactic, semantic and ontological knowledge. The extracted ACE relations and events are then mapped to KBP slot fills. In pattern matching, we extract and rank patterns based on a distant supervision approach (Mintz et al., 2009) that uses entity-attribute pairs from Wikipedia Infoboxes and Freebase (Bollacker et al., 2008). We set a low threshold to include more answer candidates, and then a series of filtering steps to refine and improve the overall pipeline results. The filtering steps include removing answers which have inappropriate entity types or have inappropriate dependency paths to the entities.

3.3.3 Document and Name Translation

We use a statistical, phrase-based MT system (Zens and Ney, 2004) to translate Chinese documents into English for Type A Approaches. The best translation is computed by using a weighted log-linear combination of various statistical models: an n-gram language model, a phrase translation model and a word-based lexicon model. The latter two models are used in source-to-target and target-to-source directions. The model scaling factors are optimized with respect to the BLEU score similar to (Och, 2003). The training data includes 200 million running words in each language. The total language model training data consists of about 600 million running words.

We applied various name mining approaches from comparable corpora and parallel corpora, as described in (Ji et al., 2009) to extract and translate names in queries and answers in Type B approaches. The accuracy of name translation is about 88%. For those names not covered by these pairs, we relied on Google Translate [2] to obtain results.

4 Analysis of Baseline Pipelines

In this section we analyze the coverage (Section 4.1) and precision (Section 4.2) results of the baseline pipelines. We then illustrate the potential for global validation from comparable corpora through a series of examples.

4.1 Coverage Analysis: Toward Information Fusion

Table 2 summarizes the Precision (P), Recall (R) and F-measure (F) of baseline pipelines and the union of their individual results.

Table 2: Baseline Pipeline Results

System		P	R	F
Mono-lingual	(1)	0.08	0.54	0.15
	(2)	0.02	0.35	0.03
	Union of (1)+(2)	0.03	0.69	0.05
Cross-lingual	(3)	0.04	0.04	0.04
	(4)	0.03	0.25	0.05
	Union of (3)+(4)	0.03	0.26	0.05
	(5)	0.04	0.46	0.08
	Union of (3)+(4)+(5)	0.03	0.56	0.05
Comparable Corpora	Union of (1)+(2)+(3)+(4)+(5)	0.02	1	0.04

[2]http://translate.google.com/

Although crosslingual pipelines used a much smaller corpus than monolingual pipelines, they extracted comparable number of correct answers (66 vs. 81) with a slightly better precision. In fact, the crosslingual pipeline (5) performs even better than monolingual pipeline (2), especially on the employment slots. In particular, 96.35% of the correct answers for Chinese-specific person queries (e.g. "*Tang Jiaxuan*") were extracted from Chinese data. Even for those facts discovered from English data, they are about quite general slots such as "*title*" and "*employee_of*". In contrast, Chinese data covers more diverse biographical slots such as "*family members*" and "*schools_attended*".

Compared to the union of Type A approaches (pipelines (3)+(4)), Pipeline (5) returned many more correct answers with higher precision. The main reason is that Type A approaches suffer from MT errors. For example, MT mistakenly translated the query name "*Celine Dion*" into "*Clinton*" and thus English slot filling components failed to identify any answers. One can hypothesize that slot filling on MT output can be improved by re-training extraction components directly from MT output. However, our experiments of learning patterns from MT output showed negative impact, mainly because MT errors were too diverse to generalize. In other cases even though slot filling produced correct results, MT still failed to translate the answer names correctly. For example, English slot filling successfully found a potential answer for "*org:founded_by*" of the query "*Microsoft*" from the following MT output: "*The third largest of the Microsoft common founder Alan Doss , aged 50, and net assets of US 22 billion.*"; however, the answer string "*Paul Allen*" was mistakenly translated into "*Alan Doss*". MT is not so crucial for "*per:title*" slot because it does not require translation of contexts.

To summarize, 59% of the missing errors were due to text, query or answer translation errors and 20% were due to slot filling errors. Nevertheless, the union of (3)+(4)+(5) still contain more correct answers. These baseline pipelines were developed from a diverse set of algorithms, and typically showed strengths in specific slots.

In general we can conclude that monolingual and crosslingual pipelines are complementary. Combining the responses from all baseline pipelines, we can get similar number of correct answers compared to one single human annotator.

4.2 Precision Analysis: Toward Global Validation

The spurious errors from baseline crosslingual slot filling pipelines reveal both the shortcomings of the MT system and extraction across languages. Table 3 shows the distribution of spurious errors.

Pipeline	Spurious Errors	Distribution
Type A	Content Translation + Extraction	85%
	Query Translation	13%
	Answer Translation	2%
Type B	Word Segmentation	34%
	Relation Extraction	33%
	Coreference	17%
	Semantic Type	13%
	Slot Type	3%

Table 3: Distribution of Spurious Errors

Table 3 indicates a majority (85%) of spurious errors from Type A pipelines were due to applying monolingual slot filling methods to MT output which preserves Chinese structure.

As demonstrated in previous work (e.g. (Parton and McKeown, 2010; Ji et al., 2009)), we also found that many (14.6%) errors were caused by the low quality of name translation for queries and answers.

For example, "麦克金蒂/*McGinty*" was mistakenly translated into the query name "*Kim Jong-il*", which led to many incorrect answers such as "*The British Royal joint military research institute*" for "*per:employee_of*".

In contrast, the spurious errors from Type B pipelines were more diverse. Chinese IE components severely suffered from word segmentation errors (34%), which were then directly propagated into Chinese document retrieval and slot filling. Many segmentation errors occurred with out-of-vocabulary names, especially person names and nested organization names. For example, the name "姚明宝/*Yao Mingbao*" was mistakenly segmented into two words "姚明/*Yao Ming*" and "宝/*bao*", and thus the document was mistakenly retrieved for the query '*Yao Ming*".

In many cases (33%) Chinese relation and event extraction components failed to capture Chinese-specific structures due to the limited size of training corpora. For example, from the context "应邀担任陈水扁经济顾问的萧万长/*Xiao Wan-chang, who were invited to become the economics consultant for Chen Shui-bian*", Chinese slot filling system mistakenly extracted "*consultant*" as a "*per:title*" answer for the query "*Chen Shui-bian*" using a common pattern "*<query><title>*".

13% of errors were caused due to invalid semantic types for certain slots. For example, many metaphoric titles such as "*tough guy*" don't match the definition of "*per:title*" in the annotation guideline "*employment or membership position*".

5 Global Validation

Based on the above motivations we propose to incorporate global evidence from a very large collection of comparable documents to refine local decisions. The central idea is to over-generate candidate answers from multiple weak baselines to ensure high upper-bound of recall, and then conduct effective global validation to filter spurious errors while keeping good answers in order to enhance precision.

5.1 Supervised Rescoring

Ideally, we want to choose a validation model which can pick out important features in a context wider than that used by baseline pipelines. Merging individual systems to form the union of answers can be effective, but Table 2 shows that simple union of all pipelines produced worse F-measure than the best pipeline.

In this paper we exploit the reranking paradigm, commonly used in information retrieval, to conduct global validation. By modeling the empirical distribution of labeled training data, statistical models are used to identify the strengths and weaknesses (e.g. high and low precision slots) of individual systems, and rescore answers accordingly. Specially, we develop a supervised Maximum Entropy (MaxEnt) based model to rescore the answers from the pipelines, selecting only the highest-scoring answers.

The rescorer was trained (using cross-validation) on varying subsets of the features. The threshold at which an answer is deemed to be true is chosen to maximize the F-Measure on the training set.

5.2 Validation Features

Table 4 describes the validation features used for rescoring, where *q* is the query, *q'* the Chinese translation of *q*, *t* the slot type, *a* the candidate answer, *a'* the Chinese form of *a*, *s* the context sentence and *d* is the context document supporting *a*.

The feature set benefits from multiple dimensions of crosslingual slot filling. These features were applied to both languages wherever annotation resources were available.

In the KBP slot filling task, slots are often dependent on each other, so we can improve the results by improving the "coherence" of the story (i.e. consistency among all generated answers - query profiles). We use feature *f2* to check whether the same answer was generated for conflicting slots, such as *per:parents* and *per:children*.

Compared to traditional QA tasks, slot filling is a more fine-grained task in which different slots are expected to obtain semantically different answers. Therefore, we explored semantic constraints in both local and global contexts. For example, we utilized bilingual name gazetteers from ACE training corpora, Google n-grams (Ji and Lin, 2009) and the geonames website [3] to encode features *f6*, *f8* and *f9*; The *org:top_members/employees* slot requires a system to distinguish whether a person member/ employee is in the top position, thus we encoded *f10* for this purpose.

The knowledge used in our baseline pipelines is relatively static – it is not updated during the extraction process. Achieving high performance for cross-lingual slot filling requires that we take a broader view, one that looks outside a single document or a single language in order to exploit global knowledge. Fortunately, as more and more large crosslingual comparable corpora are available, we can take advantage of information redundancy to validate answers. The basic intuition is that if a candidate answer *a* is correct, it should appear together with the query *q* repeatedly, in different documents, or even in certain coreference links, relations and events.

For example, "*David Kelly - scientist*", and "石原慎太郎/*Shintaro Ishihara* - 知事/*governor*" pairs appear frequently in "*title*" coreference links in both English and Chinese corpora; "*Elizabeth II*" is very often involved in an "*employment*" relation with "*United Kingdom*" in English corpora. On the other hand, some incorrect answers with high global statistics can be filtered out using these constraints. For example, although the query "唐家璇/*Tang Jiaxuan*" appears frequently together with the candidate *per:title* answer "人员/*personnel*", it is linked by few coreference links; in contrast, it's coreferential with the correct title answer "国务委员/*State Council member*" much more frequently.

We processed cross-lingual comparable corpora to extract coreference links, relations and events among mentions (names, nominals and time expressions etc.) and stored them in an external knowledge base. Any pair of <*q*, *a*> is then compared to the entries in this knowledge base. We used 157,708 documents from Chinese TDT5 and Gigaword to count Chinese global statistics, and 7,148,446 documents from DARPA GALE MT training corpora to count English global statistics, as shown in features *f12* and *f13*. Fact based global features *f14*, *f15*, *f16* and *f17*, were calculated from 49,359 Chinese and 280,513 English documents (annotated by the bilingual IE system in Section 3.3.2.

6 Experiments

In this section, we examine the overall performance of this method. We then discuss the usefulness of the individual sets of features. In

[3] http://www.geonames.org/statistics/

Characteristics			Description
Scope	Depth	Language	
Global (Cross-system)	Shallow	English	f1: frequency of <*q, a, t*> that appears in all baseline outputs
			f2: number of conflicting slot types in which answer *a* appears in all baseline outputs
Local	Shallow	English	f3: conjunction of *t* and whether *a* is a year answer
			f4: conjunction of *t* and whether *a* includes numbers or letters
	Deep	English	f5: conjunction of place *t* and whether *a* is a country name
			f6: conjunction of *per:origin t* and whether *a* is a nationality
			f7: if *t=per:title*, whether *a* is an acceptable title
			f8: if *t* requires a name answer, whether *a* is a name
			f9: whether *a* has appropriate semantic type
Global (Within-Document)	Deep	English	f10: conjunction of *org:top_members/employees* and whether there is a high-level title in *s*
			f11: conjunction of alternative name and whether *a* is an acronym of *q*
Global (Cross-document in comparable corpora)	Shallow (Statistics)	Chinese	f12: conditional probability of *q/q'* and *a/a'* appear in the same document
		English	f13: conditional probability of *q/q'* and *a/a'* appear in the same sentence
	Deep (Fact-based)	Both	f14: co-occurrence of *q/q'* and *a/a'* appear in coreference links
		English	f15: co-occurrence of *q/q'* and *a/a'* appear in relation/event links
		English	f16: conditional probability of *q/q'* and *a/a'* appear in relation/event links
		English	f17: mutual information of *q/q'* and *a/a'* appear in relation/event links

Table 4: Validation Features for Crosslingual Slot Filling

the following results, the baseline features are always used in addition to any other features.

6.1 Overall Performance

Because of the data scarcity, ten-fold cross-validation, across queries, was used to train and test the system. Quantitative results after combining answers from multiple pipelines are shown in Table 5. We used two basic features, one is the slot type and the other is the entity type of the query (i.e. person or organization). This basic feature set is already successful in improving the precision of the pipelines, although this results in a number of correct answers being discarded as well. By adding the additional validation features described previously, both the f-score and precision of the models are improved. In the case of the cross-lingual pipelines (3+4+5) the number of correct answers chosen is almost doubled while increasing the precision of the output.

Pipelines	F	P	R
Basic Features			
1+2	0.31	0.31	0.30
3+4+5	0.26	0.39	0.20
1+2+3+4+5	0.27	0.29	0.25
Full Features			
1+2	0.37	0.30	0.46
3+4+5	0.36	0.35	0.37
1+2+3+4+5	0.31	0.28	0.35

Table 5: Using Basic Features to Filter Answers

6.2 Impact of Global Validation

A comparison of the benefits of global versus local features are shown in Table 6, both of which dramatically improve scores over the baseline features. The global features are universally more beneficial than the local features, although the local features generate results with higher precision at the expense of the number of correct answers returned. The global features are especially useful for pipelines 3+4+5, where the performance using just these features reaches those of using all other features – this does not hold true for the monolingual pipelines however.

6.3 Impact of Fact-driven Deep Knowledge

The varying benefit of fact-driven cross-document features and statistical cross-document features are shown in Table 7.

Pipelines	F	P	R
Local Features			
1+2	0.34	0.35	0.33
3+4+5	0.29	0.40	0.22
1+2+3+4+5	0.27	0.32	0.24
Global Features			
1+2	0.35	0.30	0.42
3+4+5	0.37	0.36	0.38
1+2+3+4+5	0.33	0.29	0.38

Table 6: The Benefit of Global versus Local Features

While both feature sets are beneficial, the monolingual pipelines (1+2) benefit more from statistical features while the cross-lingual pipelines (3+4+7) benefit slightly more from the fact-based features. Despite this bias, the overall results when the features are used in all pipelines are very close with the fact-based features being slightly more useful overall.

Pipelines	F	P	R
Fact-Based Features			
1+2	0.33	0.27	0.42
3+4+5	0.35	0.43	0.29
1+2+3+4+5	0.30	0.27	0.34
Statistical Features			
1+2	0.37	0.34	0.40
3+4+5	0.34	0.35	0.33
1+2+3+4+5	0.29	0.25	0.34

Table 7: Fact vs. Statistical Cross-Doc Features

Translation features were only beneficial to pipelines 3, 4, and 5, and provided a slight increase in precision from 0.39 to 0.42, but provided no noticeable benefit when used in conjunction with results from pipelines 1 and 2. This is because the answers where translation features would be most useful were already being selected by pipelines 1 and 2 using the baseline features.

6.4 Discussion

The use of any re-scoring, even with baseline features, provides large gains over the union of the baseline pipelines, removing large number of incorrect answers. The use of more sophisticated features provided substantial gains over the baseline features. In particular, global features proved very effective. Further feature engineering to address the remaining errors and the dropped correct answer would likely provide increasing gains in performance.

In addition, two human annotators, independently, conducted the same task on the same data, with a second pass of adjudication. The F-scores of inter-annotator agreement were 52.0% for the first pass and 73.2% for the second pass. This indicates that slot filling remains a challenging task for both systems and human annotators—only one monolingual system exceeded 30% F-score in the KBP2010 evaluation.

7 Conclusion and Future Work

Crosslingual slot filling is a challenging task due to limited performance in two separate areas: information extraction and machine translation. Various methods of combining techniques from these two areas provided weak yet complementary baseline pipelines. We proposed an effective approach to integrate these baselines and enhance their performance using wider and deeper knowledge from comparable corpora. The final system based on cross-lingual comparable corpora outperformed monolingual pipelines on much larger monolingual corpora.

The intuition behind our approach is that over-generation of candidate answers from weak baselines provides a potentially strong recall upper-bound. The remaining enhancement becomes simpler: filtering errors. Our experiments also suggest that our rescoring models tend to over-fit due to small amount of training data. Manual annotation and assessment are quite costly, motivating future work in active learning and semi-supervised learning methods. In addition, we plan to apply our results as feedback to improve MT performance on facts using query and answer-driven language model adaptation. We have demonstrated our approach on English-Chinese pair, but the framework is language-independent; ultimately we would like to extend the task to extracting information from more languages.

Acknowledgments

This work was supported by the U.S. NSF CAREER Award under Grant IIS-0953149 and PSC-CUNY Research Program. Any opinions, findings, and conclusions or recommendations expressed in this material are those of the author(s) and do not necessarily reflect the views of the National Science Foundation.

References

K. Bollacker, R. Cook, and P. Tufts. 2008. Freebase: A shared database of structured general human knowledge. In *Proc. National Conference on Artificial Intelligence.*

Zheng Chen, Suzanne Tamang, Adam Lee, Xiang Li, Marissa Passantino, and Heng Ji. 2010. Top-down and bottom-up: A combined approach to slot filling. *Lecture Notes in Computer Science*, 6458:300–309, December.

C. L. A. Clarke, G. V. Cormack, and T.R. Lynam. 2001. Exploiting redundancy in question answering. In *Proc. SIGIR2001.*

Doug Downey, Oren Etzioni, and Stephen Soderland. 2005. A Probabilistic Model of Redundancy in Information Extraction. In *Proc. IJCAI 2005.*

Pascale Fung and Lo Yuen Yee. 1998. An ir approach for translating new words from nonparallel and comparable texts. In *COLING-ACL.*

Dilek Hakkani-Tur, Heng Ji, and Ralph Grishman. 2007. Using information extraction to improve cross-lingual document retrieval. In *Proc. RANLP workshop on Multi-source, Multilingual Information Extraction and Summarization.*

S. Harabagiu, D. Moldovan, C. Clark, M. Bowden, A. Hickl, and P. Wang. 2005. Employing two question answering systems in trec 2005. In *Proc. TREC2005.*

Ahmed Hassan, Haytham Fahmy, and Hany Hassan. 2007. Improving named entity translation by exploiting comparable and parallel corpora. In *RANLP.*

Heng Ji and Ralph Grishman. 2008. Refining Event Extraction through Cross-Document Inference. In *Proc. of ACL-08: HLT*, pages 254–262.

Heng Ji and Dekang Lin. 2009. Gender and animacy knowledge discovery from web-scale n-grams for unsupervised person mention detection. In *Proc. PACLIC2009.*

Heng Ji, Ralph Grishman, Dayne Freitag, Matthias Blume, John Wang, Shahram Khadivi, Richard Zens, and Hermann Ney. 2009. Name translation for distillation. *Handbook of Natural Language Processing and Machine Translation: DARPA Global Autonomous Language Exploitation.*

Heng Ji, Ralph Grishman, Hoa Trang Dang, and Kira Griffitt. 2010. An overview of the tac2010 knowledge base population track. In *Proc. TAC2010.*

Heng Ji. 2009. Mining name translations from comparable corpora by creating bilingual information networks. In *ACL-IJCNLP 2009 workshop on Building and Using Comparable Corpora (BUCC 2009): from Parallel to Non-parallel Corpora.*

Alexandre Klementiev and Dan Roth. 2006. Named entity transliteration and discovery from multilingual comparable corpora. In *HLT-NAACL 2006.*

K.-L. Kwork and P. P. Deng. 2006. Chinese question-answering: Comparing monolingual with english-chinese cross-lingual results. In *Asia Information Retrieval Symposium.*

Cheng-Wei Lee, Yi-Hsun Lee, and Wen-Lian Hsu. 2008. Exploring shallow answer ranking features in cross-lingual and monolingual factoid question answering. *Computational Linguistics and Chinese Language Processing*, 13:1–26, March.

B. Magnini, M. Negri, R. Prevete, and H. Tanev. 2001. Is it the right answer?: Exploiting web redundancy for answer validation. In *Proc. ACL2001.*

Mike Mintz, Steven Bills, Rion Snow, and Dan Jurafsky. 2009. Distant supervision for relation extraction without labeled data. In *ACL-IJCNLP 2009.*

Teruko Mitamura, Mengqiu Wang, Hideki Shima, and Frank Lin. 2006. Keyword translation accuracy and cross-lingual question answering in chinese and japanese. In *EACL 2006 Workshop on MLQA.*

F. J. Och. 2003. Minimum error rate training in statistical machine translaton. In *Proc.ACL2003.*

Kristen Parton and Kathleen McKeown. 2010. Mt error detection for cross-lingual question answering. *Proc. COLING2010.*

Siddharth Patwardhan and Ellen Riloff. 2009. A Unified Model of Phrasal and Sentential Evidence for Information Extraction. In *Proc. EMNLP 2009.*

Reinhard Rapp. 1999. Automatic identification of word translations from unrelated english and german corpora. In *ACL 1999.*

Li Shao and Hwee Tou Ng. 2004. Mining new word translations from comparable corpora. In *COLING2004.*

D. Shen, G. Saarbruechen, and D. Klakow. 2006. Exploring correlation of dependency relation paths for answer extraction. In *Proc. ACL2006.*

M. M. Soubbotin and S. M. Soubbotin. 2001. Patterns of potential answer expressions as clues to the right answers. In *Proc. TREC2001.*

Richard Sproat, Tao Tao, and ChengXiang Zhai. 2006. Named entity transliteration with comparable corpora. In *ACL 2006.*

Kiyoshi Sudo, Satoshi Sekine, and Ralph Grishman. 2004. Cross-lingual information extraction evaluation. In *Proc. COLING2004.*

Tao Tao and Chengxiang Zhai. 2005. Mining comparable bilingual text corpora for cross-language information integration. In *Proc. KDD2005.*

Raghavendra Udupa, K. Saravanan, A. Kumaran, and Jagadeesh Jagarlamudi. 2009. Mint: A method for effective and scalable mining of named entity transliterations from large comparable corpora. In *EACL2009.*

Alessandro Vallin, Bernardo Magnini, Danilo Giampiccolo, Lili Aunimo, Christelle Ayache, Petya Osenova, Anselmo Peas, Maaren de Rijke, Bogdan Sacaleanu, Diana Santos, and Richard Sutcliffe. 2005. Overview of the clef 2005 multilingual question answer track. In *Proc. CLEF2005.*

Roman Yangarber. 2006. Verification of Facts across Document Boundaries. In *Proc. International Workshop on Intelligent Information Access.*

Richard Zens and Hermann Ney. 2004. Improvements in phrase-based statistical machine translation. In *Proc. HLT/NAACL 2004.*

Towards a Data Model for the Universal Corpus

Steven Abney
University of Michigan
abney@umich.edu

Steven Bird
University of Melbourne and
University of Pennsylvania
sbird@unimelb.edu.au

Abstract

We describe the design of a comparable corpus that spans all of the world's languages and facilitates large-scale cross-linguistic processing. This Universal Corpus consists of text collections aligned at the document and sentence level, multilingual wordlists, and a small set of morphological, lexical, and syntactic annotations. The design encompasses submission, storage, and access. Submission preserves the integrity of the work, allows asynchronous updates, and facilitates scholarly citation. Storage employs a cloud-hosted filestore containing normalized source data together with a database of texts and annotations. Access is permitted to the filestore, the database, and an application programming interface. All aspects of the Universal Corpus are open, and we invite community participation in its design and implementation, and in supplying and using its data.

1 Introduction

We have previously proposed a community dataset of annotated text spanning a very large number of languages, with consistent annotation and format that enables automatic cross-linguistic processing on an unprecedented scale (Abney and Bird, 2010). Here we set out the data model in detail, and invite members of the computational linguistics community to begin work on the first version of the dataset.

The targeted annotation generalizes over three widely-used kinds of data: (1) simple bitexts, that is, tokenized texts and their translations, which are widely used for training machine translation systems; (2) interlinear glossed text (IGT), which adds lemmas, morphological features and parts of speech, and is the de facto standard in the documentary linguistics literature; and (3) dependency parses, which add a head pointer and relation name for each word, and are gaining popularity as representations of syntactic structure. We do not expect all texts to have equal richness of annotation; rather, these are the degrees of annotation we wish to explicitly accommodate. Keeping the annotation lightweight is a primary desideratum.

We strive for inclusion of as many languages as possible. We are especially interested in languages outside of the group of 30 or so for which there already exist non-trivial electronic resources. Optimistically, we aim for a *universal* corpus, in the sense of one that covers a widely representative set of the world's languages and supports inquiry into universal linguistics and development of language technologies with universal applicability.

We emphasize, however, that even if completely successful, it will be *a* universal corpus and not *the* universal corpus. The term "universal" should emphatically not be understood in the sense of encompassing all language annotation efforts. We are not proposing a standard or a philosophy of language documentation, but rather a design for one particular resource. Though the goals with regard to language coverage are unusually ambitious, for the sake of achievability we keep the targeted annotation as simple as possible. The result is intended to be a single, coherent dataset that is very *broad* in language coverage, but very *thin* in complexity of annotation.

Proceedings of the 4th Workshop on Building and Using Comparable Corpora, pages 120–127,
49th Annual Meeting of the Association for Computational Linguistics,
Portland, Oregon, 24 June 2011. ©*2011 Association for Computational Linguistics*

Finally, the development of the corpus is an unfunded, all-volunteer effort. It will only come about if it wins community buy-in, in the spirit of collaborative efforts like Project Gutenberg. We formulate it as a cooperation among data providers and hosting services to provide data in a manner that creates a single, seamless dataset from the user perspective. This paper is a first draft of a "cooperative agreement" that could achieve that goal.

2 A lightweight model for multilingual text

2.1 Media and annotation

In documentary linguistics, a distinction is made between language documentation, whose concern is the collection of primary documentation such as speech recordings and indigenous written works, and language description, whose concern is the annotation and organization of the primary material (Himmelmann, 1998). We make a similar distinction between media files and annotation, where "annotation" is understood broadly to include all processing steps that make the linguistic contents more explicit, including plain text rendering, sentence segmentation, and alignment of translations.

The Corpus consists of annotated documents, in the sense of primary documents with accompanying annotation. There are many efforts at collecting documentation for a broad range of languages; what makes this Corpus distinct is its focus on annotation. Accordingly, we assume that media files and annotation are handled separately.

For media, the Language Commons collection in the Internet Archive is a recently-established repository for redistributable language data that we view as the primary host.[1] For the annotation database, a primary data host remains to be established, but we have identified some options. For example, Amazon Web Services and the Talis Connected Commons have free hosting services for public data sets.

2.2 The data model in brief

In order to keep the barriers to participation as low as possible, we have made our target for annotation as simple as possible. The data model is summarized in Figure 1. We distinguish between **aligned texts** (or parallel texts) and **analyzed texts** (comparable texts).

Semantically, the entire collection of aligned texts constitutes a matrix whose columns are languages and whose rows are texts. We limit attention to three levels of granularity: document, sentence, and word. Each cell is occupied by a string, the typical length of the string varying with the granularity. We expect the matrix to be quite sparse: most cells are empty.

The collection of analyzed texts consists, semantically, of one table per language. The rows represent words and the columns are properties of the words. The words may either be tokens in a sentence analysis, as suggested by the examples, or types representing dictionary information. The tables are comparable, in the sense that they have a common format and are conducive to language-independent processing, but they are not parallel: the i-th word in the German table has nothing to do with the i-th word in the Spanish table.

The tables in Figure 1 constitute the bulk of the data model. In addition, we assume some auxiliary information (not depicted) that is primarily organizational. It includes an association between documents and sentences, the location of documents and sentences within media files (if applicable), a grouping of table rows into "files," and a grouping of files into "works." Metadata such as revision information is attached to files and works. We return below to the characterization of this auxiliary information.

In contrast to current standard practice, we wish to emphasize the status of aligned and analyzed text as annotation of primary documents represented by media files such as speech recordings or page images, and we wish to maintain explicit connections between annotations and primary documents. We do not insist that the underlying media files be available in all cases, but we hope to identify them when possible. However, we focus on storage of the annotation; we assume that media files are in a separate store, and referenced by external URIs.

2.3 Two implementations: filestore and database

The data model is abstract, and is implemented in a couple of ways for different purposes. For distribution on physical medium or by download, it is most convenient to implement the data model as actual

[1] `http://www.archive.org/details/LanguageCommons`

Aligned Texts

	deu	spa	fra	eng	...
d_1	*sie..*	*ella..*	*elle..*	*she..*	
d_2					
⋮					
s_1					
s_2					
⋮					
w_1					
w_2					
⋮					

Analyzed Texts

deu

	sent	form	lemma	morph	pos	gloss	head	rel
w_1	s_1	*Kühe*	*Kuh*	PL	*N*	*cow*	2	SBJ
w_2	s_1	*sind*	*sein*	PL	*V*	*be*	0	ROOT
⋮								

spa

	sent	form	lemma	morph	pos	gloss	head	rel
w_1	s_2	*estas*	*este*	F.PL	*D*	*this*	2	SPC
w_2	s_2	*floras*	*flora*	F.PL	*N*	*flower*	3	SBJ
⋮								

⋮

Figure 1: An overview of the targeted annotation: Aligned Texts in a single matrix having three levels of granularity (document, sentence, word), and Analyzed Texts grouped by language and annotated down to the word level with morphological, lexical and syntactic information.

files. Each file contains information corresponding to some slice of a table, and the structure of the table is encoded in the file format. On the other hand, web services are often implemented as databases, making an implementation of the abstract model as a database desirable.

A file-based implementation is most familiar, and most existing resources are available as file collections. However, even when different existing resources have similar semantics, such as different parallel text collections, there is considerable variety in the organization and representation of the information. In order to work with multiple such sources, a substantial amount of housekeeping is required. One can view our proposed filestore as a normalized form that removes the diversity that only gets in the way of efficient cross-language processing. Indeed, our proposed format for analyzed text hews intentionally close to the format used in the CoNLL dependency-parsing shared tasks, which provided a normal form into which data from multiple treebanks was mapped (Buchholz et al., 2006).

When an existing resource is included in the Corpus, we assume that it remains externally available in its original form, but a copy is imported into the Corpus filestore in which every file has been preprocessed into one of a set of simple file formats implementing the model of Figure 1, following a consistent scheme for filenames, with utf8 character encoding, and capturing any available alignment information in an auxiliary table. Distribution of the Corpus via physical media or download simply involves copying the filestore.

The filestore is organized around material provided by individual data providers, or "authors," and maintains the identity of a data provider's contribution as a distinct intellectual "work." Works provide an appropriate unit to which to attach edition and rights metadata.

In addition to the filestore, the texts and alignments are imported into a collection of database tables that can be queried efficiently.

In section 3 we describe a simple file-based implementation of the data model, and show the variety of familiar file types that find a natural place in the model. In section 4 we describe the tabular storage model.

3 Filestore implementation

Despite the simplicity of the data model, it captures a substantial, even surprising, variety of commonly-used textual data file types.

Document-aligned text. Parallel corpora are most commonly aligned at the document level. Typically, each translation of a document is contained in a file, and there is some way of indicating which files are mutual translations of the same document. The contents of a file, as a single string, represents one cell in the Aligned Text matrix in Figure 1 (at the "document" level of granularity). A document, comprising a collection of mutual translations, corresponds to a row of the matrix.

As normal form, we propose the convention of using filenames that incorporate a language identifier and a document identifier. For example, `1001-eng.txt` and `1001-deu.txt` are the English and German files representing mutual translations of some hypothetical document 1001.

Language identifiers are ISO 639-3 language code, supplemented by the Linguist List local-use codes and subgroup and dialect identifiers.

Sentence-aligned text. At a finer grain, parallel corpora may be aligned at the sentence level. Each file contains the translation of one document, segmented into one sentence per line. Our normal form uses the same filename convention as for document-aligned text, to indicate which files are mutual translations. We use the file suffix "`.snt`" to indicate a file with one sentence per line. This incidentally indicates which document a set of sentences came from, since the filenames share a document identifier. For example, the file `1001-deu.snt` contains the sentence-segmented version of `1001-deu.txt`.

In the canonical case, each file in a group of aligned files contains the same number of sentences, and the sentences line up one-to-one. The group of aligned files corresponds to a set of rows in the Aligned Text matrix, at the "sentence" level of granularity.

There are cases in which the sentence alignment between documents is not one-to-one. Even in this case, we can view the alignment as consisting of a sequence of "beads" that sometimes contain multiple sentences in one language. If we normalize the file to one in which the group of sentences belonging to a single bead are concatenated together as a "translational unit," we reduce this case to the one-to-one case, though we do lose the information about orthographic sentence boundaries internal to a bead.

Preserving the original sentences would necessitate an extension to the data model. A typical approach is to store the alignments in a table, where n-way alignments are indicated using n-tuples of integers. We leave this as a point for future consideration. We also put aside consideration of word-level document alignment.

Translation dictionaries. A translation dictionary contains word translations in multiple languages. One representation looks just like sentence-aligned text, except that each file contains one entry per line instead of one sentence per line. Each file in an aligned set contains the same number of entries, and the entries line up one-to-one across files. This is the representation we take as our normal form. We also use the same filename convention, but with suffix `.tdi` for translation dictionary.

A translation dictionary corresponds to a set of rows in the Aligned Text matrix, at the "word" level of granularity. A translation dictionary would typically be derived from a large number of text documents, so each translation dictionary will typically have a unique document identifier, and will not align with files at the sentence or document granularity.

Transcriptions and segmentations. When one begins with a sound recording or with page images from a print volume that has been scanned, a first step is conversion to plain text. We will call this a "transcription" both for the case where the original was a sound file and for the case where the original was a page image. Transcriptions fit into our data model as the special case of "document-aligned text" in which only one language is involved. We assume that the Aligned Text matrix is sparse, and this is the extreme case in which only one cell in a row is occupied. The connection between the transcript's document identifier and the original media file is recorded in an auxiliary metadata file.

After transcription, the next step in processing is to identify the parts of the text that are natural language (as opposed to markup or tables or the like), and to segment the natural language portion into sentences. The result is sentence-segmented text. Again, we treat this as the special case of sentence-aligned text in which only one language is involved.

Analyzed text. A variety of different text file types can be grouped together under the heading of analyzed text. The richest example we consider is dependency parse structure. One widely-used file representation has one word token per line. Each line consists of tab-separated fields containing attributes of the word token. There is some variation in the attributes that are specified, but the ones used in the Analyzed Text tables of our data model are typical, namely: sentence identifier, wordform, lemma, morphological form, gloss, part of speech, head (also called *governor*), and relation (also called *role*). Sentence boundaries are not represented as tokens; rather, tokens belonging to the same sentence share the same value for sentence identifier. We continue with the same filename convention as before; for Analyzed Text files, the suffix is `.tab`.

Many different linguistic annotations are naturally represented as special cases of Analyzed Text.

- Tokenized text in "vertical format" is the special case in which the only column is the wordform column. We include the sentence ID column as well, in lieu of sentence-boundary tokens.
- POS-tagged text adds the part of speech column.
- The information in the word-by-word part of interlinear glossed text (IGT) typically includes the wordform, lemma, morph, and gloss; again we also include the sentence ID column.
- A dependency parse, as already indicated, is the case in which all columns are present.

In addition, the format accommodates a variety of monolingual and multilingual lexical resources. Such lexical resources are essential, whether manually curated or automatically extracted.

- A basic dictionary consists of a sequence of entries, each of which contains a lemma, part of speech, and gloss. Hence a dictionary is naturally represented as analyzed text containing just those three columns. The entries in a dictionary are word types rather than word tokens, so the wordform and sentence ID columns are absent.
- If two or more lexicons use the same glosses, the lexicons are implicitly aligned by virtue of the glosses and there is no need for overt alignment information. This is a more flexible representation than a translation dictionary: unlike a translation dictionary, it permits multiple words to have the same gloss (synonyms), and it adds parts of speech.

4 Database implementation

An alternative implementation, appropriate for deployment of the Corpus as a web service, is as a normalized, multi-table database. In this section we drill down and consider the kinds of tables and records that would be required in order to represent our abstract data model. We will proceed by way of example, for each of the kinds of data we would like to accommodate. Each example is displayed as a record consisting of a series of named fields.

Note that we make no firm commitment as to the physical format of these records. They could be serialized as XML when the database is implemented as a web service. Equally, they could be represented using dictionaries or tuples when the database is accessed via an application program interface (API). We will return to this later.

4.1 The Aligned Text matrix

The Aligned Text matrix is extremely sparse. We use the more flexible representation in which each matrix cell is stored using a separate record, where the record specifies (index, column) pairs. For example, the matrix row

	deu	spa	fra
d_1	*Sie...*	*Ella...*	
d_2	*Mein...*		*Mon...*

is represented as

Document Table

DID	LANG	TEXT
1	*deu*	*Sie...*
1	*spa*	*Ella...*
2	*deu*	*Mein...*
2	*fra*	*Mon...*

(The ellipses are intended to indicate that each cell contains the entire text of a document.) We have also added an explicit document ID.

When we consider entries at the sentence and word levels, we require both a document ID and sentence or word IDs within the document. Figure 2 shows an example of two sentences from the same document, translated into two languages. Note that we can think of DID + LANG as an identifier for a monolingual document instance, and DID + LANG + SID identifies a particular sentence in a monolingual document.

DID	LANG	SID	TEXT
1	deu	1	Der Hund bellte.
1	eng	1	the dog barked.
1	deu	2	Mein Vater ist Augenarzt.
1	eng	2	My father is an optometrist.

Figure 2: Two sentences with two translations. These are sentence table records.

In short, we implement the Aligned Text matrix as three database tables. All three tables have columns DID, LANG, and TEXT. The sentence table adds SID, and the word table adds WID instead of SID. (The words are types, not tokens, hence are not associated with any particular sentence.)

4.2 The Analyzed Text tables

The implementation of the Analyzed Text tables is straightforward. We add a column for the document ID, and we assume that sentence ID is relative to the document. We also represent the word token ID explicitly, and take it to be relative to the sentence. Finally, we add a column for LANG, so that we have a single table rather than one per language.

The first record from the German table in Figure 1 is implemented as in Figure 3. This is a record from a dependency parse. Other varieties of analyzed text leave some of the columns empty, as discussed in the previous section.

There is a subtlety to note. In the sentence table, the entry with `DID` 1, `SID` 1, and `LANG` "deu" is understood to be a translation of the entry with `DID` 1, `SID` 1, and `LANG` "eng." That is not the case with records in the analyzed-text table. Word 1 in the English sentence 1 of document 1 is not necessarily a translation of word 1 in the German sentence 1 of document 1.

A few comments are in order about the meanings of the columns. The wordform is the attested, inflected form of the word token. The `LEMMA` provides the lexical form, which is the headword under which one would find the word in a dictionary. The `MORPH` field provides a symbolic indicator of the relationship between the lemma and the wordform. For example, "Kühe" is the `PL` form of the lemma "Kuh."

This approach encompasses arbitrary morphological processes. For example, Hebrew *lomedet* may be represented as the `PRESPTC.FEM.SG` form of *lmd,* ("to learn").

When we represent dictionaries, the records are word types rather than word tokens. We assign a document ID to the dictionary as a whole, but by convention take the `SID` to be uniformly 0.

Ultimately, the `POS` and `GLOSS` fields are intended to contain symbols from controlled vocabularies. For the present, the choice of controlled vocabulary is up to the annotator. For the `GLOSS` field, an option that has the benefit of simplicity is to use the corresponding word from a reference language, but one might equally well use synset identifiers from WordNet, or concepts in some ontology.

4.3 The auxiliary tables

The auxiliary tables were not shown in the abstract data model as depicted in Figure 1. They primarily include metadata. We assume a table that associates each document ID with a work, and a table that provides metadata for each work. The Corpus as a whole is the sum of the works.

In the spirit of not duplicating existing efforts, we "outsource" the bulk of the metadata to OLAC (Simons and Bird, 2003). If a work has an OLAC entry, we only need to associate the internal document ID to the OLAC identifier.

There is some metadata information that we would like to include for which we cannot refer to OLAC.

- Provenance: how the annotation was constructed, e.g., who the annotator was, or what software was used if it was automatically created.
- Rights: copyright holder, license category chosen from a small set of interoperable licenses.
- Standards: allows the annotator to indicate which code sets are used for the `MORPH`, `POS`, and `GLOSS` fields. We would like to be able to specify a standard code set for each, in the same way that we have specified ISO 639-3 for language codes. Consensus has not yet crystallized around any one standard, however.

The auxiliary tables also associate documents with media files. We assume a table associating document IDs with a media files, represented by

DID	LANG	SID	WID	FORM	LEMMA	MORPH	POS	GLOSS	HEAD	REL
123	deu	1	1	Kühe	Kuh	PL	N	cow	2	SBJ

Figure 3: A single word from a dependency parse. This is a record from the analyzed-text table.

their URLs, and a table associating sentences (`DID` + `SID`) with locations in media files.

Note that, as we have defined the file and tabular implementations, there is no need for an explicit mapping between document IDs and filenames. A filename is always of the form *did–lang.suffix*, where the suffix is `.txt` for the document table, `.snt` for the sentence table, `.tdi` for the word table, and `.tab` for the analyzed-text table. Each file corresponds to a set of records in one of the tables.

5 Cloud Storage and Interface

A third interface to the Corpus is via an application programming interface. We illustrate a possible Python API using Amazon SimpleDB, a cloud-hosted tuple store accessed via a web services interface.[2] An "item" is a collection of attribute-value pairs, and is stored in a "domain." Items, attributes, and domains are roughly equivalent to records, fields, and tables in a relational database. Unlike relational databases, new attributes and domains can be added at any time.

Boto is a Python interface to Amazon Web Services that includes support for SimpleDB.[3] The following code shows an interactive session in which a connection is established and a domain is created:

```
>>> import boto
>>> sdb = boto.connect_sdb(PUBLIC_KEY, PRIVATE_KEY)
>>> domain = sdb.create_domain('analyzed_text')
```

We can create a new item, then use Python's dictionary syntax to create attribute-value pairs, before saving it:

```
>>> item = domain.new_item('123')
>>> item['DID'] = '123'
>>> item['LANG'] = 'deu'
>>> item['FORM'] = 'Kühe'
>>> item['GLOSS'] = 'cow'
>>> item['HEAD'] = '2'
>>> item.save()
```

Finally, we can retrieve an item by name, or submit a query using SQL-like syntax.

```
>>> sdb.get_attributes(domain, '123')
'LANG': 'deu', 'HEAD': '2', 'DID': '123',
'FORM': 'Kühe', 'GLOSS': 'cow'
>>> sdb.select(domain,
... 'select DID, FORM from analyzed_text
... where LANG = "deu"')
['DID': '123', 'FORM': 'Kühe']
```

We have developed an NLTK "corpus reader" which understands the Giza and NAACL03 formats for bilingual texts, and creates a series of records for insertion into SimpleDB using the Boto interface. Other formats will be added over time.

Beyond the loading of corpora, a range of query and report generation functions are needed, as illustrated in the following (non-exhaustive) list:

- `lookup(lang=ENG, rev="1.2b3", ...)`: find all items which have the specified attribute values, returning a list of dictionaries; following Python syntax, we indicate this variable number of keyword arguments with `**kwargs`.
- `extract(type=SENT, lang=[ENG, FRA, DEU], **kwargs)`: extract all aligned sentences involving English, French, and German, which meet any further constraints specified in the keyword arguments. (When called `extract(type=SENT)` this will extract all sentence alignments across all 7,000 languages, cf Figure 1.)
- `dump(type=SENT, format="giza", lang=[ENG, FRA], **kwargs)`: dump English-French bitext in Giza format.
- `extract(type=LEX, lang=[ENG, FRA, ...], **kwargs)`: produce a comparative wordlist for the specified languages.
- `dump(type=LEX, format="csv", lang=[ENG, FRA, ...], **kwargs)`: produce the wordlist in comma-separated values format.

Additional functions will be required for discovery (which annotations exist for an item?), navigation (which file does an item come from?), citation (which publications should be cited in connection with these items?), and report generation (what type and quantity of material exists for each language?).

[2] `http://aws.amazon.com/simpledb/`

[3] `http://code.google.com/p/boto/`

Further functionality could support annotation. We do not wish to enable direct modification of database fields, since everything in the Corpus comes from contributed corpora. Instead, we could foster user input and encourage crowdsourcing of annotations by developing software clients that access the Corpus using methods such as the ones already described, and which save any new annotations as just another work to be added to the Corpus.

6 Further design considerations

Versioning. When a work is contributed, it comes with (or is assigned) a version, or "edition." Multiple editions of a work may coexist in the Corpus, and each edition will have distinct filenames and identifiers to avoid risk of collision. Now, it may happen that works reference each other, as when a base text from one work is POS-tagged in another. For this reason, we treat editions as immutable. Modifications to a work are accumulated and released as a new edition. When a new edition of a base text is released, stand-off annotations of that text (such as the POS-tagging in our example) will need to be updated in turn, a task that should be largely automated. A new edition of the annotation, anchored to the new edition of the base text, is then released. The old editions remain unchanged, though they may be flagged as obsolete and may eventually be deleted.

Licensing. Many corpora come with license conditions that prevent them from being included. In some cases, this is due to license fees that are paid by institutional subscription. Here, we need to explore a new subscription model based on access. In some cases, corpus redistribution is not permitted, simply in order to ensure that all downloads occur from one site (and can be counted as evidence of impact), and so that users agree to cite the scholarly publication about the corpus. Here we can offer data providers a credible alternative: anonymized usage tracking, and an automatic way for authors to identify the publications associated with any slice of the Corpus, facilitating comprehensive citation.

Publication. The Corpus will be an online publication, with downloadable dated snapshots, evolving continually as new works and editions are added. An editorial process will be required, to ensure that contributions are appropriate, and to avoid spamming. A separate staging area would facilitate checking of incoming materials prior to release.

7 Conclusion

We have described the design and implementation of a Universal Corpus containing aligned and annotated text collections for the world's languages. We follow the same principles we set out earlier (Abney and Bird, 2010, 2.2), promoting a community-level effort to collect bilingual texts and lexicons for as many languages as possible, in a consistent format that facilitates machine processing across languages. We have proposed a normalized filestore model that integrates with current practice on the supply side, where corpora are freestanding works in a variety of formats and multiple editions. We have also devised a normalized database model which encompasses the desired range of linguistic objects, alignments, and annotations. Finally, we have argued that this model scales, and enables a view of the Universal Corpus as a vast matrix of aligned and analyzed texts spanning the world's languages, a radical departure from existing resource creation efforts in language documentation and machine translation.

We invite participation by the community in elaborating the design, implementing the storage model, and populating it with data. Furthermore, we seek collaboration in using such data as the basis for large-scale cross-linguistic analysis and modeling, and in facilitating the creation of easily accessible language resources for the world's languages.

References

Steven Abney and Steven Bird. 2010. The Human Language Project: building a universal corpus of the world's languages. In *Proc. 48th ACL*, pages 88–97. Association for Computational Linguistics.

Sabine Buchholz, Erwin Marsi, Yuval Krymolowski, and Amit Dubey. 2006. CoNLL-X shared task: Multilingual dependency parsing. `http://ilk.uvt.nl/conll/`. Accessed May 2011.

Nikolaus P. Himmelmann. 1998. Documentary and descriptive linguistics. *Linguistics*, 36:161–195.

Gary Simons and Steven Bird. 2003. The Open Language Archives Community: An infrastructure for distributed archiving of language resources. *Literary and Linguistic Computing*, 18:117–128.

An Expectation Maximization Algorithm for Textual Unit Alignment

Radu Ion
Research Institute for AI
Calea 13 Septembrie nr. 13
Bucharest 050711, Romania
radu@racai.ro

Alexandru Ceauşu
Dublin City University
Glasnevin, Dublin 9, Ireland
[address3]
aceausu@computing.dcu.ie

Elena Irimia
Research Institute for AI
Calea 13 Septembrie nr. 13
Bucharest 050711, Romania
elena@racai.ro

Abstract

The paper presents an Expectation Maximization (EM) algorithm for automatic generation of parallel and quasi-parallel data from any degree of comparable corpora ranging from parallel to weakly comparable. Specifically, we address the problem of extracting related textual units (documents, paragraphs or sentences) relying on the hypothesis that, in a given corpus, certain pairs of translation equivalents are better indicators of a correct textual unit correspondence than other pairs of translation equivalents. We evaluate our method on mixed types of bilingual comparable corpora in six language pairs, obtaining state of the art accuracy figures.

1 Introduction

Statistical Machine Translation (SMT) is in a constant need of good quality training data both for translation models and for the language models. Regarding the latter, monolingual corpora is evidently easier to collect than parallel corpora and the truth of this statement is even more obvious when it comes to pairs of languages other than those both widely spoken and computationally well-treated around the world such as English, Spanish, French or German.

Comparable corpora came as a possible solution to the problem of scarcity of parallel corpora with the promise that it may serve as a seed for parallel data extraction. A general definition of comparability that we find operational is given by Munteanu and Marcu (2005). They say that a (bilingual) comparable corpus is a set of paired documents that, *while not parallel in the strict sense, are related and convey overlapping information*.

Current practices of automatically collecting domain-dependent bilingual comparable corpora from the Web usually begin with collecting a list of t terms as seed data in both the source and the target languages. Each term (in each language) is then queried on the most popular search engine and the first N document hits are retained. The final corpus will contain $t \times N$ documents in each language and in subsequent usage the document boundaries are often disregarded.

At this point, it is important to stress out the importance of the pairing of documents in a comparable corpus. Suppose that we want to word-align a bilingual comparable corpus consisting of M documents per language, each with k words, using the IBM-1 word alignment algorithm (Brown et al., 1993). This algorithm searches for each source word, the target words that have a maximum translation probability with the source word. Aligning all the words in our corpus with no regard to document boundaries, would yield a time complexity of k^2M^2 operations. The alternative would be in finding a 1:p (with p a small positive integer, usually 1, 2 or 3) document assignment (a set of aligned document pairs) that would enforce the "no search outside the document boundary" condition when doing word alignment with the advantage of reducing the time complexity to k^2Mp operations. When M is large, the reduction may actually be vital to getting a result in a reasonable amount of time. The downside of this simplification is the loss of information: two documents may not be correctly aligned thus depriving the word-alignment algorithm of the part of the search space that would have contained the right alignments.

Proceedings of the 4th Workshop on Building and Using Comparable Corpora, pages 128–135,
49th Annual Meeting of the Association for Computational Linguistics,
Portland, Oregon, 24 June 2011. ©*2011 Association for Computational Linguistics*

Word alignment forms the basis of the phrase alignment procedure which, in turn, is the basis of any statistical translation model. A comparable corpus differs essentially from a parallel corpus by the fact that textual units do not follow a translation order that otherwise greatly reduces the word alignment search space in a parallel corpus. Given this limitation of a comparable corpus in general and the sizes of the comparable corpora that we will have to deal with in particular, we have devised one variant of an Expectation Maximization (EM) algorithm (Dempster et al., 1977) that generates a 1:1 (p = 1) document assignment from a parallel and/or comparable corpus using only pre-existing translation lexicons. Its generality would permit it to perform the same task on other textual units such as paragraphs or sentences.

In what follows, we will briefly review the literature discussing document/paragraph alignment and then we will present the derivation of the EM algorithm that generates 1:1 document alignments. We will end the article with a thorough evaluation of the performances of this algorithm and the conclusions that arise from these evaluations.

2 Related Work

Document alignment and other types of textual unit alignment have been attempted in various situations involving extracting parallel data from comparable corpora. The first case study is offered by Munteanu and Marcu (2002). They align sentences in an English-French comparable corpus of 1.3M of words per language by comparing suffix trees of the sentences. Each sentence from each part of the corpus is encoded as a suffix tree which is a tree that stores each possible suffix of a string from the last character to the full string. Using this method, Munteanu and Marcu are able to detect correct sentence alignments with a precision of 95% (out of 100 human-judged and randomly selected sentences from the generated output). The running time of their algorithm is approximately 100 hours for 50000 sentences in each of the languages.

A popular method of aligning sentences in a comparable corpus is by classifying pairs of sentences as parallel or not parallel. Munteanu and Marcu (2005) use a Maximum Entropy classifier for the job trained with the following features: sentence lengths and their differences and ratios, percentage of the words in a source sentence that have translations in a target sentence (translations are taken from pre-existing translation lexicons), the top three largest fertilities, length of the longest sequence of words that have translations, etc. The training data consisted of a small parallel corpus of 5000 sentences per language. Since the number of negative instances ($5000^2 - 5000$) is far more large than the number of positive ones (5000), the negative training instances were selected randomly out of instances that passed a certain word overlap filter (see the paper for details). The classifier precision is around 97% with a recall of 40% at the Chinese-English task and around 95% with a recall of 41% for the Arabic-English task.

Another case study of sentence alignment that we will present here is that of Chen (1993). He employs an EM algorithm that will find a sentence alignment in a parallel corpus which maximizes the translation probability for each sentence bead in the alignment. The translation probability to be maximized by the EM procedure considering each possible alignment $\mathcal{A}$ is given by

$$P(\mathcal{E},\mathcal{F},\mathcal{A}) = p(L)\prod_{k=1}^{L} P([E_p^k; F_p^k])$$

The following notations were used: $\mathcal{E}$ is the English corpus (a sequence of English sentences), $\mathcal{F}$ is the French corpus, $[E_p^k; F_p^k]$ is a sentence bead (a pairing of m sentences in English with n sentences in French), $\mathcal{A} = ([E_p^1; F_p^1], \ldots, [E_p^L; F_p^L])$ is the sentence alignment (a sequence of sentence beads) and $p(L)$ is the probability that an alignment contains L beads. The obtained accuracy is around 96% and was computed indirectly by checking disagreement with the Brown sentence aligner (Brown et al., 1991) on randomly selected 500 disagreement cases.

The last case study of document and sentence alignment from "very-non-parallel corpora" is the work from Fung and Cheung (2004). Their contribution to the problem of textual unit alignment resides in devising a bootstrapping mechanism in which, after an initial document pairing and consequent sentence alignment using a lexical overlapping similarity measure, IBM-4 model (Brown et al., 1993) is employed to enrich the bilingual dictionary that is used by the similarity measure. The process is repeated until the set of identified aligned sentences does not grow anymore. The precision of this method on English-Chinese sentence alignment is 65.7% (out of the top 2500 identified pairs).

3 EMACC

We propose *a specific instantiation of the well-known general EM algorithm* for aligning different types of textual units: documents, paragraphs, and sentences which we will name EMACC (an acronym for "Expectation Maximization Alignment for Comparable Corpora"). We draw our inspiration from the famous IBM models (specifically from the IBM-1 model) for word alignment (Brown et al., 1993) where the translation probability (eq. (5)) is modeled through an EM algorithm where the hidden variable **a** models the assignment (1:1 word alignments) from the French sequence of words (' indexes) to the English one.

By analogy, we imagined that between two sets of documents (from now on, we will refer to documents as our textual units but what we present here is equally applicable – but with different performance penalties – to paragraphs and/or sentences) – let's call them **E** and **F**, there is *an assignment* (a sequence of 1:1 document correspondences[1]), the distribution of which can be modeled by a hidden variable z taking values in the set {true, false}. This assignment will be largely determined by the existence of word translations between a pair of documents, translations that can differentiate between one another in their ability to indicate a correct document alignment versus an incorrect one. In other words, we hypothesize that there are certain pairs of translation equivalents that are better indicators of a correct document correspondence than other translation equivalents pairs.

We take the general formulation and derivation of the EM optimization problem from (Borman, 2009). The general goal is to optimize $P(X|\Theta)$, that is to find the parameter(s) Θ for which $P(X|\Theta)$ is maximum. In a sequence of derivations that we are not going to repeat here, the general EM equation is given by:

$$\Theta_{n+1} = \underset{\Theta}{\operatorname{argmax}} \sum_{z} P(z|X, \Theta_n) \ln P(X, z|\Theta) \quad (1)$$

where $\sum_z P(z|X, \Theta_n) = 1$. At step n+1, we try to obtain a new parameter Θ_{n+1} that is going to maximize (the maximization step) the sum over z (the expectation step) that in its turn depends on the best parameter Θ_n obtained at step n. Thus, in principle, the algorithm *should iterate over the set of all possible Θ parameters*, compute the expectation expression for each of these parameters and choose the parameter(s) for which the expression has the largest value. But as we will see, in practice, the set of all possible parameters has a dimension that is exponential in terms of the number of parameters. This renders the problem intractable and one should back off to heuristic searches in order to find a near-optimal solution.

We now introduce a few notations that we will operate with from this point forward. We suggest to the reader *to frequently refer to this section* in order to properly understand the next equations:

- **E** is the set of source documents, $|\mathbf{E}|$ is the cardinal of this set;
- **F** is the set of target documents with $|\mathbf{F}|$ its cardinal;
- d_{ij} is a pair of documents, $d_i \in \mathbf{E}$ and $d_j \in \mathbf{F}$;
- w_{ij} is a pair of translation equivalents $\langle w_i, w_j \rangle$ such that w_i is a lexical item that belongs to d_i and w_j is a lexical item that belongs to d_j;
- **T** is the set of all existing translation equivalents pairs $\langle w_{ij}, p \rangle$. p is the translation probability score (as the one given for instance by GIZA++ (Gao and Vogel, 2008)). We assume that GIZA++ translation lexicons already exist for the pair of languages of interest.

In order to tie equation 1 to our problem, we define its variables as follows:

- Θ is the sequence of 1:1 document alignments of the form $D_{i_1 j_1}, D_{i_2 j_2}, \dots, D_{ij} \in \{d_{ij} | d_i \in \mathbf{E}, d_j \in \mathbf{F}\}$. We call Θ *an assignment* which is basically a sequence of 1:1 document alignments. If there are $|\mathbf{E}|$ 1:1 document alignments in Θ and if $|\mathbf{E}| \leq |\mathbf{F}|$, then the set of all possible assignments has

[1] Or "alignments" or "pairs". These terms will be used with the same meaning throughout the presentation.

the cardinal equal to $|\mathbf{E}|!\binom{|\mathbf{F}|}{|\mathbf{E}|}$ where $n!$ is the factorial function of the integer n and $\binom{n}{k}$ is the binomial coefficient. It is clear now that with this kind of dimension of the set of all possible assignments (or Θ parameters), we cannot simply iterate over it in order to choose the assignment that maximizes the expectation;

- $z \in \{\text{true,false}\}$ is the hidden variable that signals if a pair of documents d_{ij} represents a correct alignment (true) or not (false);
- X is the sequence of translation equivalents pairs W_{ij} from **T** in the order they appear in each document pair from Θ.

Having defined the variables in equation 1 this way, we aim at maximizing the translation equivalents probability over a given assignment, $P(X|\Theta)$. In doing so, through the use of the hidden variable z, we are also able to find the 1:1 document alignments that attest for this maximization.

We proceed by reducing equation 1 to a form that is readily amenable to software coding. That is, we aim at obtaining some distinct probability tables that are going to be (re-)estimated by the EM procedure. Due to the lack of space, we omit the full derivation and directly give the general form of the derived EM equation

$$\Theta_{n+1} = \underset{\Theta}{\text{argmax}}[\ln P(X|\Theta) + \ln P(\text{true}|\Theta)] \quad (2)$$

Equation 2 suggests a method of updating the assignment probability $P(\text{true}|\Theta)$ with the lexical alignment probability $P(X|\Theta)$ in an effort to provide the alignment clues that will "guide" the assignment probability towards the correct assignment. All it remains to do now is to define the two probabilities.

The **lexical document alignment probability** $P(X|\Theta)$ is defined as follows:

$$P(X|\Theta) = \prod_{d_{ab}\in\Theta} \frac{\sum_{w_{ij}\in X} P(d_{ab}|w_{ij})}{|\mathbf{E}||\mathbf{F}|} \quad (3)$$

where $P(d_{ab}|w_{ij})$ is the simplified lexical document alignment probability which is initially equal to $P(w_{ij})$ from the set **T**. This probability is to be read as "the contribution w_{ij} makes to the correctness of the d_{ab} alignment". We want that the alignment contribution of one translation equivalents pair w_{ij} to distribute over the set of all possible document pairs thus enforcing that

$$\sum_{d_{ab}\in\{d_{xy}|d_x\in\mathbf{E},\, d_y\in\mathbf{F}\}} P(d_{ab}|w_{ij}) = 1 \quad (4)$$

The summation over X in equation 3 is actually over all translation equivalents pairs that are to be found only in the current d_{ab} document pair and the presence of the product $|\mathbf{E}||\mathbf{F}|$ ensures that we still have a probability value.

The **assignment probability** $P(\text{true}|\Theta)$ is also defined in the following way:

$$P(\text{true}|\Theta) = \prod_{d_{ab}\in\Theta} P(d_{ab}|\text{true}) \quad (5)$$

for which we enforce the condition:

$$\sum_{d_{ab}\in\{d_{xy}|d_x\in\mathbf{E},\, d_y\in\mathbf{F}\}} P(d_{ab}|\text{true}) = 1 \quad (6)$$

Using equations 2, 3 and 5 we deduce the final, computation-ready EM equation

$$\begin{aligned}\Theta_{n+1} &= \\ &= \underset{\Theta}{\text{argmax}}\left[\ln \prod_{d_{ab}\in\Theta} \frac{\sum_{w_{ij}\in X} P(d_{ab}|w_{ij})}{|\mathbf{E}||\mathbf{F}|}\right. \\ &\left. + \ln \prod_{d_{ab}\in\Theta} P(d_{ab}|\text{true})\right] \\ &= \underset{\Theta}{\text{argmax}} \sum_{d_{ab}\in\Theta}\left[\ln \frac{\sum_{w_{ij}\in X} P(d_{ab}|w_{ij})}{|\mathbf{E}||\mathbf{F}|}\right. \\ &\left. + \ln P(d_{ab}|\text{true})\right]\end{aligned} \quad (7)$$

As it is, equation 7 suggests an exhaustive search *in the set of all possible Θ parameters*, in order to find the parameter(s) for which the expression that is the argument of "argmax" is maximum. But, as we know from section 3, the size of this this set is prohibitive to the attempt of enumerating each Θ assignment and computing the expectation expression. Our quick solution to this problem was to directly construct the "best" Θ assignment[2] using a

[2] We did not attempt to find the mathematical maximum of the expression from equation 7 and we realize that the conse-

greedy algorithm: simply iterate over all possible 1:1 document pairs and for each document pair $d_{ab} \in \{d_{xy} | d_x \in \mathbf{E},\ d_y \in \mathbf{F}\}$, compute the alignment count (it's not a probability so we call it a "count" following IBM-1 model's terminology)

$$\ln \frac{\sum_{w_{ij} \in X} P(d_{ab}|w_{ij})}{|\mathbf{E}||\mathbf{F}|} + \ln P(d_{ab}|\mathrm{true})$$

Then, construct the best 1:1 assignment Θ_{n+1} by choosing those pairs d_{ab} for which we have counts with the maximum values. Before this cycle (which is the basic EM cycle) is resumed, we perform the following updates:

$$P(d_{ab}|\mathrm{true}) \leftarrow P(d_{ab}|\mathrm{true}) + \frac{\sum_{w_{ij} \in X} P(d_{ab}|w_{ij})}{|\mathbf{E}||\mathbf{F}|} \quad (7a)$$

$$P(d_{ab}|w_{ij}) \leftarrow \sum_{d_{xy} \in \Theta_{n+1}} P(d_{xy}|w_{ij}) \quad (7b)$$

and normalize the two probability tables with equations 6 and 4. The first update is to be interpreted as the contribution the lexical document alignment probability makes to the alignment probability. The second update equation aims at boosting the probability of a translation equivalent if and only if it is found in a pair of documents belonging to the best assignment so far. In this way, we hope that the updated translation equivalent will make a better contribution to the discovery of a correct document alignment that has not yet been discovered at step $n + 1$.

Before we start the EM iterations, we need to initialize the probability tables $P(d_{ab}|\mathrm{true})$ and $P(d_{ab}|w_{ij})$. For the second table we used the GIZA++ scores that we have for the w_{ij} translation equivalents pairs and normalized the table with equation 4. For the first probability table we have (and tried) two choices:

- (**D1**) a uniform distribution: $\frac{1}{|\mathbf{E}||\mathbf{F}|}$;
- (**D2**) a lexical document alignment measure $L(d_{ab})$ (values between 0 and 1) that is computed directly from a pair of documents d_{ab} using the w_{ij} translation equivalents pairs from the dictionary **T**:

$$L(d_{ab}) = \frac{\sum_{w_i \text{ in } d_a} f_{d_a}(w_i) \sum_{w_j \text{ in } d_b} f_{d_b}(w_j)}{|d_a||d_b|} \quad (8)$$

where $|d_a|$ is the number of words in document d_a and $f_{d_a}(w_i)$ is the frequency of word w_i in document d_a (please note that, according to section 3, w_{ij} *is not* a random pair of words, but a pair of *translation equivalents*). If every word in the source document has at least one translation (of a given threshold probability score) in the target document, then this measure is 1. We normalize the table initialized using this measure with equation 6.

EMACC finds only 1:1 textual units alignments in its present form but a document pair d_{ab} can be easily extended to a document bead following the example from (Chen, 1993). The main difference between the algorithm described by Chen and ours is that the search procedure reported there is invalid for comparable corpora in which no pruning is available due to the nature of the corpus. A second very important difference is that Chen only relies on lexical alignment information, on the parallel nature of the corpus and on sentence lengths correlations while we add the probability of the whole assignment which, when initially set to the D2 distribution, produces a significant boost of the precision of the alignment.

4 Experiments and Evaluations

The test data for document alignment was compiled from the corpora that was previously collected in the ACCURAT project[3] and that is known to the project members as the "Initial Comparable Corpora" or ICC for short. It is important to know the fact that ICC contains all types of comparable corpora from parallel to weakly comparable documents but we classified document pairs in three classes: parallel (class name: **p**), strongly comparable (**cs**) and weakly comparable (**cw**). We have considered the following pairs of languages: English-Romanian (en-ro), English-Latvian (en-lv), English-Lithuanian (en-lt), English-Estonian (en-et), English-Slovene (en-sl) and English-Greek

quence of this choice and of the greedy search procedure is not finding the true optimum.

[3] http://www.accurat-project.eu/

(en-el). For each pair of languages, ICC also contains a Gold Standard list of document alignments that were compiled by hand for testing purposes.

We trained GIZA++ translation lexicons for every language pair using the DGT-TM[4] corpus. The input texts were converted from their Unicode encoding to UTF-8 and were tokenized using a tokenizer web service described by Ceauşu (2009). Then, we applied a parallel version of GIZA++ (Gao and Vogel, 2008) that gave us the translation dictionaries of content words only (nouns, verbs, adjective and adverbs) at wordform level. For Romanian, Lithuanian, Latvian, Greek and English, we had lists of inflectional suffixes which we used to stem entries in respective dictionaries and processed documents. Slovene remained the only language which involved wordform level processing.

The accuracy of EMACC is influenced by three parameters whose values have been experimentally set:

- the threshold over which we use translation equivalents from the dictionary **T** for textual unit alignment; values for this threshold (let's name it **ThrGiza**) are from the ordered set {0.001,0.4,0.8};
- the threshold over which we decide to update the probabilities of translation equivalents with equation 7b; values for this threshold (named **ThrUpdate**) are from the same ordered set {0.001,0.4,0.8};
- the top **ThrOut**% alignments from the best assignment found by EMACC. This parameter will introduce precision and recall with the "perfect" value for recall equal to **ThrOut**%. Values for this parameter are from the set {0.3,0.7,1}.

We ran EMACC (10 EM steps) on every possible combination of these parameters for the pairs of languages in question on both initial distributions D1 and D2. For comparison, we also performed a baseline document alignment using the greedy algorithm of EMACC with the equation 8 supplying the document similarity measure. The following 4 tables report a synthesis of the results we have obtained which, because of the lack of space, we cannot give in full. We omit the results of EMACC with D1 initial distribution because the accuracy figures (both precision and recall) are always lower (10-20%) than those of EMACC with D2.

cs	**P**/R	Prms.	P/**R**	Prms.	#
en-ro	1/ 0.69047	0.4 0.4 0.7	0.85714/ 0.85714	0.4 0.4 1	42
en-sl	0.96666/ 0.28807	0.4 0.4 0.3	0.83112/ 0.83112	0.4 0.4 1	302
en-el	0.97540/ 0.29238	0.001 0.8 0.3	0.80098/ 0.80098	0.001 0.4 1	407
en-lt	0.97368/ 0.29191	0.4 0.8 0.3	0.72978/ 0.72978	0.4 0.4 1	507
en-lv	0.95757/ 0.28675	0.4 0.4 0.3	0.79854/ 0.79854	0.001 0.8 1	560
en-et	0.88135/ 0.26442	0.4 0.8 0.3	0.55182/ 0.55182	0.4 0.4 1	987

Table 1: EMACC with D2 initial distribution on strongly comparable corpora

cs	**P**/R	Prms.	P/**R**	Prms.	#
en-ro	1/ 0.69047	0.4 0.7	0.85714/ 0.85714	0.4 1	42
en-sl	0.97777/ 0.29139	0.001 0.3	0.81456/ 0.81456	0.4 0.1	302
en-el	0.94124/ 0.28148	0.001 0.3	0.71851/ 0.71851	0.001 1	407
en-lt	0.95364/ 0.28514	0.001 0.3	0.72673/ 0.72673	0.001 1	507
en-lv	0.91463/ 0.27322	0.001 0.3	0.80692/ 0.80692	0.001 1	560
en-et	0.87030/ 0.26100	0.4 0.3	0.57727/ 0.57727	0.4 1	987

Table 2: D2 baseline algorithm on strongly comparable corpora

cw	**P**/R	Prms.	P/**R**	Prms.	#
en-ro	1/ 0.29411	0.4 0.001 0.3	0.66176/ 0.66176	0.4 0.001 1	68
en-sl	0.73958/ 0.22164	0.4 0.4 0.3	0.42767/ 0.42767	0.4 0.4 1	961
en-el	0.15238/ 0.04545	0.001 0.8 0.3	0.07670/ 0.07670	0.001 0.8 1	352
en-lt	0.55670/ 0.16615	0.4 0.8 0.3	0.28307/ 0.28307	0.4 0.8 1	325
en-lv	0.23529/ 0.07045	0.4 0.4 0.3	0.10176/ 0.10176	0.4 0.4 1	511
en-et	0.59027/ 0.17634	0.4 0.8 0.3	0.27800/ 0.27800	0.4 0.8 1	483

Table 3: EMACC with D2 initial distribution on weakly comparable corpora

[4] http://langtech.jrc.it/DGT-TM.html

cw	**P**/R	Prms.	P/**R**	Prms.	#
en-ro	0.85/ 0.25	0.4 0.3	0.61764/ 0.61764	0.4 1	68
en-sl	0.65505/ 0.19624	0.4 0.3	0.39874/ 0.39874	0.4 1	961
en-el	0.11428/ 0.03428	0.4 0.3	0.06285/ 0.06285	0.4 1	352
en-lt	0.60416/ 0.18012	0.4 0.3	0.24844/ 0.24844	0.4 1	325
en-lv	0.13071/ 0.03921	0.4 0.3	0.09803/ 0.09803	0.4 1	511
en-et	0.48611/ 0.14522	0.001 0.3	0.25678/ 0.25678	0.4 1	483

Table 4: D2 baseline algorithm on weakly comparable corpora

In every table above, the **P**/R column gives the maximum precision and the associated recall EMACC was able to obtain for the corresponding pair of languages using the parameters (**Prms.**) from the next column. The P/**R** column gives the maximum recall with the associated precision that we obtained for that pair of languages.

The **Prms.** columns contain parameter settings for EMACC (see Tables 1 and 3) and for the D2 baseline algorithm (Tables 2 and 4): in Tables 1 and 3 values for `ThrGiza`, `ThrUpdate` and `ThrOut` are given from the top (of the cell) to the bottom and in Tables 2 and 4 values of `ThrGiza` and `ThrOut` are also given from top to bottom (the `ThrUpdate` parameter is missing because the D2 baseline algorithm does not do re-estimation). The # column contains the size of the test set: the number of documents in each language that have to be paired. The search space is # * # and the gold standard contains # pairs of human aligned document pairs.

To ease comparison between EMACC and the D2 baseline for each type of corpora (strongly and weakly comparable), we grayed maximal values between the two: either the precision in the **P**/R column or the recall in the P/**R** column.

In the case of strongly comparable corpora (Tables 1 and 2), we see that the benefits of re-estimating the probabilities of the translation equivalents (based on which we judge document alignments) begin to emerge with precisions for all pairs of languages (except en-sl) being better than those obtained with the D2 baseline. But the real benefit of re-estimating the probabilities of translation equivalents along the EM procedure is visible from the comparison between Tables 3 and 4. Thus, in the case of weakly comparable corpora, in which EMACC with the D2 distribution is clearly better than the baseline (with the only exception of en-lt precision), due to the significant decrease in the lexical overlap, the EM procedure is able to produce important alignment clues in the form of re-estimated (bigger) probabilities of translation equivalents that, otherwise, would have been ignored.

It is important to mention the fact that the results we obtained varied a lot with values of the parameters `ThrGiza` and `ThrUpdate`. We observed, for the majority of studied language pairs, that lowering the value for `ThrGiza` and/or `ThrUpdate` (0.1, 0.01, 0.001…), would negatively impact the performance of EMACC due to the fact of *introducing noise* in the initial computation of the D2 distribution and also on *re-estimating (increasing) probabilities for irrelevant translation equivalents*. At the other end, increasing the threshold for these parameters (0.8, 0.85, 0.9…) would also result in performance decreasing due to the fact that *too few translation equivalents (be they all correct) are not enough to pinpoint correct document alignments* since there are great chances for them to actually appear in all document pairs.

So, we have experimentally found that there is a certain balance between *the degree of correctness of translation equivalents* and *their ability to pinpoint correct document alignments*. In other words, the paradox resides in the fact that if a certain pair of translation equivalents is not correct but the respective words appear only in documents which correctly align to one another, that pair is very important to the alignment process. Conversely, if a pair of translation equivalents has a very high probability score (thus being correct) but appears in almost every possible pair of documents, that pair is not informative to the alignment process and must be excluded. We see now that the EMACC aims at finding the set of translation equivalents that is maximally informative with respect to the set of document alignments.

We have introduced the `ThrOut` parameter in order to have better precision. This parameter actually instructs EMACC to output only the top (according to the alignment score probability $P(d_{ab}|\text{true})$) `ThrOut%` of the document alignments it has found. This means that, if all are correct, the maximum recall can only be `ThrOut%`.

But another important function of ThrOut is to restrict the translation equivalents re-estimation (equation 7b) for only the top ThrOut% alignments. In other words, only the probabilities of translation equivalents that are to be found in top ThrOut% best alignments in the current EM step are re-estimated. We introduced this restriction in order to confine translation equivalents probability re-estimation to correct document alignments found so far.

Regarding the running time of EMACC, we can report that on a cluster with a total of 32 CPU cores (4 nodes) with 6-8 GB of RAM per node, the total running time is between 12h and 48h per language pair (about 2000 documents per language) depending on the setting of the various parameters.

5 Conclusions

The whole point in developing textual unit alignment algorithms for comparable corpora is to be able to provide good quality quasi-aligned data to programs that are specialized in extracting parallel data from these alignments. In the context of this paper, the most important result to note is that translation probability re-estimation is a good tool in discovering new correct textual unit alignments in the case of weakly related documents. We also tested EMACC at the alignment of 200 parallel paragraphs (small texts of no more than 50 words) for all pairs of languages that we have considered here. We can briefly report that the results are better than the strongly comparable document alignments from Tables 1 and 2 which is a promising result because one would think that a significant reduction in textual unit size would negatively impact the alignment accuracy.

Acknowledgements

This work has been supported by the ACCURAT project (http://www.accurat-project.eu/) funded by the European Community's Seventh Framework Program (FP7/2007-2013) under the Grant Agreement n° 248347. It has also been partially supported by the Romanian Ministry of Education and Research through the STAR project (no. 742/19.01.2009).

References

Borman, S. 2009. The Expectation Maximization Algorithm. A short tutorial. Online at: http://www.isi.edu/natural-language/teaching/cs562/2009/readings/B06.pdf

Brown, P. F., Lai, J. C., and Mercer, R. L. 1991. Aligning sentences in parallel corpora. In Proceedings of the 29th Annual Meeting of the Association for Computational Linguistics, pp. 169–176, June 8-21, 1991, University of California, Berkeley, California, USA.

Brown, P. F., Pietra, S. A. D., Pietra, V. J. D., and Mercer, R. L. 1993. The Mathematics of Statistical Machine Translation: Parameter Estimation. Computational Linguistics, 19(2): 263—311.

Ceauşu, A. 2009. Statistical Machine Translation for Romanian. PhD Thesis, Romanian Academy (in Romanian).

Chen, S. F. 1993. Aligning Sentences in Bilingual Corpora Using Lexical Information. In Proceedings of the 31st Annual Meeting on Association for Computational Linguistics, pp. 9—16, Columbus, Ohio, USA.

Dempster, A. P., Laird, N. M., and Rubin, D. B. 1977. Maximum likelihood from incomplete data via the EM algorithm. Journal of the Royal Statistical Society, 39(B):1—38.

Fung, P., and Cheung, P. 2004. Mining Very-Non-Parallel Corpora: Parallel Sentence and Lexicon Extraction via Bootstrapping and EM. In Proceedings of EMNLP 2004, Barcelona, Spain: July 2004.

Gao, Q., and Vogel, S. 2008. Parallel implementations of word alignment tool. ACL-08 HLT: Software Engineering, Testing, and Quality Assurance for Natural Language Processing, pp. 49—57, June 20, 2008, The Ohio State University, Columbus, Ohio, USA.

Munteanu, D. S., and Marcu, D. 2002. Processing comparable corpora with bilingual suffix trees. In Proceedings of the 2002 Conference on Empirical Methods in Natural Language Processing (EMNLP 2002), pp. 289–295, July 6-7, 2002, University of Pennsylvania, Philadelphia, USA.

Munteanu, D. S., and Marcu, D. 2005. Improving machine translation performance by exploiting non-parallel corpora. Computational Linguistics, 31(4):477–504.

Building a Web-based parallel corpus and filtering out machine-translated text

Alexandra Antonova, Alexey Misyurev
Yandex
16, Leo Tolstoy St., Moscow, Russia
{antonova, misyurev}@yandex-team.ru

Abstract

We describe a set of techniques that have been developed while collecting parallel texts for Russian-English language pair and building a corpus of parallel sentences for training a statistical machine translation system. We discuss issues of verifying potential parallel texts and filtering out automatically translated documents. Finally we evaluate the quality of the 1-million-sentence corpus which we believe may be a useful resource for machine translation research.

1 Introduction

The Russian-English language pair is rarely used in statistical machine translation research, because the number of freely available bilingual corpora for Russian-English language pair is very small compared to European languages. Available bilingual corpora[1] often belong to a specific genre (software documentation, subtitles) and require additional processing for conversion to a common format. At the same time many Russian websites contain pages translated to or from English. Originals or translations of these documents can also be found in the Internet. By our preliminary estimates these bilingual documents may yield more than 100 million unique parallel sentences while it is still a difficult task to find and extract them.

The task of unrestricted search of parallel documents all over the Web including content-based search is seldom addressed by researchers. At the same time the properties of the set of potential parallel texts found in that way are not well investigated. Building a parallel corpus of high quality from that kind of raw data is not straightforward because of low initial precision, frequent embedding of nonparallel fragments in parallel texts, and low-quality parallel texts. In this paper we address the tasks of verification of parallel documents, extraction of the best parallel fragments and filtering out automatically translated texts.

Mining parallel texts from a big document collection usually involves three phases:

- Detecting a set of potential parallel document pairs with fast but low-precision algorithms
- Pairwise verification procedure
- Further filtering of unwanted texts, e.g. automatically translated texts

Finding potential parallel texts in a collection of web documents is a challenging task that does not yet have a universal solution. There exist methods based on the analysis of meta-information (Ma and Liberman, 1999; Resnik, 2003; Mohler and Mihalcea, 2008, Nadeau and Foster 2004), such as URL similarity, HTML markup, publication date and time. More complicated methods are aimed at

[1] e.g. http://opus.lingfil.uu.se/

Proceedings of the 4th Workshop on Building and Using Comparable Corpora, pages 136–144,
49th Annual Meeting of the Association for Computational Linguistics,
Portland, Oregon, 24 June 2011. ©*2011 Association for Computational Linguistics*

detecting potential parallel texts by their content. In this case mining of parallel documents in the Internet can be regarded as the task of near-duplicate detection (Uszkoreit et al., 2010). All of the above mentioned approaches are useful as each of them is able to provide some document pairs that are not found by other methods.

In our experiments, fast algorithms of the first phase classify every pair of documents as parallel with very low precision, from 20% to 0.001%. That results in a huge set of candidate pairs of documents, for which we must decide if they are actually parallel or not. For example, if we need to get 100 000 really parallel documents we should check from 500 thousand to 100 million pairs. The large number of pairwise comparisons to be made implies that the verification procedure must be fast and scalable. Our approach is based on a sentence-alignment algorithm similar to (Brown et al., 1991; Gale and Church, 1993; Chen, 1993; Moore 2002; Ma, 2006) but it is mainly aimed at achieving high precision rather than high recall. The algorithm is able to extract parallel fragments from comparable documents, as web documents often are not exactly parallel. The similarity estimate relies on probabilistic dictionary trained on initial parallel corpus and may improve when the corpus grows.

Due to growing popularity of machine translation systems, Russian websites are being increasingly filled with texts that are translated automatically. According to selective manual annotation the share of machine translation among the texts that have passed the verification procedure is 25-35%. Machine-translated sentences often demonstrate better word correspondence than human-translated sentences and are easier to align, but the longer phrases extracted from them are likely to be unnatural and may confuse the statistical translation system at the training stage. The large share of automatically translated data decreases the value of the corpus, especially if it is intended for research. Also it will make it difficult to outperform the translation quality of the system which generated those sentences.

To the best of our knowledge, there is no existing research concerning the task of filtering out machine translation. Our filtering method is based on a special decoding algorithm that translates sentence-aligned document and then scores the output against the reference document with BLEU metric. This method allows reducing the number of automatically translated texts to 5% in the final corpus.

Our final goal is to build a quality corpus of parallel sentences appropriate for training a statistical machine translation system. We evaluate the 1-million-sentence part of our corpus by training a phrase-based translation system (Koehn et al., 2007) on these sentences and compare the results with the results of training on noisy data, containing automatically translated texts as its part.

The rest of the paper is organized as follows: Section 2 provides an overview of the system architecture and addresses specific problems at the preparatory stage. Section 3 describes the sentence-alignment algorithm and the pairwise verification procedure. The algorithm makes use of statistical dictionaries trained beforehand. In Section 4 we discuss the problem of filtering out automatically translated texts. In Section 5 we evaluate the quality of the final parallel corpus and provide some statistical information about Russian-English language pair. We conclude in Section 6 with short summary remarks.

2 System description

The corpus building procedure includes several stages represented in Figure 1. Initial training provides bilingual probabilistic dictionaries which are used in sentence alignment and verification of potential parallel texts. We used Russian/English correspondent pages from a number of bilingual web-sites of good quality. We performed robust alignment based on sentence lengths as in (Gale and Church, 1993). The obtained probabilistic dictionaries were gradually improved in a sort of a bootstrapping procedure when the corpus size increased.

Our main source of Web documents are web pages from search engine database with their textual contents already extracted and sentence boundaries detected. Nevertheless documents often include sentences that are site-specific and carry some meta-information, advertising, or just some noise. When often repeated such sentences may confuse statistical training, so we choose to delete subsequent sentences that have been encountered recently.

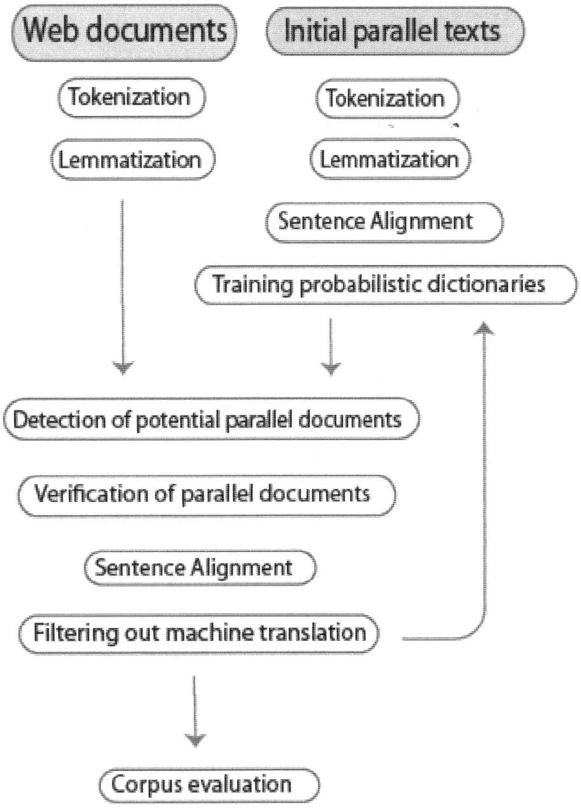

Figure 1. Corpus building procedure.

In morphologically rich languages nouns, verbs and adjectives have many different forms in text, which complicates statistical training, especially when the initial collection is comparatively small. At the same time, the task of sentence alignment relies on robust algorithms which allow for some data simplification. Word stemming, truncation of word endings and lemmatization may be used to reduce the data sparseness problem when dealing with morphologically rich languages. The accurate lemmatization algorithms for Russian language are complicated and comparatively slow because they should resolve morphological ambiguity as many word forms have more than one possible lemma. We chose a simple and fast algorithm of probabilistic lemmatization where a word is always assigned the most frequent of its possible lemmas. There are several reasons why it is appropriate for the task of sentence and word alignment:

- The algorithm runs almost as fast as the word truncation method, and in most cases it yields correct lemmas.
- Most of the information is contained in low-frequency words and those are usually less ambiguous than the frequent words.
- Individual mistakes in lemmatization do not necessarily result in wrong similarity estimation for the whole sentence.

3 Verification of potential parallel documents

Potential parallel documents are a pair of texts; each of them represents the textual content of some HTML page. The size of texts may vary from several sentences to several thousand sentences.

Our approach to the task of verification of potential parallel documents is motivated by the properties of the set of potential parallel texts, which is the output of different search algorithms including unrestricted content-based search over the Web.

The first problem is that most of the potential parallel texts on the Web, even if they prove to have parallel fragments, often contain non-parallel fragments as well, especially at the beginning or at the end. Since the parallel fragment can be located anywhere in the document pair, the verification algorithm performs exhaustive dynamic programming search within the entire document and not only within a fixed width band around the main diagonal. Our similarity measure relies heavily on features derived from the sentence alignment of the best parallel fragment and does not utilize any information from the rest of the text. We allow that the parallel fragment begins and ends anywhere in the text and also it is possible to skip one or several sentences without breaking the fragment.

We have also considered the possibility that documents can contain more than one parallel fragment separated by greater non-parallel fragments. Though such documents do exist, the contribution of lesser parallel fragments to parallel corpus is insignificant compared to much simpler case where each pair of documents can contain only one parallel fragment.

The second problem of the input data is low initial precision of potential parallel texts and the fact that there are many comparable but not parallel texts. It is worth noting that the marginal and joint probabilities of words and phrases in the set of documents with similar content may differ substantially from the probabilities obtained from the parallel corpus of random documents. For this reason we cannot completely rely on statistical models trained on the initial parallel corpus. It is important to have a similarity measure that allows for additional adjustment in order to take into account the probability distributions in the potential parallel texts found by different search algorithms.

The third problem is the large number of pairwise comparisons to be made. It requires that the verification procedure must be fast and scalable. Due to the fact that the system uses precomputed probabilistic dictionaries, each pair of documents can be processed independently and this stage fits well into the MapReduce framework (Dean and Ghemawat, 2004). For example, verification of 40 million pairs of potential parallel texts took only 35 minutes on our 250-node cluster.

The algorithm of verifying potential parallel documents takes two texts as input and tries to find the best parallel fragment, if there is any, by applying a dynamic programming search of sentence alignment. We use sentence-alignment algorithm for handling four tasks:

- Search of parallel fragments in pairs
- Verification of parallel document pairs
- Search of per-sentence alignment
- Filtering out sentences that are not completely parallel

Each sentence pair is scored using a similarity measure that makes use of two sources of prior statistical information:

- Probabilistic phrase dictionary, consisting of phrases up to two words
- Empirical distribution of lengths of Russian/English parallel sentences

Both have been obtained using initial parallel corpus. In a sort of bootstrapping procedure one can recalculate that prior statistical information as soon as a bigger parallel corpus is collected and then realign the input texts.

The algorithm neither attempts to find a word alignment between two sentences, nor it tries to translate the sentence as in (Uszkoreit et al., 2010). Instead, it takes account of all phrases from probabilistic dictionary that are applicable to a given pair of sentences disregarding position in the sentence or phrase intersection. Our probabilistic dictionary consists of 70'000 phrase translations of 1 or 2 words.

Let S and T be the set of source/target parts of phrases from a probabilistic dictionary, and $E \subset S \times T$ - the set of ordered pairs, representing the source-target dictionary entries (s,t). Let the source sentence contain phrases $S_0 \subset S$ and the target sentence contain phrases $T_0 \subset T$. Then the similarity between the two sentences is estimated by taking the following factors into account:

- $p(s \mid t)$, $p(t \mid s)$, translation probabilities;
- len_S, len_T, length of source and target sentences;
- $\log \hat{p}(len_S, len_T)$, the empirical distribution of length correspondence between source and target sentences.

The factors are log-linearly combined and the factor weights are tuned on the small development set containing 700 documents. We choose the weights so that the result of comparison of nonparallel sentences is usually negative. As a result of the search procedure we choose a parallel fragment with the biggest score. If that score is above a certain threshold the parallel fragment is extracted, otherwise the whole document is considered to be nonparallel.

Relative sentence order is usually preserved in parallel texts, though some local transformations may have been introduced by the translator, such as sentence splitting, merge or swap. Though sentence-alignment programs usually try to detect some of those transformations, we decided to ignore them for several reasons:

- Split sentences are not widely used to train a phrase-based translation system.
- One part of a split sentence can still be aligned with its whole translation as one-to-one correspondence.
- Cases of sentence swap are too rare to justify efforts needed to detect them.

4 Filtering out machine translation

After the verification procedure and sentence-alignment procedure our collection consists of sentence-aligned parallel fragments extracted from initial documents. A closer look at the parallel fragments reveals that some texts contain mistakes typically made by machine translation systems. It is undesirable to include such documents into the corpus, because a phrase-based translation system trained on this corpus may learn a great deal of badly constructed phrases.

The output of a rule-based system can be recognized without even considering its source text, as having no statistical information to rely on, the rule-based systems tend to choose the safest way of saying something, which leads to uncommonly frequent use of specific words and phrases. The differences in n-gram distributions can be captured by comparing the probabilities given by two language models: one trained on a collection of the outputs of a rule-based system and the other – on normal texts.

Our method of filtering out statistical machine translation is based on the similarity of algorithms of building phrase tables in the existing SMT systems. Those systems also have restrictions on reordering of words. Therefore their output is different from human translation, and this difference can be measured and serve as an indicator of a machine translated text. We designed a special version of phrase-based decoding algorithm whose goal was not just translate, but to provide a translation as close to the reference as possible while following the principles of phrase-based translation. The program takes two sentence-aligned documents as an input. Prior to translating each sentence, a special language model is built consisting of n-grams from the reference sentence. That model serves as a sort of soft constraint on the result of translation. The decoder output is scored against reference translation with the BLEU metric (Papineni et al., 2002) - we shall call it r-bleu for the rest of this section. The idea is that the higher is r-bleu, the more likely the reference is statistical translation itself.

The program was implemented based on the decoder of the statistical phrase-based translation system. The phrase table and the factor weights were not modified. Phrase reordering was not allowed. The phrase table contained 13 million phrases. The language model was modified in the following way. We considered only n-grams no longer than 4 words and only those that could be found in the reference sentence. The language model score for each n-gram depended only on its length.

We evaluated the method efficiency as follows. A collection of 245 random parallel fragments has been manually annotated as human or machine translation.

There are some kinds of typical mistakes indicating that the text is generated by a machine translation system. The most indicative mistake is wrong lexical choice, which can be easily recognized by a human annotator. Additional evidence are cases of incorrect agreement or unnatural word order. We considered only fragments containing more than 4 parallel sentences, because it was hard to identify the origin of shorter fragments. The annotation provided following results:

- 150 documents - human translation (64% of sentences)
- 55 documents - English-Russian machine translation (22% of sentences)
- 32 documents - Russian-English machine translation (12% of sentences)
- 8 documents - not classified (2% of sentences)

Sometimes it was possible for a human annotator to tell if a translation has been made by a rule-based or phrase-based translation system, but generally it was difficult to identify reliably the origin of a machine translated text. Also there were a number of automatically translated texts which had been post-edited by humans. Such texts often preserved unnatural word order and in that case they were annotated as automatically translated.

The annotation quality was verified by cross-validation. We took 27 random documents out of 245 and compared the results of the annotation with those performed by another annotator. There was no disagreement in identifying the translation direction. There were 4 cases of disagreement in identifying automatic translation: 3 cases of post-edited machine translation and 1 case of verbatim human translation. We realized that in case of post-edited machine translation the annotation was subjective. Nevertheless, after the question was discussed we decided that the initial annotation was correct. Table 1 represents the results of the annotation along with the range of r-bleu score.

r-bleu	Human	Automatic
0 - 5	0	0
5-10	252	0
10-15	899	0
15-20	1653	0
20-25	1762	0
25-30	1942	154
30-35	1387	538
35-40	494	963
40-45	65	1311
45-50	76	871
50-55	23	658
55-60	0	73
Total	8553	4568

Table 1. Number of parallel sentences in human/machine translated documents depending on the range of r-bleu score.

Let $C_{h\,max}$ denote the total number of sentences in all documents which were annotated as human translation. In our case $C_{h\,max} = 8553$. Let C_h denote the number of sentences in human translated documents with a r-bleu beyond certain threshold, and C_{mt} – the number of sentences in automatically translated documents with a r-bleu beyond the same threshold. Then recall(R) and precision(P) are defined as

$$R = C_h / C_{h\,max} ,$$
$$P = C_h / (C_h + C_{mt}).$$

For example, if we discard documents with r-bleu > 33.0, we get R = 90.1, P = 94.1. Figure 2 illustrates the dependency between these parameters.

The evaluation showed that parallel documents that have been translated automatically tend to get higher r-bleu scores and may be filtered out with reasonable precision and recall. As it is shown in Table 1, the total rate of machine translated sentence pairs is about 35% before the filtration. According to manual evaluation (see section 5, Table 4), this rate is reduced down to 5% in the final corpus.

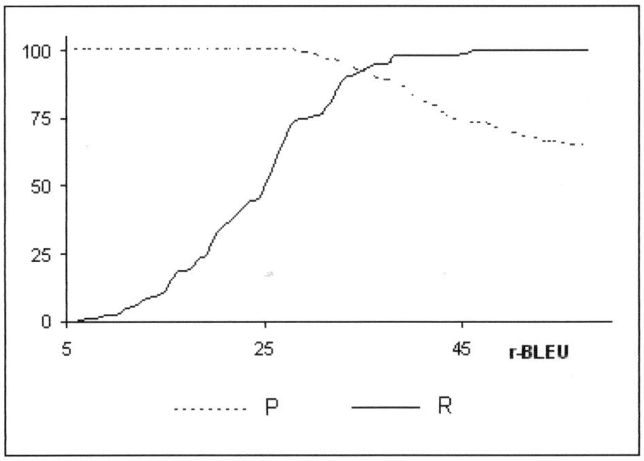

Figure 2. Dependency between r-bleu score and recall(R)/precision(P) rates of filtering procedure.

We chose the BLEU criterion partly due to its robustness. For the English-Russian language pair it yielded satisfactory results. We believe that our approach is applicable to many other language pairs as well, probably except the pairs of languages with similar word order. For those languages some other metric is possibly needed taking into account properties of particular language pair. We expect that the r-bleu threshold also depends on the language pair and has to be re-estimated.

5 Corpus of parallel sentences

After we choose a threshold value of the r-bleu criterion, we remove texts with the r-bleu score higher than the threshold from our collection of parallel fragments. Then we extract parallel sentences from the remaining texts in order to get a corpus of parallel sentences.

Sentences inside parallel fragments undergo some additional filtering before they can be included into the final corpus. We discard sentence pairs for which a similarity score is below a given threshold, or word-length ratio is less than ½. It is also useful to drop sentences whose English part contains Cyrillic symbols as those are extremely unlikely to be seen in original English texts and their presence usually means that the text is a result of machine translation or some sort of spam. All sentence pairs are lowercase and distinct. Sentences of more than 100 words have been excluded from the corpus.

In the rest of this section we estimate the quality of a 1-million-sentence part of the final parallel corpus that we are going to share with the research community. The corpus characteristics are represented in Table 2 and examples of parallel sentences are given in Table 3.

	English	Russian
Sentences	1\`022\`201	
Distinct sentences	1\`016\`580	1\`013\`426
Words	27\`158\`657	25\`135\`237
Distinct words	323\`310	651\`212
Av. Sent. Len	26.5	24.6

Table 2. Corpus characteristics: number of parallel sentences, distinct sentences, words[2], distinct words and average sentence length in words.

We evaluate corpus quality in two ways:

- Selecting each 5000-th sentence pair from the corpus and manually annotating the sentences as parallel or not. The results of the manual annotation are represented in Table 4.
- Training a statistical machine translation system on the corpus and testing its output with BLEU metric

We trained two phrase-based translation systems[3]. The first system was trained on 1 million random sentences originated in the documents which were human translations according to our r-bleu criterion. The other system was trained on the same corpus except that 35% of sentences were replaced to random sentences taken from documents which had been previously excluded as automatically translated. We reserved each 1000-th sentence from the first "clean" corpus as test data. We get word-alignment by running Giza++ (Och et al., 2000) on lemmatized texts. The phrase-table training procedure and decoder are the parts of Moses statistical machine translation system (Koehn et al., 2007). The language model has been trained on target side of the first corpus using SRI Language Modeling Toolkit (Stolcke, 2002).

в 2004 майдан прославился на весь мир благодаря оранжевой революции, которая происходила на этой площади. in 2004 maidan became-famous over all world due-to orange revolution , which took-place at this place . in 2004, maidan became famous all over the world because the orange revolution was centered here.
рассказы о народах, чей язык настолько несовершенен, что он должен восполняться жестами, - чистые мифы. stories about peoples , whose language so-much imperfect , that it should be-supplied gestures-with , - pure myths . tales about peoples whose language is so defective that it has to be eked out by gesture, are pure myths.
остальное время пусть они будут открыты, чтобы все обитатели вселенной могли увидеть тебя! the-rest-of time let they be open , so-that all inhabitants universe-of could see you ! the rest of the time, let the doors be open so that all the residents of the universe may have access to see you.
"я контролирую свою судьбу. "i control my destiny. "i control my own destiny.

Table 3. Sample parallel sentences.

Parallel	169
Parallel including non-parallel fragments	19
Non-parallel	6
English-Russian automatic[4] translation	7
Russian-English automatic translation	3
Total sentences	**204**

Table 4. Results of manual annotation of 204 sample sentences from the corpus.

[2] Punctuation symbols are considered as separate words.

[3] http://www.statmt.org/moses/

[4] Sentences containing mistakes typical for MT systems were annotated as automatic translations.

We tested both Russian-to-English and English-to-Russian translation systems on 1022 test sentences varying the language model order from trigram to 5-gram. We have not tuned the weights on the development set of sentences, because we believe that in this case the quality of translation would depend on the degree of similarity between the test and development sets of sentences and it would make our evaluation less reliable. In all experiments we used default Moses parameters, except that the maximum reordering parameter was reduced to 3 instead of 6. The results are represented in Table 5.

	Ru-En / +mt	En-Ru / +mt
3-gram	20.97 / +0.06	16.35 / -0.10
4-gram	21.04 / -0.13	16.33 / -0.13
5-gram	21.17 / -0.06	16.42 / -0.16
OnlineA[5]	25.38	21.01
OnlineB[6]	23.86	16.56

Table 5. BLEU scores measured on 1022 test sentences depending on the order of language model. The column +mt shows relative change in BLEU score of the system trained on "mt-noisy" data.

The overall system performance can be improved by tuning and/or training a bigger language model, but our goal is only to show to what extent the corpus itself is suitable for training statistical machine translation system. Online translation systems have been tested on the same test set, except that the input was detokenized and the output was lowercased. The online translation could have been better if the input text was in its original format - not lowercased.

6 Conclusion

We have described our approaches to main problems faced when building a parallel Russian-English corpus from the Internet.

We have proposed a method of filtering out automatically translated texts. It allowed us to reduce the rate of sentence pairs that originate from machine translated documents from 35% to 5%. The approach relies on general properties of the state-of-the-art statistical translation systems and therefore is applicable to many other language pairs.

We presented results of evaluation of the resulting Russian-English parallel corpus. We believe that the 1-million-sentence Russian-English corpus of parallel sentences used in this paper is a useful resource for machine translation research and machine translation contests.

[5] http://translate.google.ru/

[6] http://www.microsofttranslator.com/

References

Brown, P.F., Lai, J.C., Mercer, R.L. 1991. Aligning Sentences in Parallel Corpora. Proceedings of the 29th Annual Meeting of the Association for Computational Linguistics, Berkeley, California 169–176.

Chen, S.F. 1993. Aligning sentences in bilingual corpora using lexical information. Conference of the Association for Computational Linguistics, Columbus, Ohio, 9-16.

Dean, J. and Ghemawat, S. 2004. MapReduce: Simplified data processing on large clusters. In Proceedings of the Sixth Symposium on Operating System Design and Implementation (San Francisco, CA, Dec. 6–8). Usenix Association.

Gale, W. A., & Church, K. W. 1993. A program for aligning sentences in bilingual corpora. Computational Linguistics, 19(3), 75-102.

Philipp Koehn, Hieu Hoang, Alexandra Birch, Chris Callison-Burch, Marcello Federico, Nicola Bertoldi, Brooke Cowan, Wade Shen, Christine Moran, Richard Zens, Chris Dyer, Ondrej Bojar, Alexandra Constantin, Evan Herbst. 2007. Moses: Open Source Toolkit for Statistical Machine Translation, Annual Meeting of the Association for Computational Linguistics (ACL), demonstration session, Prague, Czech Republic, June.

Xiaoyi Ma and Mark Liberman. 1999. BITS: A method for bilingual text search over the web. Proceedings of the Machine Translation Summit VII.

Xiaoyi Ma. 2006. Champollion: A Robust Parallel Text Sentence Aligner. LREC 2006: Fifth International Conference on Language Resources and Evaluation.

Michael Mohler and Rada Mihalcea. 2008. BABYLON Parallel Text Builder: Gathering Parallel Texts for Low-Density Languages. Proceedings of the Language Resources and Evaluation Conference.

Moore, Robert C., 2002. Fast and Accurate Sentence Alignment of Bilingual Corpora. Machine Translation: From Research to Real Users

(Proceedings, 5th Conference of the Association for Machine Translation in the Americas, Tiburon, California), Springer-Verlag, Heidelberg, Germany, 135-244.

David Nadeau and George Foster, 2004. Real-time identification of parallel texts from bilingual newsfeed. Computational Linguistic in the North-East (CLiNE 2004): 21-28.

Franz Josef Och, Hermann Ney. 2000. Improved Statistical Alignment Models. Proceedings of the 38th Annual Meeting of the Association for Computational Linguistics, pp. 440-447, Hongkong, China, October.

Papineni, Kishore, Salim Roukos, Todd Ward, and Wei-Jing Zhu. 2002. BLEU: a method for automatic evaluation of machine translation. In Proceedings of the 40th Annual Meeting of the Association for Computational Linguistics (ACL), pages 311–318, Philadelphia, PA, USA.

Resnik, Philip and Noah A. Smith. 2003. The web as a parallel corpus. Computational Linguistics, 29:349–380.

Andreas Stolcke. 2002. SRILM—an extensible language modeling toolkit. Proceedings ICSLP, vol. 2, pp. 901–904, Denver, Sep.

Jakob Uszkoreit, Jay Ponte, Ashok Popat and Moshe Dubiner. 2010. Large Scale Parallel Document Mining for Machine Translation. Coling

Language-Independent Context Aware Query Translation using Wikipedia

Rohit Bharadwaj G
Search and Information Extraction Lab
LTRC
IIIT Hyderabad, India
bharadwaj@research.iiit.ac.in

Vasudeva Varma
Search and Information Extraction Lab
LTRC
IIIT Hyderabad, India
vv@iiit.ac.in

Abstract

Cross lingual information access (CLIA) systems are required to access the large amounts of multilingual content generated on the world wide web in the form of blogs, news articles and documents. In this paper, we discuss our approach to query formation for CLIA systems where language resources are replaced by Wikipedia. We claim that Wikipedia, with its rich multilingual content and structure, forms an ideal platform to build a CLIA system. Our approach is particularly useful for under-resourced languages, as all the languages don't have the resources(tools) with sufficient accuracies. We propose a context aware language-independent query formation method which, with the help of bilingual dictionaries, forms queries in the target language. Results are encouraging with a precision of 69.75% and thus endorse our claim on using Wikipedia for building CLIA systems.

1 INTRODUCTION

Cross lingual information access (CLIA) systems enable users to access the rich multilingual content that is created on the web daily. Such systems are vital to bridge the gap between information available and languages known to the user. Considerable amount of research has been done on building such systems but most of them rely heavily on the language resources and tools developed. With a constant increase in the number of languages around the world with their content on the web, CLIA systems are in need. Language independent approach is particularly useful for languages that fall into the category of under-resourced (African, few Asian languages), that doesn't have sufficient resources. In our approach towards language-independent CLIA system, we have developed context aware query translation using Wikipedia. Due to voluntary contribution of millions of users, Wikipedia gathers very significant amount of updated knowledge and provides a structured way to access it.

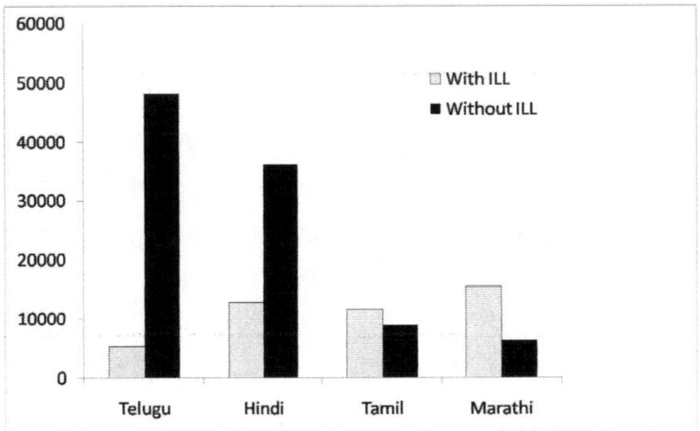

Figure 1: Number of Wikipedia pages(Y-axis) with and without Inter language link (ILL) to English in each language (X-axis)

The statistics in the Figure 1 show that it has rich multilingual content and is growing independent of the presence of English counter part. With its structurally rich content, it provides an ideal platform to perform cross lingual research. We harness Wikipedia and its structure to replace the language specific resources required for CLIA.

Our work is different from existing approaches in

Proceedings of the 4th Workshop on Building and Using Comparable Corpora, pages 145–150,
49th Annual Meeting of the Association for Computational Linguistics,
Portland, Oregon, 24 June 2011. ©*2011 Association for Computational Linguistics*

terms of

- No language resource has been used at any stage of query translation.
- Wikipedia structure has been fully utilized for achieving CLIA between English and Hindi, unlike the existing approaches, especially for query formation.

We have constructed a bilingual dictionary using cross lingual links present across the articles of same topic in different languages. As each word in the dictionary can have several translations based on various attributes like context, sense etc, we need a mechanism to identify the target word accurately based on the context of the query. To identify the context of a query, "Content Words", that are built for each Wikipedia article, are used. "Content Words" of the article are similar to the tags of the article, that reflects the context of the article in a more detailed way.

In this paper, we detail our approach in forming this "Content Words" and using them to form the query. Since our approach is language-independent and context-aware, we used a metric proposed by (Bharadwaj and Varma, 2011) to evaluate along with a dicationary-based metric. The system is built between languages English and Hindi. Hindi is selected as target language because of the availability of resources for evaluation. As our approach is language-independent, it can be used to translate queries between any pair of languages present in Wikipedia. The remainder of paper is organized as follows. Section 2 shows the related work. Proposed method is discussed in Section 3. Results and Discussion are in Section 4. We finally conclude in Section 5.

2 RELATED WORK

We discuss the related work of the two stages are involved in our system of language-independent context aware query translation,

- Resource building/ collection (Dictionaries in our case)
- Query formation

Dictionary building can be broadly classified into two approaches, manual and automatic. At initial stages, various projects like (Breen, 2004) try to build dictionaries manually, taking lot of time and effort. Though manual approaches perform well, they lag behind when recent vocabulary is considered. To reduce the effort involved, automatic extraction of dictionaries has been envisioned. The approach followed by (Kay and Roscheisen, 1999) and (Brown et al., 1990) were towards statistical machine translation, that can also be applied to dictionary building. The major requirement for using statistical methods is the availability of bilingual parallel corpora, that again is limited for under-resourced languages. Factors like sentence structure, grammatical differences, availability of language resources and the amount of parallel corpus available further hamper the recall and coverage of the dictionaries extracted.

After parallel corpora, attempts have been made to construct bilingual dictionaries using various types of corpora like comparable corpus (Sadat et al., 2003) and noisy parallel corpus (Fung and McKeown, 1997). Though there exist various approaches, most of them make use of the language resources. Wikipedia has also been used to mine dictionaries. (Tyers and Pienaar, 2008), (Erdmann et al., 2008), (Erdmann et al., 2009) have built bilingual dictionaries using Wikipedia and language resources. We have mined our dictionaries similarly considering the cross lingual links present. Our approach to dictionary building is detailed in section 3.

Wikipedia has been used for CLIA at various stages including query formation. Most recently, Wikipedia structure has been exploited in (Gaillard et al., 2010) for query translation and disambiguation. In (Schönhofen et al., 2008), Wikipedia has been exploited at all the stages of building a CLIA system. We tread the same path of (Schönhofen et al., 2008) in harnessing Wikipedia for dictionary building and query formation. Similar to them we extract concept words for each Wikipedia article and use them to disambiguate and form the query.

For evaluation purposes, we adapted evaluation measures based on Wikipedia and existing dictionaries (Bharadwaj and Varma, 2011). The authors have proposed a classification based technique, using Wikipedia article and the inter-language links present between them to classify the sentences as parallel or non-parallel based on the context of the sentences rather than at the syntactic level. We adopt a similar classification based technique and build feature vectors for classification using Support Vector Machines (SVM [1]) for evaluation.

3 PROPOSED METHOD

The architecture of the system is given in the Figure 2.

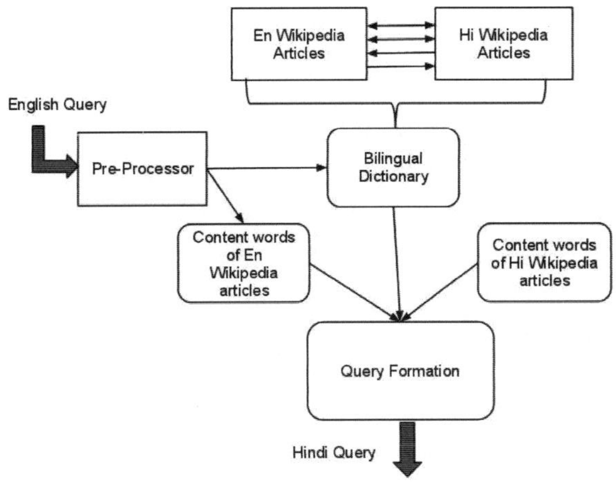

Figure 2: Architecture of the system

The following subsections describe each module in detail.

3.1 Dictionary Building

Bilingual dictionaries (English-Hindi) are built from Wikipedia by mining parallel/ near-parallel text from each structural information like title, infobox, category and abstract (initial paragraph) of the English(En) and Hindi(Hi) articles that are connected with Inter language link (ILL, arrows between En Wikipedia articles and Hi Wikipedia articles in Figure 2). The motivation for considering the other structural information of the Wikipedia article is to increase vocabulary of the dictionary both in terms of the number of words and categories of words. Titles, Infobox and Categories of the article consider only named entities that are used in the language. To increase the coverage of the dictionary and also to include other categories of words (like negations, quantifiers etc), abstract of the article is considered. Also the Inter language links between the articles are assumed to be bi-directional even if they are uni-directional. An approach similar to (Tyers and Pienaar, 2008) is followed to construct dictionaries. The dictionary is constructed iteratively by using the previously constructed dictionaries from each structure. The structural aspects of the article used are

- Title: Titles of the articles linked.
- Infobox: Infobox of the articles that are linked.
- Category: Categories of the articles linked.
- Abstract: The inital paragraph of the articles linked are considered as the article abstracts and are used for dictionary building.

A dictionary consists of word and its several possible translations, scored according to their alignment scores. Each structural information is used to enhance the dictionary built previously. Dictionary built from titles are used as starting point. As each English word is mapped to several Hindi words, filtering of words or re-ranking of the words at query formation is vital. The scoring function used for the words while building the dictionary is

$$score(w_E^i, w_H^j) = \frac{W_E^i \bigcap W_H^j}{W_E^i} \quad (1)$$

Where w_E^i is the ith word in English word list; w_H^j is the jth word in Hindi word list; $W_E^i \bigcap W_H^j$ is the count of co-occurrence of w_E^i and w_H^j in the parallel corpus and; W_E^i is the count of occurrences of the word w_E^i in the corpus.

3.2 Building Content words

The context of each English Wikipedia article A_i is extracted from the following structural information of the article.

- Title : Title of the article
- Redirect title : Redirect title of the article, if present.

[1] http://www.cs.cornell.edu/People/tj/svm_light/

- Category : Categories of the article that are predefined.

- Subsections : Titles of the different subsections of the article.

- In-links : Meta data present in the links to this article from other articles in same language.

- Out-links : Meta data of the links that link the current article to other articles in same language.

As these structural attributes are spread across the article, they help to identify the context (orientation) of the article in depth when compared with the Categories of the article. Each structural aspect described above have unique content that will help to identify the context of the article. "Content Words" are formed from each of these structural aspects. Word count of the words present in each of the above mentioned attributes are calculated and are filtered by a threshold to form the context words of the article. The threshold for filtering has been calculated by manual tagging with the help of language annotators. "Content Words" for the Hindi articles are also formed similarly. The formation of "Content Words" is similar to tagging but is not a stricly tagging mechanism as we have no constraint on the number of tags. Category alone can help to get the context but considering in-links, out-links, subsections will increase the depth of context words and will reduce the information lost by tagging the words.

3.3 Query formation

Query formation of our system depends on the context words built. For an English query (q_E) that contains the words w_E^i (i: 0 to n),

- Build W_H of size m, that contains the words returned by the dictionary for each of the words.

- For all words in (q_E), extract all the articles a_i^k (k: 0 to n) with w_E^i as one of its context word.

- Form the corresponding Hindi set of articles A_h using the cross lingual link, if present in the English article set constructed in the above step.

- For each Hindi word w_H^j (j: 0 to m), add it to Hindi query (q_H) if at least one of the articles a_i (with w_H^j as its context word) is present in A_h.

This approach helps to identify the context of the query as each query is represented by a set of articles instead of query words, that forms the concepts that the query can be interpreted to limited to Wikipedia domain. Queries are translated based on the architecture described in Figure 2.

4 Results and Discussion

4.1 Evaluation, Dataset and Results

A classification based approach and a dictionary based approach are employed to calculate the accuracy of the queries translated. 400 sentences with their corresponding translations (English-Hindi) have been used as test set to evaluate the performance of the query formation. The sentence pairs are provided by FIRE[2]. These sentences contain all types of words (Named entities, Verbs etc) and will be referred to as samples. The English language sentences are used as queries and are translated to Hindi using the approach described. Before forming the query, stop words are removed from the English sentence. The query lengths after removing stop words vary from 2 words to 8 words. The dictionary used for evaluation is an existing one, Shabdanjali[3]. In the following sections, we describe our two evaluation strategies and the performance of our system using them.

4.1.1 Dictionary based evaluation

Shabdanjali dictionary has been used to evaluate the translated queries. The evaluation metric is word overlap, though it is relaxed further. The formula

[2] http://www.isical.ac.in/ clia/

[3] Shabdanjali is an open source bilingual dictionary that is most used between English and Hindi. It is available at `http://ltrc.iiit.ac.in/onlineServices/Dictionaries/Dict_Frame.html`

used for calculating the precision is

$$precision = \frac{No.ofCorrectSamples}{TotalNumberofSamples} \quad (2)$$

A sample is said to be correct if its $overLapScore$ is greater than threshold instead of complete overlap. The $overLapScore$ of each sample is measured using Formula 3. Threshold is the average $overLapScore$ of the positive training set used for training the classifier (Training dataset is discussed in Section 4.1.2).

$$overLapScore = \frac{No.ofWordOverlap}{TotalNumberofWords} \quad (3)$$

The number of word overlaps are measured both manually and automatically to avoid inconsistent results due to varios syntactic representation of the same word in Wikipedia.

The precision for the test dataset using this approach is 42.8%.

4.1.2 Classification based evaluation

As described in Section 2, we have used a classification based technique for identifying whether the translated queries contain the same information or not. We have collected 1600 pairs of sentences where 800 sentences are parallel to each other (positive samples, exact translations) while the other half have word overlaps, but not parallel, (not exact translations but have similar content) form the negative samples. Various statistics are extracted from Wikipedia for each sentence pair to construct feature vector as described in (Bharadwaj and Varma, 2011). Each English and Hindi sentences are queried as bag-of-words query to corresponding Wikipedia articles and statistics are extracted based on the articles retrieved. The classifier used is SVM and is trained on the feature vectors generated for 1600 samples. The precision in this approach is the accuracy of the classifier. The formula used for calculating the accuracy is

$$accuracy = \frac{No.ofSamplesCorrectlyClassified}{TotalNumberofSamples} \quad (4)$$

The correctness of the sample is the prediction of the classifier. The precision for the test set is 69.75%.

4.2 Discussion

The precision achieved by classification based evaluation is higher than that of existing dictionary (Shabdanjali) primarily due to

- Dictionary (Shabdanjali) doesn't contain words of the query. (Coverage is less).

- Word forms present in the dictionary are different to that of words present in translated query. (Ex: spelling, tense etc).

To negate the effect of above factors, classification based evaluation (4.1.2) has been considered. Classification based evaluation shows that the results are better when the entire sentence and its context is considered. As there are no existing systems that translate queries based on the context and language independent, our results are encouraging to work in this direction. Since no language resources were used, our approach is scalable and can be applied to any pair of languages present in Wikipedia. The relatively low coverage of the dictionaries built using Wikipedia structure also affects the process of query translation. In future, the coverage of dictionaries can also be increased by considering other structural properties of Wikipedia.

5 Conclusion

In this paper, we have described our approach towards building a language-independent context aware query translation, replacing the language resources with the rich multilingual content provider, Wikipedia. Its structural aspects have been exploited to build the dictionary and its articles are used to form queries and also to evaluate them. Further exploitation of Wikipedia and its structure to increase the coverage of the dictionaries built will increase the overall precision. Though queries are translated in a language-independent way, using language resources of English, as it is a richly resourced language, for query formation is also envisioned.

References

Rohit G. Bharadwaj and Vasudeva Varma. 2011. Language independent identification of parallel sentences using wikipedia. In *Proceedings of the 20th international conference companion on World wide web*, WWW '11, pages 11–12, New York, NY, USA. ACM.

J. W. Breen. 2004. JMdict:A Japanese-Multilingual Dictionary. In *COLING Multilingual Linguistic Resources Workshop*, pages 71–78.

P.F. Brown, J. Cocke, S.A.D. Pietra, V.J.D. Pietra, F. Jelinek, J.D. Lafferty, R.L. Mercer, and P.S. Roossin. 1990. A statistical approach to machine translation. *Computational linguistics*, 16(2):85.

M. Erdmann, K. Nakayama, T. Hara, and S. Nishio. 2008. An approach for extracting bilingual terminology from wikipedia. In *Database Systems for Advanced Applications*, pages 380–392. Springer.

M. Erdmann, K. Nakayama, T. Hara, and S. Nishio. 2009. Improving the extraction of bilingual terminology from Wikipedia. *ACM Transactions on Multimedia Computing, Communications, and Applications (TOMCCAP)*, 5(4):1–17.

P. Fung and K. McKeown. 1997. A technical word-and term-translation aid using noisy parallel corpora across language groups. *Machine Translation*, 12(1):53–87.

B. Gaillard, M. Boualem, and O. Collin. 2010. Query Translation using Wikipedia-based resources for analysis and disambiguation.

M. Kay and M. Roscheisen. 1999. Text-translation Alignment. In *Computational Linguistics*, volume 19, pages 604–632.

F. Sadat, M. Yoshikawa, and S. Uemura. 2003. Bilingual terminology acquisition from comparable corpora and phrasal translation to cross-language information retrieval. In *Proceedings of the 41st Annual Meeting on Association for Computational Linguistics-Volume 2*, pages 141–144. Association for Computational Linguistics.

P. Schönhofen, A. Benczúr, I. Bíró, and K. Csalogány. 2008. Cross-language retrieval with wikipedia. *Advances in Multilingual and Multimodal Information Retrieval*, pages 72–79.

F.M. Tyers and J.A. Pienaar. 2008. Extracting bilingual word pairs from Wikipedia. *Collaboration: interoperability between people in the creation of language resources for less-resourced languages*, page 19.

Author Index